GLOBAL COLLECTIVE ACTION

This book examines how nations and other key participants in the global community address problems requiring coordinated efforts of two or more entities, that is, collective action. The global community has achieved successes on some issues such as eradicating smallpox, but on others, such as the reduction of drug trafficking, efforts to coordinate nations' actions have not been sufficient. This book identifies the factors that promote or inhibit successful collective action at the regional and global level for an ever-growing set of challenges stemming from augmented cross-border flows associated with globalization. The author identifies modern principles of collective action and applies them to a host of global challenges, including promoting global health, providing foreign assistance, controlling rogue nations, limiting transnational terrorism, and intervening in civil wars. Because many of these concerns involve strategic interactions where choices and their consequences are dependent on one's own and others' actions, the book relies, in places, on elementary game theory, which is fully introduced for the uninitiated reader.

Todd Sandler holds the Robert R. and Katheryn A. Dockson Professorship of International Relations and Economics at the University of Southern California. He has written or edited eighteen books, including *Economic Concepts for the Social Sciences*, *The Political Economy of NATO* (with Keith Hartley) and *Global Challenges: An Approach to Economic, Political, and Environmental Problems*, as well as numerous journal articles in economics and political science. In 2003 he was the corecipient of the National Academy of Sciences Award for Behavioral Research Relevant to the Prevention of Nuclear War.

GLOBAL COLLECTIVE ACTION

Todd Sandler

University of Southern California

CAMBRIDGE
UNIVERSITY PRESS

PUBLISHED BY THE PRESS SYNDICATE OF THE UNIVERSITY OF CAMBRIDGE
The Pitt Building, Trumpington Street, Cambridge, United Kingdom

CAMBRIDGE UNIVERSITY PRESS
The Edinburgh Building, Cambridge CB2 2RU, UK
40 West 20th Street, New York, NY 10011-4211, USA
477 Williamstown Road, Port Melbourne, VIC 3207, Australia
Ruiz de Alarcón 13, 28014 Madrid, Spain
Dock House, The Waterfront, Cape Town 8001, South Africa

http://www.cambridge.org

First published 2004

Printed in the United States of America

Typeface Times Ten Roman 10/13 pt.   *System* LATEX 2_ε [TB]

A catalog record for this book is available from the British Library

Library of Congress Cataloging in Publication Data
Sandler, Todd.
Global collective action / Todd Sandler.
p. cm.
Includes bibliographical references and index.
ISBN 0-521-83477-5 (cloth) – ISBN 0-521-54254-5 (pbk.)
1. International cooperation.   2. Alliances.   3. Globalization.   4. Public goods.
5. Game theory.   6. Decision making.   I. Title.
JZ1308.S26   2004
327.1′16 – dc22   2004040672

ISBN 0 521 83477 5 hardback
ISBN 0 521 54254 5 paperback

To Robert R. and Katheryn A. Dockson for their
generosity and friendship.

Contents

Tables and Figures

FIGURES

Preface

Globalization has increased cross-border flows beyond trade in goods and financial exchanges. Borders are porous to pollutants, diseases, terrorism, knowledge, political upheavals, conflicts, and computer viruses and worms. Unlike the nation–state where citizens can turn to a central authority to address such problems within its borders, the global community exists in a more anarchic state with independent actors who cherish their autonomy. Although these cross-border flows will continue to expand, driven by the dual forces of market globalization and technological progress, there is no movement toward global governance. Hence, one must look to nation-states, nongovernmental organizations (NGOs), multinationals, charitable foundations, and multilateral organizations as the key actors to address problems requiring coordinated efforts of two or more entities – that is, collective action.

Even in the absence of a governing body, the global community has achieved some notable successes in curbing ozone shield depletion, instituting standards of financial practices, eradicating smallpox, and regulating transit on open seas. In other areas such as the control of greenhouse gases or the elimination of transnational terrorism, the story is much different, as nations have failed thus far to coordinate their actions sufficiently. So, the real question is, what factors promote or inhibit successful collective action at the regional or global level to address an ever-growing set of challenges? This book answers this question by identifying the basic elements that affect global collective action. To do so, I rely on the modern principles of collective action and the application of some elementary game theory. The latter is necessary because collective action involves strategic interactions where choices and their consequences are dependent on one's own actions and those of others. Collective action principles and game-theoretic tools are presented in sufficient detail for the uninformed reader. Game theory is related to global collective action in a nontechnical fashion.

This book explains how some treaties and supranational institutions have achieved so much while others have accomplished so little. Very simple institutional structures that preserve nations' autonomy may, at times, coordinate participants to successfully tackle common problems where more complicated structures may fail by removing too much autonomy. In a large number of instances, incentives may be favorable for success without any explicit coordination. Incentives differ greatly among seemingly similar global collective action concerns. If these motivators are better understood, then efforts can be directed at improving incentives for just those contingencies where they are perverse. This is the approach taken here. As such, institutional design figures prominently in the analysis.

Recent books on global collective action – for example, Scott Barrett's *Environment & Statecraft* (Oxford University Press, 2003) – have focused on the use of a single tool (treaties) to address just one set of problems (the environment). My book is much broader with applications to the environment, global health, security, foreign aid, and other issues. Additionally, my book investigates various responses as well as the use of treaties. The principles necessary to understand global collective action for, say, the environment are no different than those associated with any issue requiring collective action at the transnational level. Hence, there is no reason to restrict my coverage, which is wider than any book currently available. Because the world community does not rely solely on treaties, other institutional arrangements, such as alliances and partnerships, must be investigated to analyze global collective action. Once the required principles and tools are set out in Chapters 2–4, I am able to address a wide range of global concerns in a relatively compact space.

This book combines features from my earlier books, *Global Challenges* (Cambridge University Press, 1997) and *Collective Action: Theory and Applications* (University of Michigan Press, 1992), in an entirely new presentation. This new book *is not* a rewrite of these earlier books. Many of the issues analyzed – global health, foreign aid, rogue nations, civil wars, and outer space resources – were never touched upon in either of the earlier works. Issues previously analyzed – terrorism and air pollution – are brought up to date and examined in much greater detail here. Recent events – the terrorist attacks of 9/11 and the suspected enhanced heating of the earth's atmosphere – have augmented the importance and interest in these issues. I offer many new insights on these concerns and how they may be ameliorated. In contrast to my earlier books, this book devotes whole chapters to a single application so that each can be discussed in sufficient detail. Another difference involves the theory chapters, which incorporate insights from the last decade of research on collective action where much has been written. Unlike *Collective Action: Theory and Applications*, the presentation here is devoid of mathematics to make it accessible to a broad audience. Moreover, the linkages between game theory and global collective action presented in *Global Challenges* are improved.

I owe a tremendous debt of gratitude to Carol Sandler, who read the entire manuscript and provided excellent editorial comments. She gave me crucial reactions as a nonspecialist; her feedback informed me on what interested a general reader. I have also profited from insightful comments from five anonymous reviewers on various drafts. As with my last four Cambridge University Press (CUP) books, I received excellent counsel and support from Scott Parris, the economics editor. His presence at the Press is a major factor why I have published so many of my books with CUP. I also appreciate the efforts of the production staff at CUP, who transformed the typescript into a book. I have benefited greatly from the skills, care, and patience of Christie Rainey and Sara Fisher, who typed many drafts of the chapters. I also must acknowledge my debt to my many co-authors of articles where some of these insights on global collective action were originally developed. Prominent on this list are Dan Arce, Jon Cauley, Richard Cornes, Walter Enders, Keith Hartley, and James C. Murdoch. Others include Wolfgang Buchholz, John F. Forbes, Christian Haslbeck, Wallace E. Huffman, Ravi Kanbur, Jyoti Khanna, Il-Dong Ko, Harvey E. Lapan, Kevin Morrison, Gerald F. Parise, John W. Posnett, Keith Sargent, William Schulze, Hirofumi Shimizu, Kevin Siqueira, John Tschirhart, and Wim Vijverberg. This project succeeded because of the support of my wife, Jeannie, and my son, Tristan Jon, who continue to bear much of the true costs of my books as I rummage about the house at 4:30 each morning, setting out to write or research *Global Collective Action*. I greatly appreciate their encouragement, understanding, and support.

Los Angeles
November 2003

Todd Sandler
Robert R. and Katheryn A. Dockson
Professor of International Relations
and Economics, University of
Southern California

1

Future Perfect

Suppose that we could time travel, as envisioned by H. G. Wells, to the year 2025. As we disembark the time machine, we investigate which global and transnational problems have been addressed successfully and which have not. For example, what will be the state of the HIV/AIDS epidemic by then? From 1982 to 2002, twenty million people died from AIDS and twice that number became infected.[1] Will a vaccine have been developed by 2025, or will the disease have decimated parts of Africa and Asia, thereby curtailing the projected population growth in the developing world? Will transnational terrorism by independent groups be the number one security concern in 2025 as it is today? Will so-called rogue states that operate outside of the norms of the global community have acquired weapons of mass destruction that they then use to threaten other countries? By 2025, will the corn belt of the American Midwest have moved northward into Canada as global warming heats the atmosphere? Such a visit to the future would provide insights about those problems where actions have occurred and those where they have not. For the former, one must identify what factors promoted action and, for the latter, what considerations inhibited solutions.

The greatest discovery and insights from time traveling would involve two types of observations. First, one would learn in this "future-perfect" exercise what problems will have emerged that no one foresees today. These may involve technological impacts that nobody has been clever enough to portend, or they may include stresses on the ecosphere that appear only after an unforeseen threshold has been surpassed.

---

[1] See *The Economist* (2002a) on the current state of the HIV/AIDS epidemic.

Foreknowledge of these future exigencies would allow humankind to act today either to inhibit the problem from emerging or to limit its magnitude when it eventually surfaces. In the latter case, actions today could also forestall the *onset* of the crisis. Second, the time traveler would learn which of today's problems had been exaggerated. For example, the planet may be more resilient to global warming, or perhaps other phenomena may offset the effects of greenhouse gases (GHGs) (for example, sulfur emissions may reflect sufficient solar energy to limit atmospheric heating). Moreover, the current heating trends may be due to natural cycles that are poorly understood and unrelated to global warming. Some of today's "crises" may dissipate with time because there may be the proper incentives to act so that these threats are addressed. Technological breakthroughs may handle some exigencies – new technologies may greatly curb GHGs from internal combustion engines.

In lieu of time traveling, we must use our ingenuity to leap forward in time to anticipate which challenges will be long standing and which will be self-correcting owing to appropriate incentives for action. In some instances, modest institutional changes at the supranational level may be sufficient to provide better incentives for actions; modest changes are favored because the international community has shown little capacity for a great deal of integration. An ultimate task is to ascertain global challenges not yet brought to light. The purpose of this book is to investigate a host of global challenges using modern economic reasoning and methods. In particular, I apply modern principles of collective action, where the efforts of two or more agents (e.g., individuals, firms, institutions, or nations) are required to accomplish an outcome.[2] The focus will be on global exigencies that require joint actions by nations. In a nonalarmist way, I try to identify the forces at work that either promote or inhibit action. This is an important exercise because resources are scarce and must be primarily directed to those concerns where incentives for tackling the problems are perverse. Thus, the tools of collective action serve as the time machine for shaping and predicting the prospects and realities of tomorrow's global community.

---

[2] In his seminal book, *The Logic of Collective Action*, Mancur Olson (1965) puts forth essential principles of collective action. These principles have been updated and expanded in Hardin (1982) and Sandler (1992). More recently, these principles have been applied to global contingencies by Sandler (1997, 1998) and Sandler and Hartley (2001).

Market Failures and the Need for Global Collective Action

When guided by Adam Smith's "invisible hand," the unfettered pursuit of self-interest by individuals results in an efficient outcome. This reassuring guidance hinges on many understood or unstated assumptions, which have increasingly been shown by modern-day economics not to hold.[3] In particular, markets must be *complete* in the sense that things with value must be traded competitively. Competitiveness means that there must be a sufficient number of buyers and sellers to a transaction so that no one has a measurable influence on price. For complete markets, my actions as a producer or consumer must not have negative or positive consequences on others that go uncompensated. Moreover, information on prices, workers' effort, product quality, and output must be observable with little or no search costs or bribes to those in the know. The failure of these underlying assumptions to hold is easily understood during a walk in any city when taking a deep breath or listening to the surrounding sounds – uncompensated actions of others that dirty the air and make noises abound and affect one's well-being. Information imperfections arise when workers' efforts are unobservable, but they must later be compensated for their output, which may vary owing to random events – for example, Internet outages and faulty raw materials – beyond their control. Often, information is asymmetric in that one side of a transaction is knowledgeable while the other is not. For example, a person seeking insurance coverage knows the likely risks that he or she poses but has no incentive to reveal this information to the insurer. Uncompensated interdependencies and asymmetric information lead to market failures because resources do not go to their most-valued use.

Just as market failures plague exchanges among individual agents, they also plague transactions among nations, so that resources are misallocated internationally. Such market failures take varied forms including the depletion of the ozone layer, transference of transnational terrorism, failure to contain contagious diseases, abuse of antibiotics, and underinvestment in research and development. Many such challenges confront society regarding health, security, knowledge creation, and the environment. A portion of these exigencies is related to the process of globalization, which refers to the significant rise in transboundary transactions.

---

[3] See Stiglitz's (2000, 2002a) Nobel Prize lecture and an earlier paper on the increasing importance of market failures.

Globalization is an ongoing process of increasing transnational flows that fosters greater interdependence among nations, their people, and institutions. Globalization not only takes the form of transfrontier economic flows of goods and financial instruments but also consists of noneconomic exchanges (e.g., pollution, cyber viruses, revolutions, and information). Advances in technologies have shrunk the world and accelerated these transnational flows and interdependencies. For example, the increase in commercial air travel allows passengers to carry a deadly virus to cities near and far, so that plagues can disseminate rapidly. Moreover, computers facilitate the formation of terrorist networks that can coordinate swarm attacks globally. On the positive side, medical breakthroughs can benefit patients worldwide at a much faster rate than ever before owing to enhanced communication networks. Market failures at the international level are behind the need for global or transnational collective action where nations address concerns together.

Global Action or Inaction

Global contingencies may be met with action or inaction and, in both cases, the response may be either appropriate or inappropriate. If, for example, an alleged rogue nation really has no intention to threaten other nations or does not have the means to pose a real threat, then the best response is inaction by a superpower or the global community. In studying global contingencies, one must realize that action may be automatic in some circumstances owing to incentives. Following the four simultaneous hijackings on 11 September 2001 (henceforth called 9/11), many nations acted to address the al-Qaida threat: some countries froze assets of organizations suspected of supporting al-Qaida, while others took part in the US-led attack on the Taliban and al-Qaida in Afghanistan. Still others redoubled efforts to capture al-Qaida cells or share intelligence with the United States. Many nations showed their support by not condemning the US-led attack on Afghanistan. These acts of support were quite out of character with past reactions – for example, France required US planes to avoid its airspace during the US retaliatory raid on Libya on the morning of 15 April 1986,[4] which made for a more involved and dangerous

---

[4]   The US raid on Tripoli and other Libyan targets, including Muammar Qaddafi's residence at the Azizyah barracks, was in response to Libyan involvement in the bombing of the La Belle Discothèque on 4 April 1986 in West Berlin. On the Libyan raid and the discothèque bombing, see Mickolus, Sandler, and Murdock (1989, Volume 2, 365–7, 373–4). On the effectiveness of the raid, see Enders and Sandler (1993).

mission. By the summer of 2002, this international support was waning on the part of some nations.

Another successful response to a global challenge involves actions to eliminate the use of chlorofluorocarbons (CFCs), which deplete the stratospheric ozone layer that protects living organisms from harmful ultraviolet radiation. On 16 September 1987, the Montreal Protocol was framed and set explicit limits on ozone-depleting substances such as CFCs. This treaty entered into force on 1 January 1989 after the primary consumers and producers of CFCs had ratified the Protocol.[5] In the ensuing years, amendments to the treaty made much more stringent the required limits to CFC use. The number of nations ratifying the treaty grew until most had agreed to the Protocol's provision. More than most international agreements, the Montreal Protocol demonstrates that global collective action can be achieved under the right conditions, even if nations must sacrifice some autonomy. Any cheating on the treaty can be primarily traced to individual smugglers, rather than nations, who profit by selling CFCs below their high tax-inclusive price during the phasing-out period.

As international transactions have grown in recent decades, the global community has had to provide infrastructure to facilitate these exchanges.[6] International transportation and communication networks have had to address a number of collective action issues – system interoperability, accidents and mishaps, jurisdictional rights, and competitive practices (Zacher, 1996). In international shipping, the International Maritime Organization oversees international trade and institutes conventions on accidents and their prevention, innocent passage, pollution, and other issues. The International Civil Aviation Organization enacts regulations to promote air traffic flow and to maintain safety in the skies. For telecommunications, the International Telecommunication Union (ITU) establishes practices to curb signal interference and allocates the frequency bands of the electromagnetic spectrum to various specific purposes. The ITU also promotes the adoption of standardized equipment, which fosters interoperability.

For these regulatory regimes and others, nations have cooperated in not only providing a universal set of rules, but also in sacrificing some of their autonomy. A significant factor inducing nations to establish these international institutions and to submit to their regulations involves mutual self-interest in achieving the free flow of trade and communication among

---

[5] See Benedick (1991) and Barrett (1999) on ozone diplomacy and the Montreal Protocol.
[6] See Sandler (2003a) on the need for supranational infrastructure.

countries (Zacher, 1996). Apparently, the loss of autonomy is modest, so that the gain from the conventions does not have to be large to garner each nation a net gain. Because most nations already had similar regulations at home (e.g., allocating frequencies among alternative uses, procedures to avoid accidents at sea), the adoption of universal standards did not mark much of a departure from the status quo. Such conventions have more to do with restricting the way that firms and individuals can act rather than with restricting the autonomy of the participating governments, which had to approve the conventions. Governments saw greater national income coming from their adoption of uniform standards as trade and capital flows increased. By instituting common practices, these international regimes also limited the transaction costs by removing trade and communication impediments.

These examples demonstrate the possibility of global action under fortuitous circumstances that include the recognition of a shared threat in the case of 9/11, leadership by dominant nations in the case of the Montreal Protocol, and sufficient mutual self-interest for participants in the case of transnational infrastructure. Despite numerous obstacles, sovereign nations have achieved a wide range of coordinated actions on diverse issues. These successes provide encouragement.

The continued inability of the global community to develop a plan of action with respect to curbing the accumulation of GHGs indicates that some global challenges are very difficult to address. Another seemingly intractable contingency concerns reducing the income gaps between poor and rich nations. By the late 1990s, the richest 20% of nations earned 86% of the world gross domestic product (GDP), leaving the poorest 20% of nations to earn just 1% of the world GDP (United Nations Development Program, 1999). Virtually, any measure of economic activity – for example, world export market share, foreign direct investment, and communication infrastructure investment – would reflect similar disparities between the richest and poorest countries. This disparity has worsened by many measures in recent years. As increased demands surpass an ecosphere's regenerative capacity, increased environmental degradation will become a greater concern and reality. In some cases, environmental crises and resource scarcity (for example, with respect to water, strategic metals, and energy) may even result in war owing to the large consequences for the involved nations.[7] To address such crises and scarcities may require

---

[7] Such concerns are documented and expressed by Klare (2001) and Reuveny (2002).

losses in autonomy or else a degree of cooperation that nations have, heretofore, been unwilling or unable to accomplish. The large benefits associated with avoiding conflicts may result in tighter ties among nations than seen before or thought possible.

Global inaction may be based on a number of factors. First, the country-specific costs of action may dwarf the country's share of the resulting benefits. This scenario is likely when the country's action does not provide any actor-specific benefits that bolster the agent's share of group gains. Second, an absence of information is anticipated to inhibit decisiveness especially when actions require expenditures that are unnecessary under some resolutions of uncertainty. If these costs from action today are sufficiently great, inaction may be a more desirable response until the uncertainty is resolved. Third, global inaction is difficult to overcome when there is no leader nation that plays a major role in the contingency. Fourth, global inaction is more probable when a large number of nations are required for an effective solution. Fifth, the associated loss of autonomy that action necessitates is a crucial factor behind inertia because nations are loath to give up autonomy. To limit such sacrifices, nations introduce escape clauses into collective agreements that allow them to ignore an unanticipated and costly outcome. For instance, nations have left open the option not to abide by World Court judgments that are adverse, while permanent members of the Security Council can veto resolutions. Such clauses make some agreements virtually meaningless as instruments of cooperation.

Two Extreme Scenarios in a Global Village

One extreme vision of integration might best be characterized as the "Star Trek" scenario, where nations join larger collectives until a world federation evolves. Under this scenario, nations sacrifice some autonomy and grant a global body select authority over allocative and other economic policies with global consequences. With the rise of regionalism,[8] there has been a growth of regional collectives [e.g., the Andean Community, Central American Common Market, European Union (EU), and Mercado Commún del Sur] that provide some regionwide services, such as monetary union, infrastructure, and a common trade policy. In the Star Trek scenario, these regional collectives would acquire greater power over

---

[8] On the new regionalism, see Dodds (1998), Hettne, Inotai, and Sunkel (1999), and Stålgren (2000).

more economic decisions with regionwide consequences. Thus, regional trading blocs would become custom unions with responsibility for harmonizing a wider range of trading and taxing issues. In the long run, these custom unions would be transformed into more unified regional conglomerates that supply regional public goods whose benefits are received by member nations. As their responsibilities grow, such conglomerates would also address income redistribution (as has been true of the EU), stabilization policies, and growth issues. *Networks* of these regional collectives could constitute the global governance body at the peak of the federation. The nation would focus on those issues with just national consequences, leaving decisions with wider consequences to regional institutions or their network.

At the opposite extreme to the Star Trek solution is the *anarchic* supranational community where nations act independently in a Lockean natural state. Therefore, this view of transnational collective action has nations maintaining as much autonomy as possible. This so-called realist depiction casts nations as the main players. Any treaties or international organizations will remain weak and powerless to guide collective action and address resource misallocations that stem from uncompensated interdependencies. The need for greater cooperation on some issues, raised by globalization, is met with nations shunning cooperative responses. The most powerful nations will control the agenda and will agree to join only loose arrangements that maintain their autonomy and further their agenda. The number of nations will continue to increase and this growth in the number of agents will only heighten the difficulty of cooperation and the preservation of uncoordinated pursuit of national priorities. Such an anarchic state is not an equilibrium because the most powerful nations will serve to legitimize rules and institutions to limit the need to protect one's assets from plunder through conflict, pollution, or other means.

Given these two polar scenarios, what is the likely outcome of increased transnational flows in a globalized society? Neither extreme applies in practice: although nations will stay important and essential agents, they will sacrifice some autonomy to regional partnerships and, in a few select instances, to global collectives. Past examples provide a pretty good glimpse into tomorrow, not unlike a time travel. If a nation is *not viewed* as having sacrificed much autonomy with an agreement, then the circumstances for a collective agreement is conducive even when, in fact, a good deal of autonomy has been lost. That is, appearances matter greatly.

Thus, agreements on standards of commerce that augment a country's markets is likely signed even if the nation had utilized much different standards prior to the agreement, because the nation's concessionary behavior may be characterized by the world community as not surrendering much autonomy.

To illustrate the appearance issue, consider the Basle Capital Accord of July 1988 among the Group of 10 (G-10) nations, which sought to avert a "race to the bottom" in terms of falling capital requirements and supervisory practices (Arce and Sandler, 2002, p. 25; Reinicke, 1998, pp. 103–5). Prior to the Basle Accord, international banks practiced financial regulation arbitrage to augment their lending funds through weaker capital requirements and less stringent regulatory practices. As a consequence, banks exploited differences in margin and capital requirements, thus exposing depositors to greater risks. Among G-10 countries, the Basle Accord removed *competitive deregulation* used by banks of member nations to augment their loanable reserves. Nonmember nations of the Basle Accord became compelled to adopt identical requirements and practices to maintain the appearance of solvency. Such practices served as a solvency signal so that nonmembers mimicked the signatory countries' behavior. Among G-10 countries, the Basle Accord could be viewed as little loss in autonomy because all agreed that some level of capital and margin requirements was necessary, so that it was just a matter of agreeing on an acceptable standard.

Most importantly, existing banking practices in G-10 countries meant modest change in their status quo. The Basle Accord had more effect on those non-G-10 countries that took advantage of the lack of rules. Such countries de facto have to abide by the Basle Accord to attract deposits to their banks. In essence, the Basle signatories gave up little autonomy in the hopes of constraining the nonsignatories to hold up the same standards. Such actions by G-10 countries are a clever means for imposing governance without appearing to do so. A treaty among G-10 countries would gravitate toward the lowest common denominator among member states, while the same treaty among many more countries would likewise focus on the lowest common denominator of this larger set. By deciding capital requirements among just G-10 countries, the Basle Accord achieved a greater restriction than would have been achieved had a wider consensus been sought from a more heterogeneous group. The new regulation then became de facto the standards that nonsignatories are obliged to follow to signal their creditworthiness.

This tendency for agreements to be driven by the least willing or cooperative nation means that collectives are most apt to form among a small
group of select, but similar, countries. This similarity may be founded on
geography, level of development, language, shared values and culture,
and common experiences. As such, there is a logical justification for the
regionalism and regional collectives that have appeared increasingly during the last decade. Global collectives are harder to form unless a global
contingency provides a set of essential participants with a large net gain
from cooperation.

When nations seek collective solutions for some contingencies, two
behavioral patterns are anticipated. First, new collectives may begin small,
representing regional or key interests. This local origin highlights the
need to understand the new regionalism and to bolster the capacity of
regional banks (e.g., Inter-American Development Bank, Asian Development Bank, and African Development Bank) to finance region-based
projects. Although small compared to the World Bank, these regional
banks are uniquely positioned – owing to propinquity, shared values, and
language – to support regional collectives (Sandler, forthcoming). Second, there may be continued reliance on a few global multilateral institutions (e.g., the World Bank, World Health Organization, and the United
Nations) with which client states have a great deal of past experience in
addressing collective action problems, though not always successfully.[9]
These global collectives can draw finances from a large number of rich
members, while limiting transaction costs of additional tasks by utilizing common infrastructure.[10] At the global level, collective action can
arise from either networks of regional collectives or global collectives.
The Montreal Protocol represents the latter, but one must remember
that only eleven ratifiers were initially required for this treaty to enter
into force. Fewer than twenty countries originally ratified the Protocol
(Benedick, 1991; Congleton, 1992). A common message of this book
is to begin modestly with collective institutions and to let them evolve
as a core of essential participants gains experience with cooperation.
Even very humble cooperative frameworks permit enhanced actions over
time.

---

[9] In the case of supporting development, the World Bank has met with mixed success
(World Bank, 1998).

[10] The resulting savings on common costs give rise to economies of scope or a fall in the
average cost as more tasks are done in the same institution.

Premise of the Book

There is a human proclivity to draw stark distinctions and to represent complex reality with a simple characterization. Thus, the two polar views of transnational collective action – that is, the Star Trek global federation and fully sovereign nations acting independently – are often put forward. Idealists ascribe to the former and its promise of collective optimality, while realists believe in the latter and the absence of true collective action. Neither is very descriptive of how nations have tackled collective concerns. This book focuses on how nations actually address situations where action by two or more of them is necessary – that is, how collective action is accomplished at the transnational level. Modern principles of collective action, derived from Olson (1965) and the research that his seminal work spawned, can inform us about global futures regarding a host of contingencies that are both real and imagined.

Collective action prescriptions and predictions hinge on at least six primary considerations: (1) the size of the group, (2) the composition of the group, (3) the rules governing the interaction (e.g., institutional arrangements), (4) the strategic nature of the interaction (e.g., is it recurring or once over), (5) the underlying information of the participants, and (6) the sequence of interactions. Olson investigated just the first three influences, while subsequent analyses examined all six factors.[11] As political economy becomes more interested in strategic behavior, it is inevitable that strategic interactions, information considerations, and the sequence of actions gain prominence. The classic influences of group size, group composition, and institutional rules may, at times, be turned on their head owing to these latter considerations. For example, we shall later discover that whether or not the large nation is exploited by the small in regard to collective action may hinge on who acts first. As such, additional factors enriched the study of collective action; simple rules of thumb are less apt to hold. Thus, greater group size may not be a clear recipe for collective action failure. Despite a larger number of scenarios, clear-cut cases do exist for drawing definitive conclusions. There are just more such cases.

A clear example of this enrichment has to do with the underlying games associated with collective action concerns at the national and transnational levels. Even twenty years ago, collective action problems were

---

[11] This is clear from Hardin (1982) and Sandler (1992), as well as the vast literature that these books surveyed.

equated with the Prisoners' Dilemma game, where agents are motivated by self-interest to settle on a strategy from which all players can improve their welfare had an alternative strategy been chosen (see, for example, Hardin, 1982). The study of collective action now recognizes that many game forms may apply. Moreover, some forms may be quite optimistic in their prediction of successful outcomes. In some instances, institutional rules can be tailored to induce a supportive strategic interaction, thereby eliminating the need for further policy intervention.[12]

The modern view of collective action is that not all such problems abide by the same rules or prescriptions because strategic interactions may differ drastically even when the problems appear to be very similar. Moreover, a proactive design of the rules may foster cooperation without the need for costly government intervention or structures. Any explanation of transnational collective action must account for the rich set of players, such as nongovernmental organizations (NGOs), charitable foundations, multinational firms, regional trading blocs, and multilateral development institutions. Efforts to identify some guiding principles for action and inaction are needed to deal with global contingencies. One must not lose sight that inaction may, under some circumstances, be the best response. By identifying those cases where incentives are not supportive of an effective response, analysts can direct resources to the most recalcitrant interdependencies where payoffs are high and cooperation is unlikely.

A Word of Caution

Many transnational concerns are not well understood. As already mentioned, a good example is global warming where natural cycles of atmospheric cooling and warming have not been fully identified. In addition, other factors integral to the process have not been properly explained so that the extent of global warming and its geographical distribution are still conjecture. Few people dispute that the accumulation of GHGs will eventually heat the atmosphere, other things being constant. Nevertheless, the temporal and spatial dimensions of this heating are not really known. There may even be intervening considerations that may delay global warming well into the future. Since action has some irreversible and costly implications, it may pay to delve deeper into the issue

---

[12] This is the message contained in Sandler (1998), in which institutional innovations are related to the underlying game.

before embarking on a course of action.[13] Such uncertainty is frequently an impediment to collective action.

Much uncertainty involves resource scarcity. The discovery of oil reserves during my lifetime has continuously caused oil scarcity to be revised. Even the natural cycles involving the replenishment of underground aquifers are poorly understood, so that dire predictions have been revised. I cannot overemphasize the importance of information acquisition and the need for skepticism when investigating global challenges. The reader should not conclude that I view all such global challenges as true crises. "The jury is out" on many global concerns until much more is known. For such issues, the discussion involves the prognosis for action once the uncertainty is eventually resolved.

Intended Audience

This book is intended for a fairly broad readership comfortable with elementary economic principles. This reasoning is at the level of a good introductory course where the student learns the workings of markets. Nevertheless, I will review essential concepts to ensure that readers have the same definitions in mind. In short, I do not assume much economic sophistication on behalf of the reader.

As needed, I will introduce simple notions of game theory and strategic behavior because these concepts are essential to the understanding of how independent agents interact in an interdependent world. For Adam Smith, strategic behavior was not essential because he primarily examined competitive economies where the behavior of an individual agent has no strategic value as the agent's actions are swamped by the actions of so many other agents. The workings of the invisible hand require that the actions of everyone bring about a desired outcome – the good of society – that no single individual's action can achieve or undo. When Smith's invisible hand applies, no one has a rationale to unilaterally change behavior because there are no better terms of trade. Competitive markets eliminate the strategic value of individual actions. Although Smith recognized strategic interactions for noncompetitive markets, he did not provide a careful study of such interactions. For transnational interactions, however, individual behavior – say, of a nation or a regional trade pact – has a discernible influence on the actions or reactions of similar agents. As

---

[13] On the delay of investment decisions, see Ko, Lapan, and Sandler (1992).

.

such, these strategic interdependencies are important to investigate if likely outcomes are to be anticipated. For the purposes of the book, only elementary game-theoretic notions are required in which no foreknowledge of these tools is presumed. When appropriately applied, game theory can be enlightening.

The analysis in this book should interest economists, political scientists, lawyers, social scientists, and others who want to learn about international contingencies, both real and imagined, that are newsworthy. In recent years, a host of global challenges have occupied not only policymakers but also citizens who are trying to understand the growing number of transnational exchanges. The book may also provide insights to policymakers and the many dedicated people at NGOs and multilateral aid institutions who address international problems. To be an informed citizen in today's world requires knowledge of global contingencies, their implications, and their resolution. By analyzing these issues, this book should have wide appeal.

Plan of the Book

The remainder of the book contains eleven chapters. The next three chapters are concerned with putting forth the underlying analysis that is then applied to the study of global challenges. In Chapter 2, the principles of collective action are presented in their classical and updated forms. Elementary game-theoretic notions are also introduced. Chapter 3 presents the modern analysis of market failures where the need for collective action is prevalent. Market failures involve pure public goods whose benefits are nonrival among recipients and available to payers and nonpayers alike. Other important market failures requiring transnational collective action include noncompensated interdependencies (known as externalities), open-access common property, and asymmetric information. In Chapter 4, the analysis is extended to include transnational public goods whose benefits spill over international borders so that two or more countries are affected. This chapter focuses on how these goods are financed. Jurisdictional and institutional issues are also considered. How supranational institutions are designed in practice is presented by examining how real-world institutions (for example, the International Monetary Fund and United Nations) finance their supply of transnational public goods.

The next seven chapters are devoted to the application of the analysis to specific global issues. Global health is the focus of Chapter 5. Health practices in one country can have profound implications for neighbors and even the world community; for example, global actions are needed to eradicate diseases or to redress poverty-based diseases. The need for collective action for global health transgresses both political and generational borders. In Chapter 6, the issue of foreign aid is investigated. The good intentions of wealthy countries to foster development and curb global inequality has had very mixed success. Chapter 6 evaluates past, current, and future strategies to bolster development.

Chapters 7–9 concern security worries during a time when the United States represents the only superpower. Even though the end to the Cold War promised a safer world, security risks abound with rogue nations, transnational terrorism, and civil wars. Chapter 7 addresses the issue of rogue states that allegedly pose a threat to other nations through their weapons of mass destruction. How the world community confronts such states represents a tricky collective action dilemma. In Chapter 8, the threat of international terrorism is analyzed. Although this threat has been a worldwide concern since the Israeli–Arab conflicts of the late 1960s,[14] the events of 9/11 underscore the destruction that terrorist incidents can wreak. International terrorism represents a collective action conundrum insofar as terrorists have formed effective networks while targeted nations have not. As a consequence, terrorists are able to utilize their strongest components to attack the most vulnerable points within targeted nations. Chapter 9 investigates the challenges posed by civil wars. In 2001, there were 34 armed conflicts, of which all but the India–Pakistan conflict over Kashmir were civil wars (Gleditsch et al., 2002, pp. 615–6). These conflicts present security risks not only to neighbors but also to the world at large. Global security can be affected by a disruption of the supplies of essential raw materials, the dissemination of terrorists to foreign capitals, or the spread of the conflict to other regions. The decision to intervene and the form of such intervention are difficult collective action problems that the world has increasingly had to face since the end to the Cold War (Sandler and Hartley, 1999; Shimizu and Sandler, 2002).

Chapters 10 and 11 concern the environment and resource issues. In Chapter 10, atmospheric pollution is studied so as to contrast the success

---

[14] Mickolus (1980) presents a chronology of international terrorism events for 1968–79. The birth of modern-day transnational terrorism started in 1968 (Hoffman, 1998).

of the Montreal Protocol on limiting stratospheric ozone-depleting substances and the failure of the Kyoto Protocol on stemming the rate of emission of GHGs. The comparison of these two cases illustrates that two seemingly similar global public good problems may have vastly different collective action prognoses owing to institutional and other relevant factors. By identifying these factors, I am able to isolate parameters that distinguish global action from inaction. At the end of the chapter, a similar exercise involves a comparison between the success in stemming sulfur emissions and the much more modest success in curbing nitrogen oxides emissions; both kinds of emissions lead to acid rain. Chapter 11 on the "final frontier" examines collective action problems concerning outer space and its resources, where market success and failures are relevant. From space platforms for warfare to the diversion of asteroids on a collision course with earth, outer space offers many collective action issues.

Chapter 12 not only summarizes the basic messages of the book but also looks to the future. Thus, likely institutional changes are discussed and tomorrow's global challenges are predicted. Finally, the chapter speculates on the future of globalization.

2

"With a Little Help from My Friends": Principles of Collective Action

Collective action arises when the efforts of two or more individuals are needed to achieve an outcome. From the time when humans first walked upright, individuals have relied on the actions of the group for defense, fuel, food (for example, hunting large animals), reconnaissance, charity, and safety. By its nature, collective action involves interdependency among individuals in which the contributions or efforts of one individual influence the actions of other individuals, thus implying a strategic interaction. As society becomes more complex, the need for collective action grows. Globalization has taken this need to new heights. Even the existence of well-functioning markets depends on collective action in the form of contract and regulatory law, standards of weights and measures, a justice system, police, and infrastructure (for example, transportation and communication networks) that provide for the unfettered exchange of property rights.

Collective action is partly associated with the provision of pure public goods whose benefits are nonrival *and* nonexcludable. Benefits are nonrival when a unit of the good can be consumed by one individual without detracting, in the slightest, from the consumption opportunities still available for others from the *same* unit. Like magic, a nonrival good can be used by more and more people without a noticeable degradation in quality or quantity. Reducing air pollution gives a nonrival benefit, since my breathing the cleaner air does not reduce the benefits of the improved air quality available for others. Similarly, uncovering the cure for a disease helps everyone – an application of the cure to one person does not limit the cure's application to others. If the benefits of a good are available to all once the good is supplied, then its benefits are nonexcludable. Air pollution removal is nonexcludable because it is impractical and undesirable to keep others from breathing the cleaner air. When a good's benefits are nonexcludable, many individuals will fail to contribute because they will get the good's benefits free once provided by others. Such actions permit free riders to save income that they can spend on excludable goods.

By displaying both nonrival and nonexcludable benefits, a *pure* public good presents a collective action problem. Nonexcludability will result in too little of the good being supplied owing to free riding, while nonrivalry means that exclusion, if feasible, will reduce social welfare by denying consumption to those whose derived benefits are less than the price. This welfare loss arises when there is no cost associated with extending consumption rights to anyone who derives satisfaction from the good, even when this satisfaction is rather small. The conundrum for society is how to provide a public good if it cannot recoup its costs by charging a price. Public provision may or may not be a viable alternative. Since the publication of Mancur Olson's *The Logic of Collective Action* (1965), public goods have served as the "poster-child" collective action problem. In reality, public goods are just one kind of collective action problem; others include externalities (or uncompensated interdependencies), common property, and other market failures (see Chap. 3).

Collective action failures, associated with public goods and other scenarios, rest on a single basic premise: *individual rationality is not sufficient for collective rationality*. That is, individuals who abide by the tenets of rationality[1] may make choices from which the collective is left in an inferior position. Individual rationality requires the maximization of an individual's well-being subject to a budget or resource constraint. Rationality implies predictability so that alterations to tastes or one's constraints lead to foreseeable behavioral changes. Moreover, rationality means that well-informed agents obtain their best opportunity, given their constraints; they do not choose an affordable or feasible outcome that is less desirable to other available outcomes. A collective action failure follows when the

---

[1]   This premise of individual rationality requires well-behaved tastes that are monotonic, consistent, and continuous. Monotonicity requires an individual to prefer a market basket that has more of at least one good and no less of any other goods. Consistency of tastes means that if a consumer considers bundle A to be at least as good as bundle B, and also views bundle B to be at least as good as bundle C, then this consumer must consider bundle A to be at least as good as bundle C. Taste continuity implies that all bundles can be ranked. Often, a fourth condition on individual tastes requires a person's willingness to trade one good for another to depend on his or her relative holdings of the goods: goods in relatively great supply have a lower substitution value – that is, the individual is generous in trading the abundant good for those in short supply.

rational decisions of the group's individuals result in an inefficient collective choice from which individuals are powerless to change. In the movie, *A Beautiful Mind*, John Nash indicates his recognition of the basic premise of such collective action failures when he exclaims that his dissertation "proves Adam Smith wrong." That is, the selfish pursuit of individuals' well-being may not be led, as if by an invisible hand, to the common good of society.

Imagine for a moment, a world devoid of collective action. There would be no nations, no armies, no laws, no weather forecasts, no culture, no accumulated knowledge, no roads, no governments, no police, and no charity. To protect one's belongings, each person would have to use scarce resources to build defenses or stand guard, both of which detract from productive activities. Collective action is anticipated to evolve from this natural state. Strong individuals would emerge who are specialized in providing protection.[2] If these protectors can offer their services for fewer resources than those required to defend one's own possessions, then defense would be collectivized, not unlike the services of the feudal lords. These protectors would amass weapons and armies and would eventually become the government whose legitimacy derives from its protection of lives and property. With time, this government would take on additional collective activities, such as building roads and schools. The government would enact laws and create courts to adjudicate these laws in order to limit its resource expenditures. With internal order established, governments can turn their attention to external threats. Thus, there seems to be a natural tendency for some level of collective action to emerge even in an anarchic state.

The study of collective action investigates the factors that motivate individuals to coordinate their activities to improve their collective well-being. Why are some forms of collective action (for example, a convention for which side of the road to drive on) self-enforcing, while other forms (such as contributing to a pure public good) are not? What are the underlying parameters or considerations behind people's willingness to act to achieve a collective good? What is the prognosis for global collective action in light of globalization and the increasing number of associated collective action concerns? The primary purpose of this chapter is to address these questions while displaying some general principles of collective action that

---

[2] This origin of government from an anarchic state is based on the analysis of Bush and Mayer (1974).

can be applied to a host of exigencies confronting humankind in an age of globalization. I am particularly interested in analyzing the strategic foundations for collective action with the use of some elementary game theory. General principles of collective action are derived for the interaction between two or more generic agents, which can represent individuals, firms, nations, organizations, or some combination of these agents.

I begin with an analysis of a Prisoners' Dilemma game to illustrate a pure public good, collective action scenario. An essential insight is that collective action failures need not stem from the overused Prisoners' Dilemma explanation. I then distill some general principles of collective action from Olson's (1965) seminal book. Although these principles hold in numerous applications, their validity is based on many unstated assumptions, which are highlighted. Next, I more fully relate collective action to some alternative game forms. I end with a prognosis for global collective action.

Prisoners' Dilemma

The three identifying characteristics of a noncooperative game are the set of players, their strategy sets, and the resulting payoffs for their strategic choices. In a noncooperative game, players act independently to pick strategies that appear to be best for them. Although the Prisoners' Dilemma is just one of 78 distinct 2×2 matrix forms for two-player games, it is used frequently in international relations applications. The game is illustrated for a two-agent contribution decision, in which agents A and B must each choose between two strategies: contribute one unit or no units of the public good. To get the payoffs associated with the four strategic combinations, I must specify the benefits and costs derived from the contributions to the public good. Suppose that the cost of each contributed unit is 8. Further suppose that a unit of the public good yields 6 in benefits to each player, regardless of the contributor, because of nonexclusion and nonrivalry of benefits. In Figure 2.1, the top matrix indicates the payoffs for the four possible strategy combinations: no contributions, B alone contributes a unit, A alone contributes a unit, and both players contribute a unit for a total of two units. The left-hand payoff in each cell of the matrix is that of player A, whereas the right-hand payoff in each cell is that of player B. The rows denote the two strategies of A, whereas the columns indicate the two strategies of B.

If no one contributes, then there are no benefits or costs so that each player receives 0 in the upper left-hand cell in matrix a. If, however, B

	B	
	Do Not Contribute	Contribute
Do Not Contribute	Nash 0, 0	6, –2
Contribute	–2, 6	4, 4

A is the row player.

a. Contribution Prisoners' Dilemma

	B	
	Do Not Contribute	Contribute
Do Not Contribute	Nash 2, 2	4, 1
Contribute	1, 4	3, 3

A is the row player.

b. Ordinal representation of Prisoners' Dilemma

Figure 2.1. Prisoners' Dilemma

contributes a unit and *A* free rides, then *B* receives a net payoff of –2 (= 6 – 8) as provision costs of 8 are deducted from the payoff of 6, while *A* gets 6 from the free ride supplied by *B* (see upper right-hand cell in matrix *a*). These payoffs are reversed when *B* free rides on *A*'s contribution. When both players contribute a unit of the good, each receives a net gain of 4 (= 2 × 6 – 8) as 12 in benefits, with 6 garnered from each unit, are reduced by the players' provision costs of 8. Player *A* has an obvious choice to contribute nothing, because the associated payoffs are larger than the corresponding payoffs for contributing. That is, 0 is a better payoff than –2, and 6 is a better payoff than 4. Similarly the best independent strategy for *B* is also not to contribute, insofar as the game is symmetric. A strategy, such as not contributing, that provides a greater payoff regardless of the other player's action is termed a *dominant strategy* and figures prominently throughout the book. In matrix *a* of Figure 2.1, both players' dominant strategy is not to contribute.

The mutual no-contribution strategy combination in the top left-hand cell is a *Nash equilibrium from which neither player would unilaterally alter his or her strategy* if given the opportunity. If, at this equilibrium, player A (or B) alone changes to contributing a unit, then his or her payoff is reduced by 2 (that is, from 0 to -2). A Nash equilibrium can also be described as each player choosing his or her best response to the other player's best response. In the Prisoners' Dilemma, a player's best response is the dominant strategy. As all players exercise their dominant strategy, a Nash equilibrium results.[3] Although playing one's dominant strategy in a Prisoners' Dilemma leads to an equilibrium from which neither player would regret his or her action *alone*, both players could be made better off if they *both* changed their strategy. Mutual regret is the hallmark of the Prisoners' Dilemma. If the players could agree to cooperate and contribute, then all would be better off by 4 over the Nash equilibrium. Unfortunately, such an agreement may not be honored. When, say, player A knows that B will abide by the agreement and contribute, A is better off reneging and free riding, since a payoff of 6 exceeds that of 4. The "temptation" payoff of 6 exceeds the reward of 4 from cooperating.

The Prisoners' Dilemma has a configuration of ordinal payoffs that uniquely distinguishes it from other games. To accomplish this identification, each payoff is rank ordered from highest to lowest, in which the highest payoff of 6 is assigned an ordinal rank of 4, the next best an ordinal rank of 3, the third best an ordinal rank of 2, and the lowest an ordinal rank of 1. The resulting ordinal payoff matrix is depicted in the bottom matrix of Figure 2.1. Any two-person payoff matrix that possesses the same ordinal payoff pattern as this bottom matrix is a Prisoners' Dilemma.[4] When expressed in an ordinal form, the dominant strategy remains the same – to not contribute – since $2 > 1$ and $4 > 3$. Moreover, the Nash equilibrium is also the same. Thus, many of a game's strategic features are captured by the ordinal representation.[5]

---

[3] The intersection of dominant strategies, if one exists for each player, yields a Nash equilibrium, but a Nash equilibrium need not be the intersection dominant strategies (Binmore, 1992).

[4] If the two strategies were interchanged in the rows and columns, then the distinguishing feature of the Prisoners' Dilemma would have the (3, 3) and (2, 2) payoffs switched along the main diagonal and the 1s and 4s switched along the off-diagonal. This alternative pattern also identifies the Prisoners' Dilemma.

[5] Not all strategic features are captured. For example, a mixed strategy, where probability weights are applied to pure strategies, cannot be constructed for an ordinal representation. Mixed strategies are not relevant to a Prisoners' Dilemma.

	Number of GHGs-reducing nations other than nation i							
	0	1	2	3	4	5	6	7
Nation i Does Not Cut GHGs by 10%	Nash 0	6	12	18	24	30	36	42
Nation i Does Cut GHGs by 10%	-2	4	10	16	22	28	34	Social Optimum 40

Figure 2.2. Eight-nation Prisoners' Dilemma

Next, I turn to an *n*-player Prisoners' Dilemma ($n = 8$), since this representation will make concrete some of the Olsonian principles of collective action discussed at a later point in the chapter. To give the example real-world relevance, I consider the reduction of the emissions of greenhouse gases (GHGs), which can trap solar energy in the atmosphere thereby warming the climate of the planet. Each of eight identical nations are allowed two strategies: to cut or not to cut GHG emissions by 10%. Cutting these emissions costs the reducing nation 8, while benefiting it and each of the other seven nations by 6 apiece so that benefits are nonrival. For simplicity, I assume that all eight nations are identical.

In Figure 2.2, the columns refer to the actions of the other seven nations, and the two rows denote the strategy of the *i*th representative nation. The payoffs listed in each of the sixteen cells are those of nation *i*, based on its decision to reduce GHG emissions or not and the decisions of the other nations. The payoffs in Figure 2.2 are computed as follows: Consider the top row of payoffs, representing nation *i*'s free-rider response when it relies on the emission-reducing actions of others. *Each* nation that limits pollution by 10% confers a gain of 6 on nation *i* at no expense to *i*. Thus, nation *i* gains 6 when one nation cuts its GHG emissions, 12 when two nations cut their GHG emissions, and so on. Next consider the bottom row, corresponding to nation *i* cutting its emissions by 10%, with and without similar responses from others. If nation *i* reduces emissions alone, then it achieves a net payoff of −2, equal to benefits of 6 less reduction costs of 8. If, however, another nation also reduces its emissions, then nation *i* receives 4, which equals its gross benefits of 12 ($= 2 \times 6$) less its own costs of 8. Gross benefits are 12 because the nation's reduction and that of another provide 6 in benefits apiece. The other net payoffs in the bottom row are computed in a similar fashion, where the net payoff equals 6 times the number of reducers (including nation *i*) less 8 in costs.

The dominant strategy is for nation i not to cut GHG emissions, because the net payoffs in the top row are each greater by 2 than the corresponding payoffs in the bottom row. That is, the difference in corresponding payoffs between the two rows equal the individual costs (c_i) to nation i less its derived individual benefits (b_i) from reducing its own emissions. As nation i and, therefore, the other seven nations play their dominant strategy of doing nothing, a Nash equilibrium results where no one cuts emissions. In Figure 2.2, nation i will not move unilaterally from the indicated Nash equilibrium because 0 is a preferred payoff to -2. The social optimum results only when all eight nations limit their pollution and receive 40 in benefits apiece for a total of 320. This is a better overall outcome than just seven nations reducing their emissions, in which the sole free rider receives 42 and the other seven receive just 34 for a grand total of 280. This single free rider outcome is not sustainable as an equilibrium because every nation will seek the 42 payoff of being the sole free rider and no one will cut emissions.

This game representation can accommodate any number of players. If the number is an unspecified n, then there must be $n - 1$ columns to represent the actions of the nations other than i. Not cutting emissions is still the dominant strategy, insofar as the top row's payoffs still exceed the corresponding payoffs in the bottom row by $c_i - b_i$. The Nash equilibrium continues to involve no one contributing. The social optimum involves all n nations cutting their emissions for a per nation benefit of $nb_i - c_i$ and an aggregate benefit of $n^2 b_i - nc_i$.

This n-nation scenario has many global counterparts provided that $c_i - b_i > 0$.[6] Examples may include other pollution-reducing problems, retaliating against a state-sponsor of terrorism, preempting a rogue nation, ending a foreign civil war, and redistributing income to less-developed countries. If, however, $b_i - c_i > 0$, so that the net gain from acting alone is positive, then the payoffs in the bottom row of the matrix (not displayed) would exceed the top row, and the dominant strategy would be to reduce pollutants. Moreover, the Nash equilibrium would correspond to the social optimum where every nation reduces its pollution. Action to provide the public good is then incentive compatible. Thus, the net

---

[6] In the experimental literature, the "linear symmetric variable contribution environment" assumes that $c_i - b_i > 0$, so that complete free riding characterizes the Nash equilibrium and everyone contributing represents the social optimum (Cornes and Sandler, 1996, pp. 510–13; Isaac, McCue, and Plott, 1985; Isaac, Walker, and Thomas, 1984).

payoffs from individual action is an essential consideration. Suppose that $b_i - c_i > 0$ for just a subset of nations. In this scenario, this subset will provide the public good and the others will free ride.

If each of the payoffs from the free rider can be sufficiently reduced, then pollution reduction can be transformed into a dominant strategy in Figure 2.2. Any punishment greater than 2 will work.[7] The punishment solution to free riding begs the question because the presence of an enforcement mechanism acts like a pure public good whose benefits are themselves nonexcludable and nonrival. As such, the institution of an enforcement mechanism poses its own Prisoners' Dilemma. This is well illustrated by the absence of such mechanisms to back up United Nations conventions and resolutions, which are violated daily. During 2003, North Korea's defiant violation of the Nuclear Nonproliferation Treaty has been met with universal condemnation, but no enforcer has come forward. Institutional innovations other than enforcement must be devised to promote collective action in such cases.

Collective Action and Prisoners' Dilemma Games

There is an essential insight to the relationship between collective action and the underlying game that has been frequently misunderstood in the literature; for example, Hardin (1982, p. 25) states that "Indeed, the problem of collective action and the Prisoners' Dilemma are essentially the same."[8] Mancur Olson once told me that he had also equated collective action failures and Prisoners' Dilemma until he read my earlier book on collective action (Sandler, 1992). There is no question that Prisoners' Dilemmas give rise to collective action failures. By using their dominant strategy, individuals end up at a Nash equilibrium from which all can be made better off. Rational individual action leads to an undesirable outcome for the group. Selfish pursuits do not benefit the group.

It is the reverse statement – all collective action failures are Prisoners' Dilemmas – that is false. To illustrate, consider the following scenario. Each of two individuals can supply one or no units of a public good; however, a minimal threshold must be met before a benefit of 8 is received by all. Unit provision cost is assumed to be 4. In the top payoff matrix

---

[7] Any punishment greater than $c_i - b_i$ will serve the purpose.

[8] Although this statement is incorrect, the Hardin (1982) book is excellent and is especially insightful in its extended discussion on conventions and norms.

a. Assurance game

	B: 0 units	B: 1 unit
A: 0 units	Nash 0, 0	0, –4
A: 1 unit	–4, 0	Nash 4, 4

b. Coordination game

	B: 0 units	B: 1 unit
A: 0 units	0, 0 *1, 1*	Nash 6, 2 *4, 3*
A: 1 unit	Nash 2, 6 *3, 4*	2, 2 *3, 3*

c. Chicken game

	B: 0 units	B: 1 unit
A: 0 units	–3, –3	Nash 6, –2
A: 1 unit	Nash –2, 6	4, 4

Figure 2.3. Some alternative game forms for collective action

in Figure 2.3, the resulting game is displayed. If no one contributes, then net payoffs are, of course, 0 for both players. When just one individual provides a unit, the contributor suffers the costs without any gain for a net payoff of –4, while the noncontributor receives no free-rider benefits because the threshold of two units has not been reached. In the lower right-hand cell, both players supply a unit and the threshold is attained, giving each contributor a net gain of 4 (= 8 − 4). There is no dominant strategy in this game, since from either player's perspective, 0 > −4, but

$0 < 4$. There are two Nash equilibriums if both players choose the same strategy.[9] These equilibriums are along the main diagonal where matching behavior is practiced – that is, either both individuals provide a unit or neither supplies a unit. An assurance game applies if two nations have insufficient firefighters to suppress a forest fire on their common border, but together they possess sufficient firefighters to put out the fire. Some security or pollution pacts may abide by this minimal threshold scenario so that an assurance game is germane. In one Star Trek episode, two enemy ships had to work in unison to defeat a common threat that neither could defend alone; thus, an assurance game applied.

The assurance game has vastly different collective action implications than the Prisoners' Dilemma.[10] Although the collective action prognosis is more encouraging with an assurance game since one of the Nash equilibriums is also the social optimum, collective action failures may still occur if either the other Nash equilibrium is chosen or else the off-diagonal cells are chosen in the top matrix. Because there is no dominant strategy, the required coordination may not be achieved as players act independently. One means for assuring the optimal outcome is to take a leadership role by contributing. Once a player either sees the leadership or believes the other player's stated intention to lead, he or she will also contribute because a payoff of 4 is better than a payoff of 0 from free riding. Unlike a Prisoners' Dilemma, the sequence of moves matters in an assurance game where the first mover provides incentives for the other player to copy the displayed behavior. As a would-be leader, one can demonstrate intentions by taking actions beforehand to bind oneself to a strategic choice – say, through a public announcement or instituting an automatic punishment mechanism for reneging. Contracts or agreements to cooperate under assurance scenarios are self-enforcing, unlike Prisoners' Dilemmas where abiding by an agreement tempts the other player to cheat so as to achieve the highest payoff.[11]

Consider next a slight, but important, variant displayed in matrix *b* in Figure 2.3 where *only* the first unit supplied yields benefits of 6 to everyone. This scenario applies to uncovering intelligence, finding cures,

---

[9] These are the "pure-strategy" equilibriums, where each player chooses a single strategy and does not randomize between strategies. The mixed-strategy Nash equilibrium for this game has each player choosing each strategy half of the time – that is, with a probability of 50%.

[10] On *n*-person versions of the assurance game, see Sandler (1992, pp. 44–9).

[11] On self-enforcement, see Barrett (1994), Runge (1984), Sandler (1997, 1998), and Sen (1967).

isolating bacteria, or neutralizing a terrorist group; once the chore is accomplished, additional efforts provide no further benefits. The per-unit cost of supply is now assumed to be 4. Absence of any contributions means zero payoffs in the upper left-hand cell of matrix *b*. If just one player contributes or accomplishes the task, then this contributor nets 2 $(= 6 - 4)$ and the free rider receives 6 in the two off-diagonal cells. When both players contribute, each receives 2, equal to the difference between the benefits of 6, derived from just the first unit supplied, less the pro-vision cost of 4. This *coordination* game, as it is called, has no dominant strategy but possesses two pure-strategy Nash equilibriums in which one person contributes and the other free rides. Collective failure may result because an absence of successful coordination may end with the socially inferior diagonal cells being reached.

The bottom matrix represents a *chicken game* in which the absence of action can lead to dire consequences. Consider a city threatened with a flood whose residents must decide whether to sandbag the river banks prior to an impending (certain) flood. The height of the sandbags is a pub-lic good. Providing no sandbags whatsoever will result in harm to every-one when the flood comes, so that the payoffs from collective inaction are negative rather than zero. These dire consequences can be avoided if someone acts. The game is named chicken because each player would like to hold out so that the other player acts (or "chickens out"). Similarly, doing nothing about a pollution threat may give negative, not zero, pay-offs and a chicken game scenario. To illustrate the chicken game, suppose that the underlying contribution game is the same as the upper Prisoners' Dilemma game of Figure 2.1, except that a harm of −3 befalls both players if nothing is contributed. Otherwise, the payoffs in matrix *c* of Figure 2.3 are those in the top matrix of Figure 2.1. The chicken game is a type of coordination game with no dominant strategy and two pure-strategy Nash equilibriums, where a single player contributes. The chicken game's Nash equilibriums are not social optimums because mutual contributions imply 8 in aggregate benefits, which exceed those of 4 at the equilibriums.[12] A collective failure is ever present because the chicken game may result in an even worse outcome if each player does nothing by assuming that the other will act, so that each ends up with −3. Leadership will result in a Nash equilibrium but not the social optimum, which requires even more

---

[12] If the payoffs in the chicken game are ordinally ranked, then the ordinal pattern would resemble the Prisoners' Dilemma, except that the 1s and 2s in the bottom matrix of Figure 2.1 would be interchanged.

coordination than merely taking the initiative. In a chicken game, leadership involves not contributing and trying to stick the other player with the action.

One Size Fits All?

These alternative game forms indicate that collective action problems need not be associated with a Prisoners' Dilemma. In fact, most collective action problems are not Prisoners' Dilemmas but some other relevant game. There are many other germane game forms than the four depicted thus far. This insight has important policy implications. To prescribe the right remedy, the strategic aspects of a collective action problem must be identified: one size does *not* fit all. Effective solutions for some collective action failures may be ineffective for others; for example, leadership works for the middle matrix but not for the bottom matrix of Figure 2.3. Although general principles of collective action encapsulate useful rules of thumb, the richness of underlying game forms means that any general principles must have many exceptions. The study of collective action permits far less generalization than usually presupposed. This is a recurring theme of this book. Because the rules of the game, as embodied by institutions, determine the underlying strategic form, institutional change can, at times, circumvent collective action difficulties.

Longer Viewpoints

Let us return to the Prisoners' Dilemma scenario, but one in which the interaction is repeated. Suppose that two nations border a common lake, befouled by discharges from firms. Further suppose that the net difference between individual benefits and costs from curbing pollution is negative so that a classic Prisoners' Dilemma applies. If the interaction occurs just once, then the expected outcome is that nothing is done to ameliorate the pollution. Even if the interaction occurs twice, still nothing is anticipated to be done, because far-sighted players who look ahead to the second period realize that the dominant strategy is to do nothing given that there is no tomorrow. With no action anticipated in the second period, the dominant strategy is also for neither to act in the first period. In fact, there should be no action in any period when there are a fixed, known number of interactions at the outset.

Things may change drastically when there are many tomorrows – either an unknown number or too many to count – then each player's dominant strategy may be to reduce pollutants, especially when each applies a *tit-for-tat* strategy of continuing these reductions until one's opponent stops limiting pollution. Following such a transgression, the tit-for-tat player will begin curbing again once the opponent does so.[13] In general, the tit-for-tat strategy is to copy the opponent's strategy from the previous period. Such dynamic strategies, with their threat-backed inducement to cooperate, may result in successful collective action. No wonder that successful societies and institutions try to instill a sense of permanency among members. The saying "long live the king" has real importance for successful collective action. Institutions (or universities) where a large number of administrators are temporary or acting will be plagued by all kinds of ineffective collective action. Governments try to give the impression of being everlasting through their monumental buildings, harking back to a classical age. This same air of longevity is fostered by organizations as they try to instill in their members norms of behavior, meant to further the well-being of the group. Long-lived institutions display their date of founding prominently and often.

Each of the other game forms – for example, assurance, chicken, and coordination – can be analyzed as repeated games. Tit-for-tat as well as other dynamic strategies, including less-forgiving ones, may result in Nash equilibriums for repeated plays of these other game forms. Repeated interactions bolsters collective action success. This holds not only based on strategic factors, but also based on social considerations. When agents interact repeatedly, norms and social conventions evolve whose legitimacy rests on their ability to limit transaction costs (as roles are learned and expectations are formed) and their effectiveness to promote the group's well-being (Hardin, 1982; North, 1990). The importance of repeated interactions highlights that these institutions must be first formed if their advantages are to be exploited. Thus, institutional formation becomes a beacon for successful collective action, but this formation may be problematic, particularly at the regional and global level.

General Principles of Collective Action

Many pathbreaking works in economics faced obstacles to their publication because they broke with tradition and treaded on vested interests.

---

[13] On repeated plays of the Prisoners' Dilemma, see Axelrod (1984) and Sandler (1992, Chapter 3).

After more than three decades of publishing, I discovered that my articles with the greatest number of citations invariably received the largest number of rejection letters. Those articles with no rejections went into immediate obscurity even when they appeared in top journals. Olson's (1965) famed dissertation on collective action also confronted roadblocks after the original director of the dissertation, Edward H. Chamberlin, took ill, and Thomas Schelling took over the task. Olson needed to redraft the dissertation under Schelling's excellent guidance. In the last four decades, few books in economics have achieved the wide-ranging, lasting, and profound impact of *The Logic of Collective Action* (hereafter called *Logic*). Its analysis of collective action problems has transcended economics and has altered thinking about group behavior in sociology, anthropology, law, and political science (especially international relations). Prior to *Logic*, groups and political collectives were viewed as furthering their members' and/or constituency's well-being. Olson showed that actions by group members may worsen, rather than enhance, collective or group well-being. That is, an individual's pursuit of his or her well-being might not augment the aggregate benefit of the group and, in a large number of reasonable scenarios, could lead to an inferior outcome.

Mathematical economists who read *Logic* will surely be disappointed and annoyed by poorly formed models with unstated assumptions and incomplete proofs. Olson's sweeping maxims of collective action will surely irritate modelers who are careful to make clear the general applicability of their propositions. Nevertheless, his bold propositions became the strength, rather than the weakness, of *Logic*. First, the simple statement of these propositions meant that people from a wide range of disciplines could read and profit from Olson's work. Economists' reliance on sophisticated mathematics, not found in *Logic*, usually excludes all but the well-trained economist from their works. Second, Olson's general propositions challenged, even taunted, the readers to find exceptions, which indeed they did. These challenges to Olson generated a vast literature that continues to grow today, thus making *Logic* one of the most cited economics books in recent decades. Third, Olson's propositions, while not universally true, are valid in numerous specific cases that apply to real-world problems that arise daily. That is, as rough rules of thumb, Olson's propositions engendered useful principles that do more to further, rather than hinder, understanding. Had Olson qualified his propositions, *Logic* would not, I am convinced, have generated the interest that it has. Fourth,

Table 2.1. *Collective Action: General Rules of Thumb*

Size propositions:
- Large groups may not provide themselves with a collective good; that is, large collective action groups will have difficulty forming.
- The larger the group, the greater the inefficiency associated with individual uncoordinated (Nash) behavior.

Group composition propositions:
- Larger members (those with the greater endowments) bear a disproportionate burden of collective provision. This is the so-called exploitation hypothesis.
- Heterogeneous groups are more likely to achieve some collective action.
- Homogeneous groups are more apt to form.

Institutional recommendations:
- Collective failures may be overcome through selective incentives that augment individual gains.
- Collective failures may be overcome through institutional design – for example, a federated structure.

Source: Olson (1965) and Sandler (1992)

the appearance of Olson's work coincided with the emerging interest of economists to study market failures, which *Logic* focused on.

From Olson's *Logic*, we can glean at least seven general rules of thumb for collective action, which are displayed in Table 2.1 for convenience. These can be partitioned into three categories based on group size, group composition, and institutional recommendations.

The first size proposition indicates that the larger the number of agents, the more inertia to overcome for the group to provide itself with any of the collective good. Olson (1965, pp. 32–4, 48) argued that larger groups are less likely to supply any of the collective good when compared with smaller groups, because the share of the group's benefit going to an individual or a subset of individuals (known as a coalition) declines with group size. Olson's argument follows from considering a group with, say, 10 versus 100 individuals. In the former case, one-tenth of the collective benefit might warrant an individual to foot the cost of provision, while one-hundredth of the *same* collective benefit is less apt to justify an individual to cover this same cost of provision. Based on this reasoning, the larger the group, the less motivated are individuals to provide the collective action as their share drops proportionately. As overall group size increases, the incentives of any given sized coalition to supply the collective good would likewise decline. This proposition is highly dependent on *aggregate* collective benefits and provision costs remaining unchanged as group size increases; neither may hold in practice. For example, the aggregate benefits of a pure public good may increase proportionately to group size, so that an individual's derived benefits remain unchanged, regardless of group size. Suppose that a pure public good provides 5 in benefits for each group member, so that five members receive an aggregate benefit of 25 and ten members gain an aggregate benefit of 50. In either case, the contributor receives 5 regardless of group size owing to the nonrivalry of benefits.

For this example, the crucial factor for motivating contributions is not group size or the contributor's share of the collective gain per se, but whether one or more individuals achieve a net benefit, $b_i - c_i$, that exceeds zero. In the Prisoners' Dilemma depicted in Figure 2.2, it is negative net benefits associated with contributing a unit that keep players from contributing and not a declining share of benefits. Olson's proposition focuses on shares without being sufficiently clear about how group size influences an individual's benefits, costs, and, hence, net benefits. His emphasis on declining shares of benefits seemed to dismiss the pure publicness of the collective good.

In practice, many large special interest groups have more difficulty forming than do their smaller counterparts. This is less due to Olson's share argument than to the organizing costs that surely increase with group size. Numerous large groups surmount this problem by starting small at a local level (for example, labor unions) and then linking geographically.

The second size principle concerns allocative efficiency, where uncoordinated action by larger groups are anticipated to depart further from the social optimum when compared with the outcome from a smaller group.[14] The principle is elementary to establish for the Prisoners' Dilemma representation of pure public good provision, displayed earlier in Figure 2.2 for eight players. Uncoordinated individual optimizing behavior results in no contributions for a total benefit of 0, whereas the social optimum requires everyone to contribute for an aggregate net gain of 320 ($= 8 \times 40$). For group size n, the optimality shortfall is $n(nb_i - c_i)$, which increases with n.

[14] A third size proposition – the larger the group, the smaller the collective provision level – has been left out because it is false for normal goods, the consumption of which increases with an individual's income (see Chamberlin, 1974; McGuire, 1974; Sandler, 1992, pp. 49–50).

In general, this positive association between suboptimality and increased group size can be shown for other (for example, chicken), but not all, underlying games. Other essential collective action problems, such as the tragedy of the commons, also adhere to this size proposition (Sandler and Arce, 2003). The validity of this size principle hinges on the publicness of the collective action, the difference $c_i - b_i$, the number of interactions, the players' taste, and the behavior of provision costs, most of which are left unspecified by Olson (1965). This proposition has been influential because it is descriptive of many relevant scenarios.

The next three collective action principles involve the composition of the group's membership. Collectives may be homogeneous in that all members possess identical tastes and income, or collectives may be heterogeneous in that members have different tastes and/or different incomes. In the real world, both kinds of collectives exist. The members of prestigious neighborhoods or exclusive country clubs are often homogeneous, while the users of national parks or defense are heterogeneous.

The most celebrated of these three "composition" propositions is the *exploitation hypothesis*, where the large (rich) players carry the burden for the smaller players. A classic instance is an alliance that contains a large and small ally that face the same unit cost of defense. Given that the large ally has more to lose from an attack and more income to use for protection, the larger ally will choose a greater provision level. If defense is purely public among allies, then the small ally can have its entire defense needs covered by the large ally (Olson and Zeckhauser, 1966; Sandler, 1993). Consequently, the large ally shoulders the burden for the small. Consider a more generic pure public good provision scenario. Suppose that the public good is normal so that its purchase rises with income. If tastes are identical, then the richest individual will supply the most public good. In fact, contributors can be rank ordered from highest to lowest based solely on income.[15] Once again, the large carries the burden of collective provision for the small. The validity of this principle depends on the tastes for the public good correlating with income. If, however, a poorer individual has a greater taste for a collective good than a richer counterpart, then the small could conceivably carry the burden for the large. Other issues with this important proposition are considered in the ensuing section.

---

[15] This is established by Andreoni (1988) and Bergstrom, Blume, and Varian (1986). Also, see Andreoni and McGuire (1993).

The second composition principle hinges on heterogeneity, which allows some members to gain either sufficiently large shares or amounts of the collective benefit that they will provide the good for the group. That is, great disparity among potential contributors may ensure that one or more individuals (probably the richest) derive sufficient gains to bear the entire cost of collective provision. The US Centers for Disease Control (CDC) tracks plagues worldwide because of US self-interest in promoting world health, especially against contagious diseases. If the disease can be contained at its place of outbreak, then it will not come to US soil. This monitoring has great enough payoffs for the United States that its CDC provides this vigilance for the world. The presence of highly interested and well-endowed potential contributors can lead to some of the good being provided. To paraphrase Olson, a large participant may "privilege" the rest of the group.

For initial formation, group homogeneity proves helpful because common tastes mean that agreements can be reached with minimal transaction costs. If, for example, all potential members have the same tastes and income, then all desire the same provision level and there is little to barter over. Such homogeneity facilitates potential members identifying one another at the formation stage. In the real world, people do tend to join groups where members have similar views for the collective activity and similar means.

The third set of principles involves overcoming collective action failures. In Olson's *Logic*, two pathways are suggested. First, selective incentives can be applied to motivate individual action by tying private inducements to collective action. These selective incentives for charitable activities may take the form of recognition or special dispensation or privileges (for example, season tickets to supporters of the opera company or one's name on a plaque). For international relations, a hegemon may become the world's cop because it then has more input in setting the world's agenda. A tropical country receives private inducements for preserving its rain forest owing to ecotourism, watersheds, and other localized benefits. This preservation also provides global collective benefits from sequestering carbon and preserving biodiversity. The greater is the portion of these private inducements as a share of total benefits, the greater will be the agent's motivation to contribute to the collective action. Second, the design of institutional rules can provide the proper incentive to surmount collective action impediments. In *Logic*, Olson focused on the use of federated structures that foster closer contact among participants and reduce the size of subgroups so that individual actions are more readily noticed. Federal structures characterize environmental lobbies and some charities (for example, the United Fund). The choice of institutional design can also influence the underlying strategic interaction or game form. If a game form can be instituted that is more supportive of collective action, then more favorable collective action outcomes can be engineered. The study of these design principles have figured prominently in recent analyses of collective action.

Some Collective Action Updates

The propositions presented in the last section remain essential guiding principles for collective action even though there can be many qualifiers that change their validity. Some of the more important ones are now considered.

The Role of Costs

In *Logic*, all agents are assumed to face the same cost function so that there is no comparative advantage.[16] The cost function is also assumed to have constant marginal cost. In addition, costs are independent of group size. If comparative advantage is allowed, then cost advantages may reverse some of the general principles. For example, suppose that a small ally has a cost advantage over its larger counterpart, so that the former's marginal costs are less than those of the latter. This cost advantage will increase the small ally's optimizing defense level, where the ally equates its marginal benefits and marginal costs of defense. If this augmentation is sufficiently large, then the small ally's defense burden may rival or even exceed that of the large ally, thus reversing the exploitation hypothesis. Israel has a comparative advantage in enhancing the performance of some high-technology conventional arms. Additionally, differences in costs may create sufficient asymmetry for some provision of the collective good even when tastes and income are identical among individuals.

If costs are no longer linear, then marginal costs rise with output. As a larger provider is confronted with increasing marginal costs, he or she will supply less than had marginal cost been constant. Thus, increasing

---

[16] The same assumptions on costs hold in Olson and Zeckhauser (1966), but not in their follow-up paper on alliances where cost differences are allowed (see Olson and Zeckhauser, 1967; Sandler and Hartley, 2001).

marginal cost limits exploitation, though it is not anticipated to reverse exploitation. If costs depend on collective membership, then the group size propositions may change. When, for example, costs increase with the size of the collective owing to congestion or crowding, clubs can form where nonmembers are excluded and members are charged for the marginal congestion costs that they impose on the membership. Club goods that are partially rival and excludable – for example, communication networks, irrigation systems, electric grids, common markets, the electromagnetic spectrum, and nature preserves – can be provided by members financed through toll proceeds.

Unlike pure public goods, club goods can be allocated efficiently by members regardless of group size since the toll mechanism can force payments that "internalize" or account for the crowding externality.[17] In so doing, club tolls direct resources for providing club goods to their most-valued use. Even taste differences among members are taken into account: members with a stronger preference for the club good will visit more often and will thus pay more in total tolls. For example, users of a communication network that gain the most from signals sent or received will utilize the network most often and pay the greatest charges. In contrast, nonexcludable public goods (for example, better air quality) do not provide a means for monitoring preferences (that is, we all breathe equally) and charging for the good's use according to tastes (our derived benefit from cleaner air).

Selective Incentives and Joint Products

In recent times, selective incentives have been discussed in terms of *joint products* (see Chap. 3), which occur when a collective activity yields two or more outputs that may vary in their degree of publicness.[18] The direct analogy with selective incentives arises when one of these jointly produced outputs is private to the provider. For example, because an ally's arsenal and troops can also be used to provide disaster relief, coastal protection, and anti-insurgency protection at home, ally-specific benefits are jointly derived from a country's military assets. These same assets also yield deterrence from attack; this deterrence is a jointly produced, alliancewide pure public good.

---

[17] The principles of club theory are presented in Buchanan (1965), Cornes and Sandler (1996), Sandler (1992), and Sandler and Tschirhart (1980, 1997).
[18] On joint products, see Cornes and Sandler (1984, 1994).

The greater is the share of jointly produced *excludable* benefits to all benefits associated with the collective activity, the more successful will be the collective action. Private joint products, when bundled with purely public joint products, represent a private inducement to participate and contribute. A potential contributor can free ride on the jointly produced pure public goods, but *not* on the bundled private goods. If individuals want these latter goods, they must contribute.

On Aggregation Technologies

In recent years, a third property of public goods has figured into the analysis of collective action in terms of the provision of public goods.[19] The *aggregation technology* indicates how individual contributions to the collective action influence the total quantity of the public good. Olson implicitly assumed a summation technology where each individual's or nation's unit of contribution adds equally to the good's total level and benefits. The overall level of the public good is merely the sum of individual contributions. For example, the accumulation of greenhouse gases (GHG) abides by a summation technology. If 200 nations each emit 1,000 metric tons of GHGs into the atmosphere, 200,000 metric tons result, with each ton having the same marginal effect on heating the atmosphere. Similarly, the total effort to limit GHG emissions equals the sum of individual cutbacks. Because each unit has the same marginal effect, every unit is a perfect substitute for other units in a summation technology. This perfect substitutability of effort drives the motivation to free ride and leads to the principle of undersupply of collective action increasing with group size.

The analysis in Figures 2.1 and 2.2 that supported the size principle of suboptimality is dependent on the summation technology. This is why per-person gross benefits in the n-person matrix in Figure 2.2 equal nb_i. Multiplying the number of units contributed by the per-unit benefits is indicative of the summation technology. As a general rule, the aggregation technology determines the manner in which per-unit benefits are transformed into groupwise benefits. As such, the aggregation technology influences the strategic underpinnings of the collective action and, hence, the underlying game form.

---

[19] The aggregation technology or the technology of public supply aggregation was first introduced by Hirshleifer (1983) and Cornes and Sandler (1981, 1984). Also, see Cornes and Sandler (1996), Kanbur, Sandler, and Morrison (1999), Sandler (1997, 1998) and Vicary (1990).

The message to convey is that many other aggregation technologies exist (see Chap. 3 for details). Furthermore, many of these technologies are more supportive of successful collective action. In some situations, institutions can be designed to draw on a more favorable aggregation technology. For example, treaty wording may do this, as well as the contribution mechanisms in supranational organizations.

Strategic Assumption: Nash or Something Else

Another implicit assumption behind the general principles of collective action is that of Nash behavior, where actions are simultaneous and each player chooses a best response to the anticipated best response of others. To illustrate how an alternative strategic assumption makes a difference, I briefly consider leader–follower behavior in which one player (the leader) moves first and then the other player (the follower) optimizes in light of the leader's choice.[20] In this scenario, the follower still adheres to Nash behavior, while the leader is able to exploit this knowledge of the follower's behavior. In the pure public good scenario, the leader reduces its provision of the public good because the leader accounts for the anticipated increase by the follower that the leader's strategic reduction will induce.[21] If, say, the leader is the large ally and the follower is the small ally, then the leader's cutbacks in defense provision can conceivably reverse exploitation, with the small being more burdened than the large. The underlying strategic assumption, therefore, matters greatly for the validity of the general principles of collective action. Once again, our general intuition about collective action hinges on unstated assumptions.

More on Collective Action and Game Forms

At the time that Olson wrote *Logic*, game theory did not hold sway over economics. Hence, Olson's seminal work understandably did not incorporate strategic aspects into the analysis. This is particularly unfortunate because collective action is integrally dependent on game theory owing to the interaction among rational individuals that characterizes every facet

[20] For technical details, see Sandler (1992, pp. 56–8) and Bruce (1990).

[21] The leader chooses the point on the follower's downward-sloping reaction path that maximizes the leader's well-being. In total, the aggregate provision for leader–follower behavior is less than for Nash, so that suboptimality is even worse.

	B	
	Do Not Contribute	Contribute
Do Not Contribute	0, 0	2, 2
Contribute	2, 2	Nash 4, 4

A appears on the left labeling the rows.

Figure 2.4. Cost sharing and Prisoners' Dilemma

of collective action. The study of public goods, and other market failures where collective action is required is all about how a rational individual will act in regards to how he or she thinks rational others will behave.

To find solutions to collective failures, one must look to institutional engineering that yields strategic interactions more conducive to cooperation. This is aptly illustrated by returning to the voluntary contribution to a pure public good example, depicted earlier in Figure 2.1, where each unit contributed yields 6 in benefits to each of two individuals at a per-unit cost of 8 to just the contributor. The collective action failure arises because the consequences of the individual's decision on the group's well-being are not part of the decision maker's calculus. Suppose that an institutional arrangement is introduced where provision costs are shared regardless of the provider. Figure 2.4 depicts the impact of this institutional adjustment. The two diagonal cells' payoffs are unchanged, because cost sharing has no impact on net payoffs when either no one contributes or both contribute a unit of the public good. In the latter scenario, contributors must still deduct costs of 8 from their aggregate benefits of 12. The real consequences of this institutional innovation are felt in the off-diagonal cells, where just player *A* or *B* contributes. Now, each must pay 4 ($= 8/2$), so that the contributor and the noncontributor both receive 2 ($= 6 - 4$). The dominant strategy is to contribute, and there is no longer a free ride available. The Nash equilibrium in the lower right-hand cell is the social optimum. By introducing cost sharing, the social implications of one's decisions are internalized. This can also be accomplished by sharing benefits.

The proposed mechanism works like the so-called preference-revelation mechanisms whereby the social consequences of one's actions are imposed on the individual (that is, "internalized") through side payments that make "doing the right thing" a dominant strategy.[22] Cost-sharing would also transform the n-person Prisoners' Dilemma of Figure 2.2 into a game where contributing is the dominant strategy for all n players and the Nash equilibrium is the social optimum.[23] Throughout this book elementary institutional innovations, unexplored in *Logic*, can transform failed collective action into successful action. A real-world instance of a cost-sharing arrangement is UN assessment accounts for sharing peacekeeping expenses. These accounts were established by Resolution 3101 of the UN General Assembly to create a more permanent funding source to cover the annual expenses of peacekeeping, which had formerly strained the UN regular budget.[24] Prior to these cost-sharing accounts, the United Nations unsuccessfully relied on voluntary contributions from members to defray peacekeeping expenses. Cost-sharing arrangements are also used by the North Atlantic Treaty Organization (NATO) and the European Union (EU) to finance infrastructure projects that have alliancewide or EU-wide benefits. Even the Montreal Protocol on reducing ozone-depleting substances relies on cost assignments to underwrite its multilateral fund for assisting developing countries to make the transition to ozone-friendly substances.

To further illustrate the importance of strategic interactions, I consider the situation where two nations are threatened by a common state-sponsor of terrorism. The importance of this example is to demonstrate how changes in circumstances can alter game forms and the prognosis for collective action. In the top matrix of Figure 2.5, the traditional Prisoners' Dilemma representation of this scenario is displayed in ordinal form. Under the standard storyline, each nation is best off when free riding on the retaliatory actions of the other targeted nation and is worse off when providing the free ride. The next-worst outcome is the status quo of no action whatsoever, while the second-best outcome is mutual retaliation. As depicted, each nation is anticipated to play its dominant strategy, thereby ending up with the Nash equilibrium where the state-sponsor operates with impunity.

Next suppose that a horrendous terrorist incident, such as 9/11, takes place. If the two nations that lose the most citizens in the attack are

---

[22] On preference-revelation mechanisms, see Cornes and Sandler (1996, Chap. 5) and the citations therein.

[23] This statement holds provided that $n > c_i/b_i$.

[24] On Resolution 3101 and its implications, see Khanna, Sandler, and Shimizu (1998, 1999) and Shimizu and Sandler (2002).

	B	
	Do Not Retaliate	Retaliate
Do Not Retaliate	Nash 2, 2	4, 1
Retaliate	1, 4	3, 3

A

a. Retaliation as a Prisoners' Dilemma

	B	
	Do Not Retaliate	Retaliate
Do Not Retaliate	Nash 2, 2	3, 1
Retaliate	1, 3	Nash 4, 4

A

b. Retaliation as an assurance game

Figure 2.5. Retaliation against a state-sponsor of terrorism

considered (that is, the United States and the United Kingdom in the case of 9/11), then free riding is apt to meet with sufficient public opprobrium that it is now less desirable than being part of the collective retaliation. This is true even though retaliation places the country's armed forces in harm's way. In the bottom matrix of Figure 2.5, the game has been changed to an assurance game with two Nash equilibriums. If one country takes a leadership role in retaliating – say, the United States – then the other country will surely join since an ordinal payoff of 4 is better than a payoff of 3. If, moreover, the mutual free ride is sufficiently repugnant to countries' citizens, then the 2s and 1s are switched in the game matrix and the Nash equilibrium in the bottom matrix would be mutual retaliation.

The transformation of a Prisoners' Dilemma into an assurance game also aptly characterizes the arms race between the United States and Russia toward the end of the Cold War. In such an arms race, the strategic choices are to escalate or limit arms. Toward the end of the Cold War,

Russia and the United States better understood the economic attrition caused by their arms race. Once the adversaries viewed mutual nuclear disarmament as having an even greater payoff than arming unilaterally, the ordinal 3 and 4 payoffs changed position in the arms race matrix (not displayed), thereby changing the game to that of assurance. When Gorbachev took the disarmament lead, the best option for the United States was to follow and the Cold War swiftly ended.

Globalization and Global Collective Action

Globalization has enhanced not only cross-border flows of private goods but also the transfer of public good spillovers and externalities. Therefore, the need for transnational collective action has heightened at the regional and global level. All of the collective action principles for two or more agents also apply for nations as agents. Thus, for example, the larger the number of nations influenced by a transnational public good spillover, the greater the anticipated suboptimality.

The primary feature that needs to be remembered when studying global collective action is the institutional environment. Compared with a nation, the global community is not too far removed from the natural anarchic state with every nation out for itself. There are no strong supranational bodies with comparable enforcement capabilities to those of a national government within the nation-state. The main supranational organizations are the United Nations, World Bank, International Monetary Fund, NATO, the EU, and their component suborganizations. The continued reliance on these loose supranational institutions is predicted to be the main mechanism for addressing transnational collective action as nations resist losing sovereignty to tighter institutions with greater enforcement powers. If, however, exigencies create sufficiently large benefits from collective action, then nations will either rely on the wealthiest nation or empower an institution to address the concern. Cataclysmic events – dire consequences from global warming, an approaching asteroid on collision course, or terrorist possession of nuclear weapons – would induce nations to sacrifice autonomy to a powerful nation or supranational entity *if time were to permit a response.*

Each need for regional and global collective action differs in terms of the number of essential participants, leadership possibilities, net benefits of individual action, associated uncertainty, intertemporal aspects, and other strategic considerations. Thus, policy recommendations for transnational collective action must be tailored to adjust for strategic factors. The view that there is a common fix, institutional innovation, or blueprint treaty is doomed to failure.[25] For some contingencies, the required loss of autonomy is so small and the resulting benefits so large that nations cooperate with little prodding. For example, the adoption of conventions to avoid accidents at sea or the institution of standard weights and measures took place quickly. These successes highlight that, even at the global level, collective action is feasible under some circumstances.

Concluding Remarks

By presenting the general principles of collective action, this chapter and the next provide the theoretical foundation for my study of global collective action. This study goes beyond Olson's *Logic* by stressing the strategic game-theoretic factors. In so doing, I identify implicit assumptions behind Olson's general propositions so that the reader gains an appreciation that Olson's general principles, while of great importance, have many essential exceptions. Understanding such exceptions can enlighten policymakers to engineer effective institutional innovations that foster collective action at the local, regional, or global level.

---

[25] Benedick (1991) believes that the Montreal Protocol on ozone-depleting substances is a "blueprint treaty for other transnational problems." The international community appears to agree by using the Protocol as a template for subsequent treaties.

3

Absence of Invisibility: Market Failures

How does economic thinking differ today from fifty years ago? There are at least three main differences. In the last twenty years, strategic interactions play a much greater role, with the application of game theory to virtually every aspect of economics. During the decades prior to the 1980s, economists focused on general-equilibrium analysis, which undoubtedly represented the most important development in economics during the last century.[1] If the interest in strategic interactions continues to hold sway over the profession, then strategy-based theories are apt to represent the greatest achievement of economics in the current century. Ironically, the earlier fixation on general, and often competitive, equilibriums eliminated interest in strategic interactions, insofar as any individual's actions are inconsequential in light of those of everyone else in aggregation. A second key difference is today's recognition of market failures and their prevalence. These market failures are often, but not always, associated with collective action failures. A third essential difference is the importance of information and the realization that information may be incomplete or costly to acquire. As such, information may also result in market failures sometimes in the form of missing markets that may necessitate the need for collective action. These differences are behind the growing need for collective action within and among nations.

---

[1] Certainly, Arrow (1974) and Starr (1997) would agree with this statement, but others might not. I make this statement owing to the status afforded to the pioneers of general-equilibrium theory and their dominance in the literature throughout much of the twentieth century. These pioneers include the following Nobel Prize recipients: Paul Samuelson in 1970, Kenneth Arrow and John Hicks in 1972, Wassily Leontief in 1973, Leonid Kantorovich and Tjalling Koopmans in 1975, and Gerard Debreu in 1983. For further discussion on these three differences, see Sandler (2001).

Adam Smith's invisible hand, mentioned in Chapter 1, indicates that well-functioning and complete markets (that is, a price for every transaction of value) will result in a social optimum from which no one can be helped without causing harm to someone. If markets are competitive and complete, then uncoordinated selfish pursuits of individuals will be guided as if by an invisible hand to this glorious outcome. Changes in tastes and technologies will be taken into account automatically as prices and profits direct individual actions to a new optimum.

So what can go wrong with this seemingly flawless ideal? A crucial element in the operation of markets is the presence of property rights or recognized claims of ownership, written or implicit, to an activity's benefits or costs. If these property rights are neither recognized nor enforced, there may be little incentive to pay for the particular good, so that markets no longer operate properly. With the failure of markets, prices and profits do not provide proper signals and resources do not gravitate to their best-valued use. Markets fail when self-interested actions of independent agents result in socially inferior outcomes from which a resource reassignment can improve some individuals' welfare, but not at the expense of other individuals.

The main purpose of this chapter is to review some of these market failures where conscious policy may be required – that is, the visible hand – to ensure society's well-being. A second purpose is to show that many market failures may imply collective action failures. In so doing, I emphasize that diverse market failures need alternative remedies that may include doing nothing at all. In the case of public goods, the collective action implications and the need, if at all, for corrective policy can only be understood by investigating the three dimensions of publicness – nonrivalry of benefits, nonexcludability of nonpayers, and aggregation technology. Collective action concerns that arise with externalities, common property, and asymmetric information are also analyzed.

In a globalized world, market failures are ubiquitous as technology creates novel failures and the division of nations adds still further failures. At the transnational level, such failures are especially troublesome because the required infrastructure to address them may not exist. The creation of this infrastructure is a transnational public good and represents its own potential market failure.

If there is a single message to underscore, it is that one must resist the temptation to generalize too much when it comes to market failures and the need for collective action that they might imply. For some public goods, almost no guidance is required because incentives implied by the associated strategic interaction is conducive to acceptable results – that is, the invisible hand may still operate. In other cases, necessary actions may range from light to heavy handed.

Pure Public Goods versus Private Goods

In Chapter 2, pure public goods are defined to provide nonrival benefits that are nonexcludable to everyone – contributors and noncontributors – in the goods' range of spillovers. Examples of pure public goods include global warming reduction, basic research findings, a thicker stratospheric ozone shield, safer air corridors, and monitoring of the planet's atmosphere. Nonrivalry of benefits is often equated with a zero marginal cost of extending consumption to additional users, meaning that no crowding costs or other associated expenses – such as capacity building or a "hook-up" fee – are implied by additional consumers (Bruce, 2001, Chap. 3). If, however, some consumers must be given the ability to enjoy the good's benefits through requisite supportive activities, nonrivalry is not satisfied in this zero marginal costs sense. For a thicker ozone shield, there is no required capacity building to allow people globally to benefit from the protection against harmful ultraviolet (UV) radiation, so there are no marginal costs in extending its consumption. When these marginal costs are zero, exclusion may lead to a welfare loss whenever people who derive a positive benefit are excluded. Thus, nonrivalry may be associated with a market failure.

Nonexclusion poses a free-rider problem for a pure public good because a provider cannot keep noncontributors from consuming the good's benefits. If the good is provided and contributions solicited afterward, people have a strong incentive to understate or hide their true derived benefits so that contributions are meager compared with benefits received. There is no reason to reveal one's true gains through payment since the money can be used to purchase other goods whose benefits are not freely available. Even if the potential recipients are polled prior to provision, there are no incentives to be forthright: If respondents believe that subsequent charges will be based on their response, then they will understate their derived benefits; if, instead, respondents believe that subsequent charges will not be based on their response, then they will overstate their derived benefits. Complicated preference-revelation mechanisms can be designed to make truth telling the dominant strategy, but such mechanisms are costly

	B	
	0 units	1 unit
A 0 units	0, 0	6, 2
1 unit	2, 6	8, 8 Nash

Figure 3.1. Public goods where $b_i - c_i > 0$

to administer and only work if bothersome income or purchasing-power influences, associated with the procedure, are sanitized.[2] The costs and the complexity of these mechanisms mean that they are no panacea to free-riding problems.

In Chapter 2, the free-rider problem is depicted in game form and is shown to be particularly acute when the overall level of the public good abides by a summation technology, so that one agent's contributions are completely substitutable for those of another. Moreover, the problem is associated with the per-unit costs (c_i) being larger than per-unit benefits (b_i), thereby resulting in a dominant strategy to not contribute. Suppose that this latter assumption is changed, so that $b_i - c_i > 0$ for agent i. Specifically, assume that each of two agents can contribute no units or 1 unit of the pure public good, where each unit contributed yields a benefit of 6 to both players at a cost of just 4 to the provider. The associated game in normal form is displayed in Figure 3.1, where in each cell the payoff on the left (right) is that of agent A (B). If only one player contributes a unit, the contributor receives 2 ($= 6 - 4$) and the noncontributor gets the free-rider gain of 6; if both players provide a unit, then each contributor receives 8 ($= 2 \times 6 - 4$). Now there is a dominant strategy to give a unit because each player's payoff from providing a unit is greater than that of not contributing ($2 > 0, 8 > 6$), so that each agent uses its dominant strategy and the Nash equilibrium of mutual provision results. This Nash equilibrium is also the social optimum, demonstrating that the invisible hand may guide action even in a pure public good scenario under fortuitous circumstances. When $b_i - c_i > 0$, contributing is *incentive compatible* if benefits from contributing on one's own exceeds the

---

[2] On these preference-revelation mechanisms, see Clarke (1971), Cornes and Sandler (1996, Chap. 7), and Green and Laffont (1977).

associated costs. Examples include efforts by the main consuming nations to curb ozone-depleting chlorofluorocarbons and the actions by nations to devise accident-preventing conventions on the open seas. Too much pessimism may thus lead to erroneous conclusions for a pure public good.

A private good is the polar opposite to a pure public good in the sense that the good's benefits are fully rival and completely excludable to non-payers at virtually no costs. To receive the private good, an agent must pay for the units consumed. Because no units, and therefore no benefits, are received without paying for them, the dominant strategy is to purchase the good as long as $b_i - c_i > 0$. As such, private goods are incentive compatible. An individual stops purchasing additional units once b_i has been driven down to c_i by an individual's diminishing marginal willingness to pay, in which case $b_i - c_i = 0$.

The nomenclature of public good is misleading because a public good may be publicly or privately provided, while a private good may be privately or publicly supplied. The prefix of public refers to the publicness properties of nonrivalry and nonexcludability and not to its form of provision. Clearly, incentive-compatible public goods as well as others (see next section) can be privately provided, while some private goods (for example, school lunches or vaccinations) are publicly provided because society deems that their consumption merits public support or some societywide gains are perceived, as in the case of vaccines. Public provision of any kind of good presents its own difficulties in terms of transaction costs, government officials' own motives, and information difficulties.[3]

Other Kinds of Collective Goods

To illustrate the importance of the two standard properties of publicness, I will examine the collective action implications of five classes of collective goods. These classes are by no means exhaustive, but they do represent the primary ones.

Impurely Public Goods: Some Rivalry but No Exclusion

Partly rival benefits lead to congestion or crowding costs in which an additional user decreases the quantity or quality of a good's benefits available to others, so that the costs to extend consumption to

---

[3] For starters, a government must ascertain the preferences of its constituency for the public or private good, and the incentives to respond truthfully are perverse.

another individual is not zero. As a consequence, there are grounds to limit group size of consumers so that it is not inclusive of everyone.[4] Unfortunately, nonexclusion does not permit this limitation by assumption, and this results in overuse and a market failure. Individual consumers do not account for the crowding that their use creates for others. Along the electromagnetic spectrum, for example, congestion takes the form of interference or noise as the utilization of a given bandwidth increases. When controlling a pest that threatens alternative locations, actions to inhibit the pest in one area limits these actions elsewhere as a given amount of inhibiting resources is thinned. Police raids and network infiltrations to curb organized crime can also result in some rivalry, because actions directed at one network limit operations against other networks. For both pest and crime control, the derived benefits go to anyone at risk, so benefits are nonexcludable though partly rival. Both of these activities may give rise to a coordination game, akin to that associated with a chicken game, where some action is anticipated, but who will act among multiple potential providers must be worked out.

Group size is still a bane for successful collective action. Increased group size now adds to suboptimality in two ways: overutilization and undersupply. Moreover, greater group size may inhibit any collective action, as crowding truly means that an individual's share of the collective benefits goes down with group size in keeping with Olson's (1965) original formulation. If a congestible impure public good possesses nonexcludable benefits, then the exploitation hypothesis may be turned on its head. That is, the larger agents may utilize the good more often and, thus, be responsible for more congestion. If these greater users are not the providers, then they place a larger burden, in terms of crowding, on the smaller agents. When these larger agents are also the supplier, the utilization burden must be compared with the opposite supply burden to determine exploitation, if any.

Impurely Public Good with Full Exclusion but No Rivalry

Impure public goods may vary according to the degree of rivalry and/or the extent of excludability. At the other extreme to the kind just

---

[4] Olson (1965) distinguishes between inclusive groups, where everybody receives the good's benefit, and exclusive groups, where a limited number of people receive the good's benefits. For a pure public good, the group should be inclusive, while for an impure public good with partly rival benefits, the group should be exclusive.

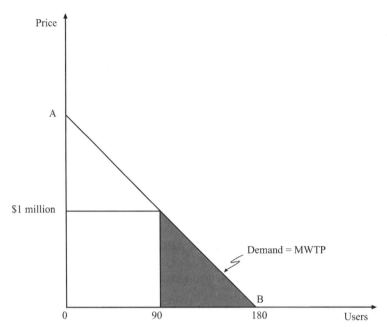

Figure 3.2. Welfare loss associated with a nonrival, excludable public good

considered, an impure public good can be excludable while displaying no rivalry among users. For transnational public goods, a relevant example is the provision of satellite-based weather forecasts for different countries. Another example is intelligence gathered on organized crime. At the national level, pay-per-view television is an appropriate example. Nonpayers can be excluded in each of these instances from the good's benefits, which are nonrival among consumers. Only those agents whose marginal willingness to pay (MWTP) is at least as great as the price charged will utilize the forecast service, intelligence, or television program. Some inefficiency remains because the marginal cost of additional users is negligible, yet some agents' MWTP is greater than zero but less than the price charged. Social welfare can, consequently, be augmented by including such agents.

This inefficiency is displayed in Figure 3.2, which shows the demand of 180 countries for satellite-based weather forecasts.[5] Line AB denotes the aggregate demand or MWTP to subscribe to these forecasts. Suppose that the marginal costs of providing the forecasts to a subscriber are zero

---

[5] The area under the demand for MWTP curve in Figure 3.2 represents potential consumers' total willingness to pay or derived benefits.

once the satellite is deployed at a provision and launch cost of $90 million. Each nation's choice is to subscribe or not to subscribe. If the provider charges $1 million per subscriber, 90 countries will subscribe (those whose MWTP equals or exceeds $1 million), thereby generating $90 million in revenues for the provider to cover provision and launch cost. Those countries whose MWTP is less than $1 million will not subscribe. This results in a welfare loss (collective failure) of $45 million [= $1 million × (180–90)/2], represented by the shaded triangle, because providing the service to additional countries would be costless to achieve. A dilemma arises since the revenue is required to finance the good's provision, but exclusion results in welfare losses. A solution is supranational provision financed by taxes, but this raises other problems in terms of the absence of such supranational structures with taxing powers.

Once an exclusion mechanism is employed, strategic considerations are eliminated; individuals are forced to reveal their preferences or go without the public good. Exclusion limits the associated noncooperative aspects. A collective action failure still applies in terms of the welfare loss. Group size remains a determinant of the extent of suboptimality because a larger group size shifts out the demand curve in Figure 3.2, thereby leading to a greater shaded loss. Group composition is, however, less of a concern since those with greater demand – large or small agents – are charged accordingly. If anyone assumes a disproportionate burden, it is the excluded individuals who tend to be small owing to insufficient income. Group asymmetry may identify a provider or the supplier may be the government, a firm, or some collective of agents. Subsidies to those whose MWTP is too small can help limit the inefficiency, but such mechanisms are more tenuous at the transnational level. In aid programs, donors can subsidize poor countries so that they can partake in these excludable public goods (Kanbur, Sandler, and Morrison, 1999).

Club Goods

Club goods are not only excludable but also partly rival. Examples include the International Telecommunications Satellite Organization (INTELSAT), a satellite-based communication network that carries most transcontinental phone calls and television transmissions (see Chap. 11), and international airports that are used by commercial airliners. Even the air corridors above 31,000 feet for airliners traveling between countries are club goods whose use can be monitored and tolls charged according to utilization. Club goods can be provided by members financed through tolls imposed on users based on the crowding costs that their use creates. In a club, members cooperate to provide a shared good, so that strategic considerations are not necessarily relevant. Club goods can be allocated efficiently through the toll mechanism that accounts for the crowding that each visit imposes on the members.

As discussed in Chapter 2, taste differences among members are taken into account by clubs: members with a stronger preference for the club good will visit more often and will thus pay more in *total tolls*. A club represents a low-cost institutional arrangement for the collective provision. The partial rivalry of club goods means that exclusion is not welfare reducing when those excluded do not receive sufficient benefits to cover the crowding costs that their consumption creates. Such individuals need to be left out because they cannot compensate others for the harm that their use causes. Multiple clubs can form when a single club cannot accommodate everyone. Clubs can contain just members from the same nation or can have an international membership. INTELSAT is a transnational club that is a private consortium of nations and firms as members. Even the deployment of crisis-management squads to a terrorist incident or a regional instability can be operated as a club. At the transnational level, clubs economize on transaction costs, while they minimize members' losses of autonomy. The presence of club goods reminds us that some collective goods can be provided privately and that such goods need not be associated with market or collective action failures.

Joint Products

Another essential type of collective good includes those activities that yield two or more outputs or *joint products* that may vary in their degree of publicness (Sandler, 1977). As such, jointly produced outputs may be purely public, private, a club good, or something else. Joint products imply bundling where two or more outputs occur simultaneously. Foreign aid, especially when tied, is associated with joint products. Welfare improvement for recipient nations gives a purely public altruistic gain to all nations that care for those less fortunate. If, moreover, the aid provider has stipulated conditions – for example, the purchase of technical assistance from the donor or the leasing of military bases to the donor – then donor-specific private benefits are also derived. Aid may also yield such donor gains from a more stable resource supply, trading opportunities, or greater prestige in the world community.

Joint products also characterize the rain forests whose preservation generates purely public benefits worldwide owing to carbon sequestration and biodiversity. Host-country and regional benefits from these forests include erosion control, localized climate effects, watersheds, and eco-tourist sites. These localized benefits give these tropical countries a stake or ownership in their forest preservation and, in so doing, should motivate some preservation. When determining development assistance to preserve these forests, donors must remember that these host-country benefits also motivate preservation on the host country's own behalf. Joint products also characterize peacekeeping and many other transnational collective activities.

With joint products, the prognosis for collective action hinges on the collective activity's ratio of excludable benefits (that is, contributor-specific benefits and club goods) to total benefits. As this ratio approaches one, the share of excludable benefits dominates, enabling markets and clubs to efficiently allocate resources to the good's provision. As the ratio approaches zero, the share of purely public benefits increases, making it likely that the activity will be undersupplied (or oversupplied if public spillovers are negative). Joint products encompass a wide variety of scenarios and may include underprovision (when the share of purely public benefits dominates), overprovision (when the share of purely public negative spillovers dominates), or nearly efficient provision (when the share of contributor-specific or club outputs, or both, dominate).[6]

Institutions can be designed to bolster the share of contributor-specific joint products so as to motivate more effective collective action. For example, voting shares in the International Monetary Fund (IMF) are based, in part, on a country's share of support for IMF loans. If a country's support is 19% of the IMF quota, then this country possesses roughly 19% of the voting privileges in the IMF (see Chap. 4 for more details). This voting structure emphasizes supporter-specific benefits to entice nations to give to IMF activities that also give purely public global benefits from greater financial stability. Similarly, to motivate countries to pay the greater peacekeeping assessments and UN membership fees levied on Security Council permanent members, the UN gives these countries a

---

[6] On the influence of this ratio on optimality, see Sandler and Forbes (1980), Sandler and Hartley (2001), and Sandler and Murdoch (2000). Also, see Sandler (2003b).

veto over security matters, which is not provided to other UN member countries.

If the jointly produced contributor-specific benefits are *complementary* to the purely public benefits when contributors desire to consume these derived outputs in conjunction,[7] then increased spillovers of the purely public component may encourage more, rather than less, collective provision by recipients. In this case, bundling is important because spillover recipients cannot receive the complementary contributor-specific benefit unless they support the collective action. The presence of a jointly produced private benefit acts like property rights that motivate action; complementarity reinforces this desire to support the collective action.

From a strategic vantage, joint products include a wide range of game forms depending on the mix of excludable to total benefits. If this ratio is close to one, then the dominant strategy is to contribute and an incentive-compatible contribution game applies. With sufficient complementarity, an assurance game can result as an agent is better off contributing when others contribute, leading to matching-behavior equilibriums. The relevant collective action principles also hinge on this mix of benefits. If the ratio is zero so that the activity is purely public, then Olson's general principles apply for a summation aggregator. If, however, the ratio is one, then markets or clubs can take over and there are no collective action worries. A whole range of collective action outcomes are possible for ratio values between zero and one.

Open-Access Commons

The open-access commons is another polar case of impurity in which the benefits to the shared good is wholly or partially rival but nonexcludable. This nonexcludability may be culturally based (for example, the common heritage of the ocean beyond some coastal resource zone), physically determined (for example, the accessibility of airsheds), or institutionally fixed (for example, the use of air corridors or airwaves according to rules set by an international body). For some open-access commons (henceforth, called commons), a fixed input may be jointly utilized by exploiters; for example, fishing boats ply a fishery. The fishery is the fixed input, while the boats, crew, and equipment are the variable inputs.

---

[7] Goods are complementary when each good enhances the marginal derived benefits of the other good.

Number of contributors other than i

	0	1	2	3	4
→ i Does Not Contribute	Nash 0	5	10	15	20
i Contributes	−3	2	7	12	Social Optimum 17

a. Five-person contribution game

Number of farmers other than i whose cattle graze in commons

	0	1	2	3	4
i Does Not Graze	Social Optimum 0	−5	−10	−15	−20
→ i Grazes	3	−2	−7	−12	Nash −17

b. Five-person commons game

Figure 3.3. Five-person symmetric representations

As more boats populate the fishery, the crew of each boat must expend more effort to land a given catch. Each boat creates crowding costs on others that are not taken into account by the boat owner when allocating resources.

In the literature, the commons problem is typically treated as being identical to the pure public good contribution dilemma (Ostrom, Gardner, and Walker, 1994). That is, both are characterized as Prisoners' Dilemmas that allegedly abide by the canonical principles of collective action. This characterization is quite misleading as can be seen in Figure 3.3, which contains two five-player game matrices.[8] In matrix *a* at the top of the figure, each of five identical agents must decide whether or not to contribute one unit to a pure public good. Each unit contributed costs the contributor 8 and gives 5 in benefits to each of the five agents regardless of whether

---

[8] The analysis in this subsection comes from Sandler and Arce (2003).

they contribute. The *ith* representative agent's payoffs are displayed in the cells. The two rows correspond to *i*'s two strategies, and the five columns refer to the number of contributors other than *i* who contribute a unit. If *i* does not contribute, then *i* gets a free-rider benefit of 5 times the number of other contributors – for example, 5 for one other contributor, 10 for two other contributors, and so on. If, in contrast, *i* contributes, then *i* receives $(nb_i - c_i)$, where n is the number of contributors including *i*, $b_i = 5$, and $c_i = 8$. When, for instance, *i* and two others contribute, the net payoff for *i* is 7 $(= 3 \times 5 - 8)$. The arrow indicates the dominant strategy is for *i* to not contribute, because each entry in the top row is greater than the corresponding entry in the bottom row (for example, 0 > –3, 5 > 2, and so on). Insofar as everyone views the game in the same fashion, everyone applies this dominant strategy and no one contributes, which is the Nash equilibrium from which no one would unilaterally alter his or her strategy if given the opportunity. The social optimum with the greatest total payoff to society is for all to contribute with a net per-person payoff of 17. Although the payoff for *i* is higher when *i* is the sole free rider, this outcome is not the social optimum because the other four players receive just 12 apiece. Society nets 85 $(= 5 \times 17)$ for universal contributions, and society receives just 68 $[= 20 + (4 \times 12)]$ for a lone free rider.

In matrix *b* in Figure 3.3, an analogous five-agent commons game is depicted in which five farmers graze their cattle on a commons pasture. Now, each farmer whose cattle grazes imposes a *public* cost of 5 on everyone, including himself or herself. If *i* does not graze his or her cattle but two others graze their cattle, then *i* experiences a cost of 10. When *i* also grazes his or her herd, then *i*'s payoff is $(b_i - nc_i)$, where n is the number of grazers including *i*, $b_i = 8$, and $c_i = 5$. If, therefore, *i* and three others graze their cattle, then *i* nets -12 $[= 8 - (4 \times 5)]$. The dominant strategy for *i* and thus everyone is to graze their cattle, resulting in the Nash equilibrium with a per-person payoff of -17. The social optimum with payoffs of 0 is for no one to use the commons for grazing.

There are some fascinating similarities and differences between the contribution and commons games. In their most stylized forms in Figure 3.3, both games are Prisoners' Dilemmas where the extent of suboptimality (that is, the difference between the payoffs for the social optimum and the Nash equilibrium) equals $n(nb_i - c_i)$ for the contribution game and $n(nc_i - b_i)$ for the commons. Suboptimality increases with group size for both scenarios, so that Olson's prediction regarding group size and inefficiency holds. The games, however, differ because benefits are public

Table 3.1. *Collective Goods: Examples, Strategic Implications, and Provision Prognosis*

Good Type	Examples	Strategic Implications	Provision Prognosis
Pure Public	• curbing global warming • basic research findings	Prisoners' Dilemma if $c_i - b_i > 0$ and summation technology. If some action is required to avoid dire consequences, then chicken game applies.	Undersupplied and need for public provision. General collective action principles hold for special cases.
Impurely public with some rivalry but no exclusion	• controlling pests • curbing organized crime	A wide variety of game forms apply, including a coordination game, where some provision is anticipated if the agents can decide who will supply the good.	Some supply is anticipated, but the good is still undersupplied. Size principles hold, but not all of the composition principles hold. Some public provision needed.
Impurely public with full exclusion but no rivalry	• weather forecasts • intelligence on organized crime	Exclusion eliminates strategic considerations and forces some individuals to reveal a preference. Those whose willingness to pay is too small are excluded even though there are no crowding costs.	Inefficiency results because people with positive benefits are excluded. Size principles remain a concern, but composition principles are less relevant. Public subsidies of the poor may reduce inefficiency.

Club goods	• INTELSAT • international airports	In an ideal club, there are no strategic considerations. Members cooperate to provide a shared good, where use is monitored. Congestion tolls are used to internalize these costs and finance the good.	Optimal provision results as externality is internalized. Taste differences are revealed through visitation. Heavier users pay more in total tolls. Collective action principles do not hold.
Joint products	• foreign aid • preservation of rain forests	A wide variety of game forms are relevant including assurance, depending on the mix of excludable to total benefits. Dominant strategy may even be to contribute if share of private benefits is sufficiently large.	Ratio of excludable to total benefits is the key consideration. As this ratio approaches one, markets and clubs work more fully. General collective action principles hold more fully as this ratio approaches zero. Institutional design can promote these excludable benefits
Open-access commons	• high seas • atmosphere	Prisoners' Dilemma with a dominant strategy to exploit the commons.	Size principles apply; however, exploitation is turned on its head – the large exploits the small.

and received by all for the contribution game, while costs are private to the contributor. The roles of benefits and costs are reversed in the commons for which the costs are public, while benefits are private to the exploiter. This role reversal switches the relative positions of the Nash equilibrium and the social optimum in two scenarios, so that inaction is the problem for the public good scenario, while action is the difficulty for the commons. Another essential difference involves group composition and the so-called exploitation hypothesis, where the large is exploited by the small (Olson, 1965; Sandler, 1992). This hypothesis would hold for the contribution game if asymmetry is introduced for identical tastes but different income levels among agents. In this scenario, the richer agent will provide more units of the public good if this good is normal with contributions increasing with income. As such, the small, poor agents are afforded an easy or free ride at the larger agents' expense. For the commons, the anticipated exploitation is just the opposite with the larger agents utilizing the commons more frequently, thereby creating a greater negative externality on the small players who are being exploited (Sandler and Arce, 2003).

Myriad other differences can follow as the aggregation technology is allowed to vary for the contribution game and the crowding-cost technology is permitted to change for the commons. Thus far, these technologies are captured by the n, indicating a summation technology for the public good and constant costs for the commons. As these technologies differ from the canonical case, the underlying game form for the two games can also vary and part company.

Summary

Table 3.1 displays the six cases of collective goods. For each type, two examples are listed along with strategic implications and provision prognosis. Collective action concerns are included with the provision prognosis. This table serves as a ready reference for the specific applications discussed in the remainder of the book.

Third Property of Publicness

A third essential characteristic of publicness involves how individual contributions to the collective good determine the total quantity of the good available for consumption, a relationship known as the *aggregation technology*.[9] This aggregation property influences the incentives that potential contributors possess and, in so doing, affects the strategic aspects surrounding the provision of the collective good. Each of the first five sub-classes of collective goods in Table 3.1 can be further subdivided by the aggregation technology (Sandler, 2003b). Although there are numerous variants of the aggregation technology, we consider just five important ones here.

Before Hirshleifer (1983) introduced other aggregation technologies, the only one was that of *summation* where each unit contributed to the public good adds identically and cumulatively to the overall level of the good available for consumption. Money given to a charitable cause abides by a summation technology because the sum of the contributions determines the overall resources for alleviating poverty. In the case of peacekeeping, each country's contribution of troops to a rapid reaction force adds in a cumulative fashion to the overall size of the force and its peacekeeping potential. Other examples involve the curbing of ozone-shield-depleting substances and the size of a rain forest tract set aside for conservation.

The primary distinguishing feature of summation is that every contributor's efforts are perfectly substitutable for those of others; that is, my unit of provision has the same impact on the total level of the public good as a unit supplied by anyone else. Thus, everyone's marginal influence is the same. Summation is a necessary ingredient to the *neutrality theorem*, which indicates that a redistribution of income among contributors (whose tastes can differ) has no net effect on the level of the public good.[10] Those receiving income increase their public good contributions by precisely the amount that those losing income decrease their contributions. Because one contributor's provision of the pure public good is a perfect substitute for that from another contributor under a summation technology, increased provision through redistribution replaces the need to contribute these units on one's own on a dollar-for-dollar basis. Neutrality also applies if some authority – say, a government – *taxes contributors* to

---

[9] Hirshleifer (1983) and Cornes and Sandler (1984) introduced the notion of an aggregation technology. Also, see Arce and Sandler (2001), Cornes (1993), Kanbur, Sandler, and Morrison (1999), Vicary (1990), and Vicary and Sandler (2002).

[10] Neutrality and its requirements are discussed in Bergstrom, Blume, and Varian (1986), Cornes and Sandler (1984, 1985), Sandler and Posnett (1991), and Warr (1983). The neutrality theorem was first discovered by Shibata (1971).

try to bolster supply. These taxes merely replace private provision with public supply without any increment in the overall supply. Summation is an important factor in the validity of the negative influence of group size on suboptimality and group formation.

Two game forms typically underlie the summation representation of a public good. The first is the Prisoners' Dilemma where each agent's dominant strategy is to not contribute when $b_i - c_i < 0$. Each agent considers his or her net gain from contributing while ignoring benefits conferred on others. The second relevant game form is a chicken game where per-unit benefit is again less than per-unit cost when viewed from an individual contributor's perspective. The added feature in the chicken representation is that doing nothing at all, or doing too little, results in negative payoffs; that is, some of the public good must be provided or everyone suffers. The status quo of no provision has dire consequences,[11] so that not contributing is no longer a dominant strategy. If, for instance, nothing at all is done about a plague, the consequences may be dire. One or more nations will have incentives to accomplish some minimal sufficient effort to forestall the disaster. The trick is to coordinate among nations to achieve such minimal levels since free-riding incentives are still present. The most likely contributors are the best-endowed nations or a multilateral agency that can direct efforts. In either case, the exploitation hypothesis is a real concern.

If a *weakest-link* aggregation technology applies, then the smallest contribution fixes the quantity of the public good for the entire group receiving benefits. When airport security against skyjackings is provided, the least-secure airport determines the level of safety, especially in a globalized world where a nation's citizens can be targeted at home or abroad. Terrorists will probe airport security to locate the least-fortified point. Another example of weakest link is limiting the diffusion of a pest or disease, which will spread through the least-effective barrier. Other instances include tracking the diffusion of diseases or curbing the spread of revolutions.

With a weakest-link public good, *matching behavior* is anticipated because there is no return from providing beyond the smallest contribution level. This follows because larger contributions use up scarce resources without adding to the amount of the public good consumed. The incentive to free ride is effectively eliminated; giving nothing means

---

[11] These consequences must be greater in absolute value than the absolute value of $b_i - c_i$.

		q_B	
	0	1	2
0	Nash 0, 0	0, −2	0, −4
q_A 1	−2, 0	Nash 2, 2	2, 0
2	−4, 0	0, 2	Nash 4, 4

Figure 3.4. Weakest-link public good with three contribution strategies

that the smallest contribution is zero, so the public good is effectively nonexistent. If tastes and endowments are identical, a social optimum results from independent choice as each person's choice is best for all (Sandler, 1992). In this extreme scenario, the invisible hand guides agents to an optimum. To understand the possibility for global action, one must recognize that the right combinations of public characteristics can mean success without explicit coordination. With identical tastes but different incomes, the poorer agents may possess insufficient capacity to provide a level of the public good acceptable to the more wealthy agents who are motivated to augment these poorer agents' contributions to the public goods through in-kind or money transfers (Vicary and Sandler, 2002). This behavior is directed by an inherent complementarity among contributions that fosters more optimal outcomes.

The matching equilibriums are well illustrated in the 3×3 game matrix in Figure 3.4 where two agents, A and B, can choose to contribute 0, 1, or 2 units of the weakest-link public good, denoted by q_A and q_B for agent A and B. Suppose that each unit of the good costs the provider 2. If the smallest contribution is one unit, then each player receives 4 in benefits (prior to the costs of 2 being deducted); if, however, the smallest contribution of the players is two units, then each player receives 8 (or 4 per unit) in benefits [prior to the costs of 4 ($= 2 \times 2$) being deducted]. If, say, one individual provides two units and the other provides just one unit, the larger provider gets 0 ($= 4 - 4$), which equals the benefits from the one matched unit minus the provision costs of 4 from the two units, while the smaller provider gets 2 ($= 4 - 2$), which equals the net benefits from one unit. Other payoffs are computed in a similar fashion for the other cells. In this assurance game, there are three Nash equilibriums along the diagonal where *both* players give 0, 1, or 2 units apiece; that is, players match one another's contributions as hypothesized. This scenario is generalizable to more units, in which all equilibriums will be along the diagonal. In practice, the resulting equilibrium depends on the relative endowments of the agents with the poorest individual determining the level of the weakest-link public good, unless the richer players choose to support the poorest individuals' contribution.

A third aggregation technology is that of *threshold* where the overall level of the public good must surpass a set level for any benefits to be received.[12] How this level is achieved involves an aggregator – for example, summation or weakest-link. Moreover, the set threshold value is a second component of the aggregation technology. For example, suppose that the level of the good abides by summation, but at least two units must be provided before benefits of 4 per unit are received by both agents. Further suppose that each unit costs 6 to supply. With a single contributor, the contributor nets minus six from the costs of providing a unit while the noncontributor receives nothing. There are no benefits for either agent when a single unit is provided because the threshold of two units is not achieved. If both agents contribute, the threshold is attained and each agent receives $2 (= 2 \times 4 - 6)$ as the agent's costs of 6 on the one unit contributed are deducted from the benefits of 8 derived from the two units available for consumption. This scenario translates into the 2×2 matrix *a* in Figure 3.5, where the Nash pure-strategy equilibriums involve an assurance game with matching behavior along the diagonal. In this game, leadership can result in an optimal outcome. If, for example, agent *A* takes the lead and contributes a unit, agent *B* is then better off following *A*'s lead – a payoff of 2 is better than nothing. Institutional design – in terms of cost sharing and refundability of contributions – can create threshold situations to entice members to view contributing as a dominant strategy. As such, game forms other than assurance may apply. These institutional considerations are taken up in Chapter 4.

A threshold aggregator has many transnational public good counterparts. Peacekeeping is an instance where the threshold is determined by the sizes of the opposing armies or rebels that must be kept apart

---

[12] On threshold contribution games, see Bagnoli and McKee (1991), Palfrey and Rosenthal (1984), and Sandler (1992, 1998).

		B	
		0 units	1 unit
A	0 units	Nash 0, 0	0, −6
	1 unit	−6, 0	Nash 2, 2

a. *Public good: threshold aggregator*

		B	
		0 units	1 unit
A	0 units	0, 0	Nash 6, 2
	1 unit	Nash 2, 6	2, 2

b. *Public good: best-shot aggregator*

		B	
		0 units	1 unit
A	0 units	0, 0	3, −1
	1 unit	Nash 1, 4	4, 1

c. *Public good: weighted sum*

Figure 3.5. Three alternative aggregators for public good contributions

(see Chap. 9). Experience has taught (for example, the Congo in the 1960s) that peacekeepers must present sufficient forces and firepower to maintain separation and peace. When the need arises, as in Kosovo and East Timor, the peacekeeping force is not dispatched unless a sufficient capacity is surpassed. Another example is forest-fire suppression for which the conflagration determines the required threshold. Unless the firefighting force exceeds a required threshold depending on the size of the blaze, firefighters are at grave risk and may make no headway in containing the blaze.

A fourth useful and prevalent aggregator is *best shot* for which the overall level of the public good equals the largest single individual provision level. To find a cure for Ebola, AIDS, or antibiotic-resistant tuberculosis, the research team with the greatest effort is typically the one that meets with success. For a discrete best-shot good, whoever is first to supply the good provides it for everyone. There may be some randomness for some discovery scenarios so that additional research teams beyond the one expending the greatest effort may be required to increase the probability of success. Another best-shot example would be the provision of a missile defense system to destroy incoming missiles.

In matrix *b* of Figure 3.5, a best-shot, public good contribution game is displayed for agents A and B, who can contribute 0 or 1 unit to the public good. The first unit contributed, which is the best shot, provides 6 in benefits to both agents at a cost of 4 to just the provider. If, for example, A free rides on best-shooter B, then A gains 6, while B nets 2 ($= 6 - 4$) as costs of 4 are deducted. When both agents contribute a unit, the second unit is redundant and provides no benefits, so the payoff in the right-hand bottom cell of matrix *b* is 2 ($= 6 - 4$) for both agents. The resulting game is a coordination game with two pure-strategy equilibriums with a single contributor and a free rider. Coordination requires that the agents do not assume the same roles. In the simple game in matrix *b*, the Nash equilibriums are social optimums with maximum gains of 8, therefore underscoring that the prognosis for efficiency is very dependent on the characteristics of the public good. The game depicted is a discrete-choice situation where the good is either provided or not – for example, the disease is cured or not. If the choice is continuous with a variable level of the maximum provision being chosen, then a less than optimal outcome is likely as the best shooter fails to account for the benefits derived by others from his or her provision level choice. A less extreme form of best shot is better shot, where contributions below the greatest also provide benefits with the largest provision level giving the greatest benefits, followed by the next largest level, and so on.

Another aggregator technology of public supply is *weighted sum*, for which weights are applied to the individual contributions before summing them to ascertain the overall level of the public good available for consumption. This technology generalizes summation, which results when all of the weights are one. Acid rain deposition and its reduction adhere to this technology at the regional level. The sulfur deposition on country i is the weighted sum of the country's own emissions and those of the other countries, where these weights are the share of the emitting countries' pollution deposited on country i.[13] Corresponding weights depend on wind direction, the countries' relative locations, their sizes, and other considerations. Controlling a pest may also follow a weighted-sum technology owing to barriers and other natural considerations that may make some pathways more likely, so that efforts are not equally as effective everywhere.

When the weights are not one, individual contributions are no longer perfect substitutes, thereby curbing some free riding. This lack of substitutability also makes neutrality less of a concern, so that corrective action may not crowd out or replace individual voluntary efforts. With weighted sum, the country's derived share of its own contribution is often high, this motivates supply efforts because this share reflects the country's "ownership" to the consequence of its public good contribution. For example, over 60% of a country's sulfur emissions is on average deposited on itself, so that it is highly motivated to curb such emissions. This relatively large self-pollution provides localized benefits that promote action.

Matrix c in Figure 3.5 applies to a weighted-sum technology in which a unit provided by agent A gives 7 in benefits to himself and just 4 in benefits to agent B, while a unit provided by agent B yields 5 in benefits to herself and just 3 in benefits to agent A.[14] The per-unit provision cost of the public good is 6. The payoffs listed in the matrix are easy to compute based on these data. Agent A has a dominant strategy to contribute because $1 > 0$ and $4 > 3$, while B has no dominant strategy. Given A's dominant strategy, agent B is best off free riding so that the Nash equilibrium is the bottom left-hand cell. Since a wide variety of payoff patterns exist for weighted sum, there are consequently a large number of game forms consistent with this technology – there is no hallmark game form for weighted sum. As a generalization, it follows that the greater is the share of benefits going to

---

[13] These spatial models of acid rain are analyzed by Murdoch, Sandler, and Sargent (1997) and Murdoch, Sandler, and Vijverberg (2003). Also, see atmospheric references in these articles.

[14] In this example, A's contribution yields 11 in benefits with A receiving 7/11 of the total and B receiving 4/11 of the total. A similar calculation applies for B's contribution, which gives 8 in total benefits.

Table 3.2. *Alternative Aggregation Technologies for Pure Public Goods*

Aggregation Technology	Examples	Strategic Implications	Provision Prognosis
Summation: public good levels equal the sum of individual contributions	• charitable activities • rapid reaction force	Prisoners' Dilemma or chicken if $b_i - c_i < 0$	Undersupply or the need to coordinate efforts to avoid dire consequences.
Weakest link: only the smallest effort determines the public good level	• security against hijackings • limiting the diffusion of a pest	Assurance	Matching behavior with optimal results if tastes and endowments are the same.
Threshold: good must surpass a threshold for benefits to be received	• peacekeeping • fire suppression	Assurance	Threshold often reached and outcome may be near to optimal.
Best shot: only the largest effort determines the public good level	• discovering cures • infiltrating terrorist networks	Coordination	Discrete goods may be efficiently supplied, but continuous goods are unlikely to be efficiently supplied.
Weighted sum: each contribution can have a different additive impact	• cleanup of sulfur emissions • controlling a pest	Wide variety of game forms	A wide variety of outcomes are possible, with suboptimality being less of a concern.

a contributor, the more likely the agent is to contribute. With weighted sum, collective action may have a reasonably optimistic prognosis in many cases.

Table 3.2 summarizes the five aggregation technologies, complete with examples, strategic implications, and the provision prognosis. The main message here is that aggregation technologies other than summation often present a more hopeful indication of some collective action. Given that Olson's *Logic* assumed a summation technology, it is no wonder that Olson's prognosis for collective action was so grim. Policy must adjust for the underlying aggregation technology if it is to be effective.

Externality

Another market failure that is behind many global exigencies is an *externality*, which is an interdependency among two or more agents (for example, individuals, firms, or nations) that is not taken into account by a market transaction. Myriad externalities can arise when actions by one nation creates an uncompensated interdependency for other nations. If, for example, a nation's coal-fired electric-power plants emit sulfur or nitrogen oxides that are later deposited abroad, then a *transnational externality* is present. Unless the emitter is made to compensate its downwind neighbor for damages, the emitter would have no incentive to curb its polluting activity. From a social viewpoint, too much production is taking place unless the externally imposed costs are included in the producer's operating expense. An external benefit or positive externality may result, for example, when one nation eliminates a terrorist group that targets many nations. In the case of positive externalities, too little of the action is expected unless the generator of the externality is compensated for its good deed.

An externality implies the absence of a price or market for an action that imposes costs or benefits on others. As such, decision makers must make choices when confronted with actions of others that are beyond their control. These externality-based quantities represent constraints that limit one's choices and, thus, result in a loss of allocative efficiency. Thus, externalities may be referred to as quantity-constrained behavior,[15] where some agents' quantity choices are not directed by prices. Without the proper price signals, markets cannot serve their invisible-hand function and, consequently, they fail to achieve allocative efficiency. Moreover, the presence of one agent's quantity choice influences the well-being and action of other agents so that strategic interactions, irrelevant in an ideal competitive market scenario, become relevant.

There is also the issue of the relationship between pure public goods and externalities. For public goods, the actions and contributions of each provider clearly affect the other agents' well-being and also act as a quantity constraint; thus, the two problems are clearly related. The easiest

[15] This is the approach of Cornes and Sandler (1996, Chap. 3). They show that the indirect utility function for consumers and the indirect profit function cannot be expressed solely in terms of market datum – prices, income, and technology – because some quantities remain as constraints in these functions. The inability to express these quantities in terms of prices imply the absence of key markets.

way to characterize this correspondence is to view externalities as the broader problem that includes public goods as a subset – that is, every public good problem is an externality, but not every externality is a public good. For public goods, the contributions of others enter, say, the utility of an agent in a particular way vis-à-vis the aggregation technology that indicates how individual contributions determine the overall level of the good. In the case of an externality, there is no need for an aggregation technology; the actions of an agent simply affect the other persons' well-being – this influence can be local (one other person) or far-reaching like a public good. Both problems stem from quantity constraints beyond an agent's control and the absence of a relevant market and its price signals. Externalities, like public goods, may be related to a wide variety of alternative game/strategic forms and corrective prescriptions. Furthermore, there may be alternative collective action implications for different kinds of externalities. A classic instance of this is the *reciprocal externality* where agents impose externalities on one another. Suppose that two nations create differing external costs on one another – nation A pollutes the air of nation B, while nation B pollutes a river passing through nation A. Such a scenario is apt to result in each nation curbing some of its externality-generating activity as a bargained output since each nation has leverage over the other. Unlike public goods, externalities may involve sufficiently small numbers of agents (even two) that bargaining may be practical, leading to successful collective action. Moreover, exploitation need not adhere to size considerations; rather, the externality generator – large or small – will possess the exploitative advantage.

Corrections to externalities assume many forms. In the case of a small number of agents, bargaining can successfully address the externality, thus "internalizing" it in which the external implications of an agent's actions are included in his or her decision calculus. Ownership arrangements can also correct the externality in which the externality recipient and generator combine as a single entity – for example, a sod ranch next to a chicken farm can become a single entity to account for the smell external costs and the fertilizer external benefits. Another internalization scheme or solution – particularly suited to small-numbers externalities – is for a court to assign a liability assignment to the generator of a negative externality or to imbue the recipient with the rights to demand compensation. In either case, the parties are anticipated to bargain to an optimal outcome. This insight is known as the Coase (1960) theorem.

In a large-numbers situation, bargaining is not an option owing to prohibitive transaction costs. A Pigouvian tax/subsidy program in the case of external costs/benefits can force the generator to include the external costs/benefits imposed on others when deciding allocative decisions.[16] For a Pigouvian tax/subsidy, two wrongs make a right as the price is distorted by a tax in the case of external costs, so that the additional costs imposed on a nonconsenting party is made part of the price of the externality generator. This external-cost-inclusive price sustains a socially optimal activity level where social benefits and social costs are equated at the margin. Other solutions may involve quotas where only a limited amount of the activity, consistent with the social optimum, is allowed. If quotas take the form of permits to impose external costs (say pollution permits) that can be traded, then a pseudo market can achieve an efficient outcome as the permits are auctioned to those who most value the ability to pollute.

Asymmetric Information

Asymmetric information involves one party to a transaction being more informed than another. A market failure results as some costs and benefits are inevitably left out of the market price. Suppose that the manufacturer of guidance systems for cruise missiles knows that its system has a 20% failure probability leading the missile to veer off course. In fact, this risk may be due to faulty batteries that would be relatively cheap to replace – say, for $100. From the manufacturer's viewpoint, this recall would cut into its profit, so it says nothing and the faulty guidance system remains on the million-dollar missiles. The missiles are thus sold at too high of a price given that one in five will fail in their intended missions. In some cases, this failure may result in a catastrophic outcome when the missile targets one's own assets and soldiers, making the missile worth much less than four-fifths of its selling price. If, in another instance, the unrevealed information may bolster the value of the product for some buyers and lower its value for others, then the product will sell at prices both too low for some and too high for others, given their marginal willingness to pay. As a consequence, some people will stay out of the market who would

---

[16] In the case of external costs (benefits), the tax (subsidy) is set equal to the marginal external costs (benefits) at the point where marginal social costs equal marginal social benefits.

have entered if better informed, while other people will enter the market who would have stayed out if better informed. Asymmetric information limits price as a signaling mechanism and this curbs the operation of the invisible hand.

Asymmetric information comes in two distinct forms – hidden action and hidden type. Imagine a situation where your actions, which are unobservable, can help determine an outcome. For example, suppose that nations within a region form an insurance scheme whereby forest fires, earthquakes, or other natural disasters are jointly covered. This coverage involves not only a response to manage the crisis after the fact, but also partial compensation for the losses. Having this insurance *alters* each country's incentives to exercise care, and such care-taking actions are unobservable to the collective insurers. For forest fires, risks can be limited by cleaning up undergrowth and brush, while, for earthquakes, risks can be reduced by proper construction of buildings. *Moral hazard* is the situation where insurance curtails actions to minimize risk. As such, the collective insurance scheme may fail as the first disaster exhausts funds, because the required compensation is so great owing to the failure to minimize losses. If actions to limit risks were easily observed, then the insurance premiums could be suitably tailored to these actions; therefore, the moral-hazard problem stems from unobservability.

Moral hazard may result in the absence of an insurance market – for example, there is no privately provided market for unemployment insurance since the moral-hazard problem is so great. If you know that poor performance will lead to being fired and subsequent payments for doing nothing, then some workers are induced to underperform on the job. The absence of such markets is a market failure. In international relations, moral-hazard problems abound as national sovereignty limits information. For example, actions to curb transfrontier pollutants are often unobservable unless nations agree to monitoring stations. In the case of sulfur emissions in Europe, the installation of monitoring stations by the Cooperative Programme for Monitoring and Evaluation of the Long-Range Transmission of Air Pollutants in Europe (EMEP) in 1979 eventually led to treaties reducing these emissions (see Chap. 10). The invisibility of the invisible hand hinges on the visibility of information.

The second form of asymmetric information involves the presence of two or more types of agents to a transaction or two or more qualities of goods offered for sale, where the true type is known to one side of the transaction but not to the other. Suppose that two nations are negotiating a treaty. Further suppose that nation *A* does not know whether nation *B* possesses a high or low value for the public good being negotiated. If this information were known, then the treaty could be consummated easily. Obviously, if nation *B* highly values the public good, it may not be in its interest to reveal this information because it will have to grant greater concessions for the treaty. Unless there are ways to identify the types through actions (screening) or signals given off, the treaty may not be formulated.

In some situations, hidden type results in the *adverse-selection* problem in which bad risks drive good risks out of an insurance market, thereby leading to a market failure. Suppose that countries in a region again try to form an insurance pact or even an alliance against a common threat. The membership fees will be determined by the highest risk (that is, the weakest link) if the individual risks cannot be properly assigned. Therefore, nations that view themselves as a lower risk will exit the pact, thereby leaving only the highest-risk nations. Like moral hazard, adverse selection involves a failure to account for external costs that an agent's action places on others. For example, the presence of a high-risk nation in a proposed pact affects how low-risk nations view the average net benefits of the collective. The high-risk nation lowers these net benefits and distorts the incentives for other potential participants. This kind of externality occurs whenever more than two types coexist and their differences are not apparent to one side of the transaction.

To address moral hazard, the agent must be responsible for a greater share of the consequences of its inappropriate behavior of failing to take adequate precautions. In insurance markets, this is accomplished with deductibles or copayments to *privatize* some of the external costs that moral hazard implies. Similar design principles can be used in treaties or other transnational collectives to encourage global action over inaction, which moral hazard induces. By admitting more homogeneous members, transnational collectives can circumvent the adverse-selection problem, provided this homogeneity of risk can be observed. When this homogeneity is less apparent, monitoring devices can be collectively supplied as a first step in promoting subsequent collective action. The practice of approving a convention to study a pollution problem prior to instituting a protocol (for example, the Vienna Convention before the Montreal Protocol for limiting the use of CFCs and other ozone-depleting substances) supplies the required information to sidestep the adverse-selection problem. In some cases, the international community can encourage actions that might screen a would-be participant in terms of its type.

Basic Insights

Not all public goods imply the same collective action prognosis. Transnational club goods can, for example, be efficiently supplied with tolls that account for congestion and preference differences through visitation charges. Moreover, the presence of jointly produced provider-specific benefits and club good benefits can also encourage voluntary contributions if the share of these excludable benefits is sufficiently great. The difference between per-unit benefits and costs is also an essential consideration for the possibility of global or transnational collective action. Additionally, the third property of publicness – the aggregation technology – also figures prominently in the prognosis for collective action with weakest-link and weighted-sum aggregators as encouraging action with less need for explicit policy inducements. With so many different scenarios, generalizations are only possible for specific classes of collective goods. When policy is required to prompt collective action, the support must be tailored to the market failure and its strategic implications. Because institutional choice can determine the properties of publicness, institutional design is an essential tool that will be addressed in the next chapter. Other potential collective action difficulties are also examined in terms of strategic consideration – a wide range of remedies are relevant.

4

Transnational Public Goods: Financing and Institutions

In 1976, I submitted a paper on transnational public goods (TPGs) to a top economics journal. This paper investigated the growing collective action difficulties posed by such goods and used examples that included transfrontier pollution, transnational terrorism, infectious diseases, satellite networks, and a Chunnel linking France and the United Kingdom. I was especially interested in how novel institutional and financial arrangements were slowly evolving to address these TPG contingencies. Although the paper went successfully through two rounds of refereeing, the extremely favorable recommendations of the referees were dismissed as "patronizing" by the editor, who said that such an established journal should not be publishing "avant-garde science fiction" articles.[1] For the first and last time in my life, the term avant-garde was applied to me or my work. That paper, which never saw the light of day in its original form, spawned a whole research agenda for me during two decades. Fortunately, I have lived long enough to see that everything in that paper was spot on. With new books appearing yearly,[2] there is no question that interest in TPGs is here to stay.

Why have TPGs grown in importance so that they now interest even the gatekeepers of the exalted journals, where academics turn to discover acceptable research topics? First, and foremost, the current fixation on globalization has underscored the importance of TPGs. Globalization emphasizes cross-border flows of all kinds including the spillovers of benefits and costs associated with TPGs and transnational externalities.

---

[1] The journal will remain nameless; I saved the rejection letter to remind myself to have faith in my ideas.

[2] Examples of recent books include Sandler (1997), Kaul, Grunberg, and Stern (1999), Kanbur, Sandler, and Morrison (1999), Ferroni and Mody (2002), Arce and Sandler (2002), Kaul et al. (2003), and the current book.

Additionally, globalization underscores the importance of a new set of institutions (for example, regional pacts, global governance networks, and multilateral agencies) and agents [for example, public-private partnerships, nongovernmental organizations (NGOs), and charitable foundations] that address the ever-increasing transfrontier flows. These same institutions and agents figure prominently in allocative and distributional aspects of TPGs and transnational market failures. Second, the Balkanization of nations in Africa, Asia, and Europe following the end of colonization and the breakup of the Soviet Union has created TPGs out of national public goods (NPGs). Third, technology continues to create novel TPGs and transnational public bads (TPBs). Fourth, monitoring capabilities have educated humankind to interdependencies previously unknown – for example, slipstreams transporting sulfur emissions from Asia to the United States and large holes opening in the protective stratospheric ozone layer each spring.

At the outset, an important distinction must be drawn between TPGs and global public goods (GPGs). TPGs are public goods whose benefits and costs reach beyond one country and, in some instances, beyond the current generation. If this reach is virtually worldwide, then the good is a GPG. TPGs may be further subdivided based on reach; for example, regional public goods (RPGs) influence countries within an identified area, while transtropical public goods impact countries in and around the equator. When examining the collective action prognosis for RPGs and GPGs, a researcher can easily draw the wrong conclusion if he or she fixates on the number of participants and ignores other relevant institutional considerations. That is, one may falsely conclude that RPGs are less problematic to provide than GPGs because the number of participants is smaller for RPGs (Barrett, 2002; Ferroni, 2002). This conclusion fails to account for inhibiting factors associated with RPGs – for example, regional rivalries or the absence of leader countries in some regions.

Relevant questions addressed in this chapter include: How are the basic principles of public finance being applied in practice in the allocation of resources to myriad TPGs that vary along the three dimensions of publicness? The absence of a supranational government with taxing authority makes the standard tools of public finance – that is, the ability-to-pay and benefit principles of taxation – more difficult to apply at the transnational level. Given this difficulty, should the world community rely on voluntary efforts to finance TPGs at the national level, or should it instead engineer collective responses guided by the multilateral institutions [that is, the United Nations, World Bank, and the International Monetary Fund

(IMF)]? Would a combination of national and collective provision be best? How have real-world institutions evolved in their provision of TPGs, and has this evolution promoted allocative efficiency?

With mission creep a concern for multilaterals, subsidiarity is analyzed where the jurisdictional range of the relevant institution is chosen so as to match the corresponding spillover range of the TPGs. A prevalent feature of the allocation of TPGs today is that numerous institutional arrangements have emerged as varied as the TPGs that they supply. To explain this institutional variation, I present simple design principles that not only save on transaction costs but also promote the right incentives. Proper institutional design makes the difference between global collective action and inaction on a host of exigencies. For some TPGs, regional institutions may be a better alternative than relying on action at either the national or global level. If the TPGs involve more than one region, then a network of regional institutions can coordinate actions among regions without having to resort to a world body with many unaffected (uninterested) parties and high transaction costs.

In this chapter, the analysis is at the transnational level where agents are national governments or other international players such as NGOs. At this level of abstraction, I ignore the public-choice problem as to whether a national government is really maximizing its constituents' well-being. Implicitly, I assume that these governments have their citizens' well-being in mind as they *strategically respond* to the other international agents. If, instead, I were concerned with decision making solely at the national level, then I would have greater interest in these public-choice issues. Good strategic behavior at the international level conserves on scarce resources and, in so doing, can better enable a national government to augment not only its constituents' well-being but also its officials' welfare. Thus, the analysis here is incentive compatible with a national government's actions to look out for its officials.

Basic Taxation Principles for Financing Public Goods

In industrial countries, the public sector on average accounts for between 30% and 60% of gross domestic product (GDP); in 1999, the public sector averaged 43.5% of GDP for the Organization of Economic Cooperation and Development (OECD) countries (Bruce, 2001, p. 7). Public-sector expenditure serves two main purposes: redistribution of income and the provision of public goods. Although these activities are conceptually separated, they are interrelated because the provision of public goods has distributional impacts on individuals (for example, laborers earn income by producing public goods) as resources are allocated to these goods. Efficient provision of public goods may potentially improve the well-being of everyone, thereby engineering a better distribution of income which may itself be viewed as a public good with nonrival and nonexcludable benefits for all.

Two essential principles guide taxation at the national level and can be applied to TPGs at the supranational level. The *benefit principle* requires that a good's recipients pay their marginal willingness to pay (MWTP), which consists of the value that they gain from another unit of the good. When all consumers of a pure public good pay their MWTP and this sum of MWTPs equals the good's marginal cost of provision, an optimal amount of the good is supplied. The trick is to learn consumers' true MWTPs for a public good because they may be able to consume it while underreporting the good's true worth to them. At the transnational level, these same perverse incentives exist and so nations are unlikely to be forthright about their MWTPs if they believe that fees are later tied to their reported MWTPs.

Clubs that charge users of an excludable good based on their frequency of use (see Chaps. 2 and 3) are applying the benefit principle. Members who value the good more will visit more often and will pay more in total charges; that is, their MWTPs are sufficiently great to justify many visits at the set user fee. If, for example, nations share a disaster-relief team during natural catastrophes, nations with greater need for the team's deployment would have a greater derived benefit than would other nations less prone to earthquakes and other such events. While efficiency is promoted through such club arrangements, equity is a clear concern because some potential users' MWTPs are low owing to limited income. Thus, a reliance on a club scheme at the supranational level raises the need for underwriting some countries' participation. The benefit principle also applies when a healthy share of private benefits is attached to a collective good from joint products. These supporter-specific benefits motivate contributions.

The second principle of taxation is based on an agent's ability to pay; a higher GDP indicates a greater such ability. This second principle is easier to administer because the supplying institution only needs to ascertain a recipient's income and not its derived benefits. Taxes based on ability to pay are not necessarily benefit based; rather, such taxes provide a means for promoting equity but not necessarily efficiency unless derived benefits and income are perfectly matched. Because public goods are often normal goods whose effective demand rises with income,[3] ability-to-pay schemes may partly account for some benefits received. The actual relationship between ability to pay and assigned tax burdens reflects alternative notions of equity. One such concept is horizontal equity, which requires agents with the same income or wealth to assume identical burdens for financing the public good. When financing UN peacekeeping, burdens are not only based on income but also on permanent membership on the Security Council (Durch, 1993; Mills, 1990). Such additional criteria violate horizontal equity. Alternatively, fairness may be based on vertical equity in which individuals with higher incomes are made to finance a larger amount of the public good through taxes or assigned assessments. These principles are derived from the notion of a diminishing marginal utility of income, where each additional dollar of income adds less to a person's well-being.[4] With diminishing marginal utility of income, a dollar taken from a rich agent has less of an impact on the agent's well-being than a dollar taken from a poor agent. Progressive taxation, where tax burdens increase as income rises, is based on vertical equity. When a supranational institution must be proactive in providing a TPG, usually vertical equity is applied to the ability-to-pay instrument.

There is a huge political difference in instituting these principles at the supranational, rather than national, level. For GPG financing, there is no recognized supranational government that can tax nations based on either principle of taxation. Since the early 1990s, the growth of regionalism is beginning to give rise to regional collectives that can impose some taxes to redistribute income or to provide RPGs – the EU is the prime example. The ability of regional collectives to tax is rather limited, especially when compared with government spending at the national level by member states. The situation is unlikely to change in the foreseeable future, as nations view control over their revenue sources as a key symbol of autonomy, which they have no intention to dilute or sacrifice.

The financing of GPGs or TPGs with a large spillover range is typically accomplished, if at all, on an ad hoc basis through a number of channels.[5]

---

[3] For example, defense is usually measured to be a normal good in empirical studies (Sandler and Hartley, 2001).

[4] While most economists accept the concept that the additional satisfaction derived from a good eventually displays diminishing marginal utility, the notion of diminishing marginal utility of income is more controversial.

[5] On the political aspects of financing TPGs, see Held and McGrew (2003), Kaul and Le Goulven (2003), and Sandler (forthcoming).

First, nations funnel money through multilateral and regional institutions to finance TPGs through membership, contributions, or fees. Second, a rich nation privileges the rest of the nations with the good, because the provider's derived benefits justify the associated costs even if it must solely supply the TPG. Two instances are the US Centers for Disease Control and Prevention (CDC) monitoring of disease outbreaks or the US weather satellite tracking of hurricanes in the Caribbean, Gulf of Mexico, and the Atlantic Ocean. Since infectious diseases and hurricanes pose a significant threat to the United States, it has an incentive to invest in infrastructure that monitors outbreaks worldwide as well as major storms in the region. Sharing this information with other countries is virtually costless. Unilateral provision is particularly germane to best-shot public goods. Third, specialized agencies of multilaterals support select TPGs [for example, global health by the World Health Organization (WHO)] from membership assessments (based on ability to pay), fees for services (for example, payments for reports or data), and donated trust funds. Fourth, nations can combine efforts to provide a TPG, such as NATO's efforts to address peacekeeping needs. In some cases, neighbors can jointly finance infrastructure (for example, the Chunnel joining France and the United Kingdom) or address a common crisis. Fifth, a club can collect fees and charge members to support some excludable, rival TPGs. The financing of TPGs is essentially at the national level through coordination orchestrated by regional and multilateral institutions.

An international tax, such as a Tobin tax on currency transactions, while feasible, is unlikely because its impact will be greater on the rich nations, which have powerful incentives to disapprove the tax. Additionally, a Tobin tax will distort investment incentives by discouraging transnational investments and, in so doing, imply an efficiency loss. It is important to remember that taxes on chlorofluorocarbons (CFCs) under the Montreal Protocol are collected at the national, not the supranational, level so that nations are not sacrificing any of their taxation authority to an international body. The same would be true of a carbon tax on greenhouse gas emissions.

TPG Categories and Financing

In Chapter 3, public goods are distinguished by three properties of publicness. Based on nonrivalry and nonexcludability considerations, a TPG may be purely public, impurely public, a club good, or a joint product activity. Even impurely public goods may be further subdivided into classes depending on the degree of nonrivalry or nonexcludability – for example, an impure public good may be nonrival and excludable, partially rival and excludable, partially rival and nonexcludable, or some other combination. An alternative classification scheme involves the manner in which individual contributions determine the overall level of the public good available for consumption. In addition to the five primary aggregators of summation, weighted sum, threshold, weakest link, and best shot, there are two further classes: weaker link and better shot. Both of these aggregation technologies are less extreme than their weakest-link and best-shot counterparts. For weaker link, the smallest contribution has the greatest marginal influence on the overall level, followed by the next smallest, and so on. Weaker-link TPGs include pest containment because efforts above the least may still provide some additional protection from the invaders. Another weaker-link TPG involves the enforcement of some transnational treaties (for example, actions to stem trade in endangered species), where efforts beyond the smallest may achieve a net gain. Other examples include maintenance of sterilization in a region's hospitals or network redundancies to increase reliability. With weaker link, action may not settle on matching provision levels as there are some gains with exceeding the minimal provision level (Arce and Sandler, 2001). As a consequence, a better-endowed country may be somewhat less interested in the capacity of the poorest country because some shortfall of a minimal standard by the smallest contributor may be made up by greater actions abroad.

For a better-shot TPG, the largest contribution has the greatest marginal impact on the overall consumption quantity, followed by the second-largest contribution, and so on. The discovery of new antibiotics is a better-shot public good because generally less effective new antibiotics may be more tolerated by some patients not able to take the more effective medicine. Moreover, the less effective antibiotic may provide a line of defense as the bacteria gain immunity over time to the first line of defense. Similarly, efforts below the largest to monitor the atmosphere may still provide protection, though at a diminished level to the greatest provision level. Other better-shot examples include the collection of databases and BL-4 laboratories used to isolate and study the most infectious diseases. Better-shot TPGs imply outcomes where more than one nation supplies the good but in unequal quantities. Because provision is anticipated to be spread over more agents, coordination and pooling issues are less of a concern with better-shot TPGs.

As shown in Chapter 3, the properties of publicness have strategic implications that influence the need for policy intervention. In Table 4.1,

Table 4.1. *Taxonomy Based on Three Dimensions of Publicness: Supply Prognosis*

Aggregate Technology	Pure Public Good (nonrival and nonexcludable)	Impure Public Good (partial rivalry and partial excludability)	Club Good (partial rivalry and excludable)
Summation	undersupplied *curbing ozone shield depleters*	overuse/undersupplied *deterrence against terrorism*	efficient supply *transnational parks*
Weighted sum	undersupply dependent on agent-specific benefits and actions *reducing sulfur depositions*	overuse/undersupplied with agent-specific benefits important *curbing the spread of AIDS*	efficient supply *INTELSAT*
Weakest link	efficient for a homogeneous group; capacity issue *disease containment*	overuse/some undersupply even for homogeneous groups owing to crowding *monitoring disease outbreaks*	externality-based undersupply *air traffic control*
Weaker link	efficient for a homogeneous group; less capacity issue *pest containment*	overuse/some undersupply owing to crowding *maintaining sterilization*	some externality-based undersupply *network with redundancies*
Best shot	undersupply or efficient supply coordination and pooling issues *neutralizing a rogue nation*	overuse/some undersupply coordination and pooling issues *intelligence on terrorists*	efficient supply *rapid reaction force*
Better shot	undersupply or efficient supply coordination and pooling issues are less of a concern *discovering new antibiotics*	overuse/some undersupply coordination and pooling issues are less of a concern *databases*	efficient supply *BL-4 laboratory*

Note: Examples are in italics.

three categories of public goods – pure, impure, and club – are further subdivided by six of the seven aggregation technologies. That is, a pure public good can abide by any of the six aggregators, as can an impure public or a club good. A generic impure public good, characterized by partial rivalry and partial excludability, is represented in the third column. For each of the eighteen categories displayed, the supply prognosis and a TPG example (in italics) is given. When moving away from the summation aggregator, the supply prognosis for a pure public good generally improves. If, for example, a weighted-sum technology applies and a relatively large weight is placed on the agent's own provision, then the agent is apt to contribute a more efficient quantity, insofar as the agent's effort is less substitutable for the contributions of others. For example, sulfur emissions tend to fall closer to the emitting country than some other emissions, so that more action to curb emissions are anticipated and experienced (Murdoch, Sandler, and Sargent, 1997). With a weakest-link TPG, nations that are homogeneous in terms of tastes and endowments will match one another's efficient responses. In a less homogeneous group, the better-endowed nations may have to bolster the capacity of those that cannot meet the efficient level. The other entries in the pure public good column have been discussed in the last chapter or here and require no further discussion.

Impure public goods display less drastic changes in their supply prognosis in Table 4.1 as the aggregation technology alters. Overuse is prevalent throughout because partial rivalry implies crowding costs, while partial excludability means that fees will not fully account for the crowding inconvenience imposed on others. Partial excludability also leads to undersupply that is attenuated, but does not disappear, for weakest-link, weaker-link, best-shot, and better-shot public goods. This follows because whatever is supplied is overutilized as exclusion and tolls are only partial in their remedy. The influence of the aggregator on the supply prognosis and the ability to finance an efficient provision (without a costly intervention by a supranational institution) hinges on all three properties of publicness. The need and nature of corrective policy depend on these properties.

In the right-most column of Table 4.1, club goods are distinguished according to the six aggregators. Except for weakest-link and weaker-link TPGs, the supply prognosis is excellent, since a club can use tolls to finance the club good without resorting to intervention. For a weakest-link club good, there are potential externalities that may not be completely addressed by the individual suppliers. For example, one country's less reliable air traffic control infrastructure can create ripple effects and disruptions through the network when it fails. Uniform tolls to air carriers for using the network may not account for differential reliabilities. Similarly, a security weak point in an airport network can place all air travelers at greater jeopardy from terrorist attacks. The only fix to these efficiency problems is to bring more of the shared parts of the network under general club control so that a common standard is maintained. If a club arrangement is instituted for sharing air corridors, then the same arrangement must also be instituted for security, traffic control, and other aspects jointly consumed with the utilization of air corridors.

Based on Table 4.1, a number of institutional conclusions follow. First, supranational intervention in the form of multilateral institutions, treaties, or specialized agencies is primarily needed for pure and impure public goods that adhere to a summation technology or a weighted-sum technology, where weights on one's own provision are relatively small. Second, economists' long-standing fixation on the summation aggregator has meant that the need for proactive policy for providing and financing TPGs has been exaggerated. Many TPGs abide by more agreeable aggregators that may require little or no explicit intervention. Third, club structures work well for a wide range of aggregators with the exception of weakest-link and weaker-link club goods, where additional externalities must be taken into account by a multipart toll. Fourth, financial capacity is an issue for weakest-link pure and impure public goods if adequate minimal standards of supply are to be met. Therefore, some nations or donors – charitable foundations, NGOs, and multilateral institutions – may have to finance the TPGs either through direct provision or money transfers. Partnerships with such institutions may play a role in bolstering the financial capacity of some nations to meet acceptable provision standards. For example, WHO assisted poor nations to do their part in eradicating smallpox from the world, which was accomplished in 1977. Fifth, leadership by a dominant nation or institution may be needed to provide some best-shot TPGs; pooling and coordination are associated with select best-shot TPGs. In practice, partnerships among diverse participants can draw on their comparative advantage to surpass thresholds and other impediments of best-shot TPGs. Sixth, weaker-link and better-shot TPGs are anticipated to require less policy intervention than their extreme forms.

Thus, I contend that institutional innovations in the form of the development of partnerships, the emergence of new participants, and the creation of specialized multilateral agencies are evolving to meet the challenges posed by many TPGs. These innovations can do much to foster the financing and supply of essential TPGs. Those cells in Table 4.1 where the supply prognosis is grim are where the world community must concentrate its effort.

On Subsidiarity and Jurisdictional Responsibility

The principle of subsidiarity supports the match between the coordinating jurisdiction and the spillover range of the public good. Therefore, NPGs should be allocated by a national government, RPGs by a regional institution, and GPGs by a multilateral organization. Subsidiarity rests, in part, on the notion of *fiscal equivalence*, first formulated by Breton (1965) and Olson (1969), which states that the political jurisdiction should coincide as closely as possible with the region of spillovers so that those affected by the public good determine its provision decision.[6] By matching the decision-making jurisdiction and the good's economic interests, subsidiarity seeks to foster allocative efficiency where the sum of the derived marginal benefits of those affected by a public good is equated to the marginal cost of provision. When the coordinating jurisdiction reaches beyond the range of the public good spillovers, fees or other financial burdens may then be placed on some agents who do not benefit, thus resulting in the possibility of oversupply. If, instead, the coordinating body's jurisdiction fits well within the spillover range of the public good, then decision makers will likely fail to include benefits conferred on others outside of the jurisdiction so that too little of the public good is supplied. Suppose that a pest or disease indigenous to Asia must be addressed. Without other considerations, subsidiarity indicates that an Asian institution is most appropriate to coordinate national actions to curb the pest or disease. Subsidiarity is also supported because it curtails transaction costs by reducing the number of participants to just those with a stake in the activity. This focus on essential decision makers bolsters repeated interactions, which, in turn, furthers learning and curtails asymmetric information. At the minimalist level of interactions determined by spillovers, the presence of localized benefits supports the evolution of institutions based on shared culture, norms, and values (North, 1990).

---

[6] Subsidiarity is also addressed in Arce and Sandler (2002), Kanbur (2002), Kanbur, Sandler, and Morrison (1999), and Sandler (forthcoming).

Within a country, subsidiarity holds greater sway as there are a wide variety of political jurisdictions with unique public good spillover ranges; in the United States alone, there are over 87,000 city, county, and district governments owing, in large part, to diverse spillover ranges of public goods (Bruce, 2001, p. 4). Beyond the nation-state, there are many fewer political institutions for providing public goods. A common feature is that a successful supranational body coordinates efforts over many TPGs where the body's authority does not match the benefit range of the goods. The United Nations provides numerous TPGs that include peacekeeping, global health (for example, efforts to fight HIV/AIDS in Africa and Asia), knowledge creation (population control and studies), environmental protection (treaty formulation and administration), and governance (regimes for telecommunication, transportation, and postal services). Given the wide variety of spillover ranges of TPGs supplied by multilaterals and other supranational bodies, we must look for detracting factors of subsidiarity that can explain the institutional reality that confronts us.

Economies of scale may justify using institutions with a larger jurisdictional mandate than a good's spillover range to provide a TPG, because greater production levels can lower unit costs. Thus, two or more nations may combine their wastewater treatment facilities to reduce unit costs. When the reduced costs from scale economies more than cover any loss in efficiency from the noncoincidence between the political and economic domains, the use of a larger jurisdiction is justified.

Economies of scope arise when the costs of providing two or more public goods jointly in the same institution is less expensive than supplying them in different organizations, better tailored to match the goods' spillover range. Since the spillover ranges of two or more TPGs are unlikely to coincide, the provision of multiple TPGs by the same supranational body is not expected to abide by subsidiarity. As the number of jointly supplied public goods increases, the violation of subsidiarity strengthens. Economies of scope may be traced to cost savings stemming from common costs attributable to the shared use of some inputs when allocating resources to multiple public goods. Such common inputs may extend to administrative staff, communication networks, meeting facilities, research personnel, transportation networks, and scientific staff. These scope economies cannot persist forever: as the number of TPGs supplied by the same multilateral or supranational body grows, the capacity of the infrastructure and/or cost savings from common inputs must eventually be exhausted. Once such savings are exploited, an institutional decision must be made whether to expand the infrastructure and facilities to accommodate yet more TPGs or to assign new TPGs to specialized agencies. Both practices are observed: the World Bank's interest in global health is the former, while the creation of the International Maritime Organization (IMO), WHO, and the International Telecommunication Union (ITU) represents the latter.

Another obstacle to applying the principle of subsidiarity involves the absence of the requisite institution with a jurisdiction that matches the TPG spillovers. For transtropical public goods, the world community has to either rely on a multilateral institution or engineer a patchwork of regional institutions and agents that spans the public good's range of spillovers. Along such lines, global networks – for example, the Consultative Group on International Agricultural Research (CGIAR) and the Global Environment Facility (GEF) – have emerged. Each of these programs addresses research and environmental concerns that involve similar problems (for example, sustainable agriculture and biodiversity) in widely dispersed regions. In other instances, the proper institution may exist, but it lacks sufficient capacity or finances to handle the problem. Financial capacity presents a concern for the regional development banks that currently do not have financial backing to provide for a growing number of RPGs (Kanbur, 2002; Sandler, forthcoming).

Yet another inhibiting factor to subsidiarity stems from the aggregation technology. For best-shot and better-shot TPGs, a sufficiently large effort may be required in which resources may have to be pooled beyond the jurisdiction identified with subsidiarity. Foreign assistance in the form of grants and loans to developing countries in their fight against some noncommunicable diseases is an example. A similar situation applies to some threshold TPGs that must surpass a requisite level of supply before benefits are realized.

In Table 4.2, supporting and detracting factors associated with subsidiarity are listed for ready reference. The choice of the appropriate jurisdiction for any TPG must weigh the net influences of these opposing considerations.

On Regionalism and Region-Based Collective Action

With the rise of regionalism and the consequent growth of regional collectives [for example, Andean Community (AC), Central American

Table 4.2. *Supporting and Detracting Influences on Subsidiarity*

- *Supporting factors for subsidiarity*
  - ➤ Matching economic and political domains fosters efficiency by equating the good's marginal cost of provision and the recipients' marginal benefits.
  - ➤ Limits transaction costs by reducing the number of participants, augmenting repeated interactions, and curtailing asymmetric information.
  - ➤ The presence of localized benefits promotes the evolution of the institution based on shared culture, norms, and values.
- *Detracting factors of subsidiarity*
  - ➤ Economies of scale may favor serving a larger community.
  - ➤ Economies of scope from reduced unit cost endorse providing two or more public goods in the same jurisdiction. If these economies of scope are sufficiently large, then subsidiarity may lose its sway when the goods' spillover ranges differ.
  - ➤ The requisite subsidiarity institution may not exist nor possess sufficient capacity.
  - ➤ Best-shot and better-shot technology may favor pooling beyond the jurisdiction identified by subsidiarity. The same may be true for some threshold aggregators.

Common Market (CACM), EU, North American Free Trade Association (NAFTA), Mercado Commún del Sur (MERCOSUR), and the Group of Temperate Southern Hemispheric Countries on Environment (Valdivia)], there is enhanced demand for RPGs.[7] The spillover range of RPGs includes a well-defined region that includes the territory of at least two countries. For health, environment, governance, knowledge, and security, RPGs are becoming a more important component of development and, as such, require support from multilaterals, bilateral donors, and others (Cook and Sachs, 1999; Arce and Sandler, 2002). Despite a growing demand for RPGs in the developing and developed world, RPGs tend to receive relatively little attention and inadequate support. The rise of regionalism may change this pattern with the strengthening of regional institutions that can coordinate provision of RPGs.

Traditionally, the international community supports NPGs through bilateral aid, multilaterals, and other donors, and provides TPGs through multilaterals and their specialized agencies. During 1996–98, support for NPGs was 29.4% of foreign aid contributions of the OECD; during 1996–98, support for TPGs (which includes RPGs) was just 8.79% of the

---

[7] On regionalism, see Devlin and Estevadeordal (2001), Dodds (1998), Mansfield and Milner (1999), and Padoan (1997).

foreign aid contributions of the OECD. Since 1980–82, the percentage of foreign aid for NPGs has grown from 11.24%, while this percentage for TPGs has grown from 4.98% (Willem te Velde, Morrissey, and Hewitt, 2002, pp. 126–7).

As a territorial subset, a region may be defined geologically (based on plains, mountains, or other features), geoclimatically, geographically (in terms of global placement – for example, sub-Saharan Africa), culturally (founded on a common language), or politically (for example, members of the EU). Nations may have a regional identity that is not based on contiguity (for example, Brazil and Portugal). These same considerations may define an RPG, whose benefits are distributed based on regional factors. For instance, agricultural crop research findings tend to be geo-climatic specific, because differences in temperature, rainfall, humidity, or soil affect the needs of crops, so that a research breakthrough for one geoclimatic area may have little knowledge spillovers for another area (Khanna, Huffman, and Sandler, 1994). The cleanup of many pollutants – sulfur, nitrogen oxides, and other particulates – are regional owing to their limited reach once emitted from their sources. Pollution distributed by lakes, underground water, river, or other local conveyance are necessarily regional. Infrastructure can yield regional spillovers, which is the case for waterways, communication systems, transportation networks, and fire suppression capabilities.

RPGs can pose collective action concerns that make their support, at times, more problematic than NPGs or GPGs. NPGs are provided by the country itself, while GPGs are supplied by multilateral institutions or nations adhering to international treaties. For developing countries, NPGs and GPGs are financed by bilateral donors, charitable founda-tions, NGOs, multilaterals, and other institutions. Even though GPGs involve more benefit recipients than RPGs, the latter often must surmount more formidable collective action difficulties that arise from a number of political and institutional considerations. First, regional institutions that champion RPGs are much weaker than their global counterparts. For example, the World Bank has a much greater capacity to channel support to GPGs and TPGs than the regional development banks have to finance RPGs. Second, this needed inflow is hampered by a tradition to rely on the multilateral institutions. Third, many RPGs' spillovers may not benefit large donor countries so that their motivation to underwrite these goods is limited. Fourth, many regions – especially those in the developing world – lack a dominant nation that can provide the necessary leadership. Fifth, competitive forces among regional members may inhibit provision of the needed RPGs (Cook and Sachs, 1999). Sixth, the absence of a political identity or institution at the regional level can inhibit the receipt of grants and loans for supporting RPGs. A regional collective may be needed to offer collateral for loans and to account for their disbursements. Sixth, a host of nongeographical barriers – involving language, geology, or trade bloc membership – may hamper the provision and effective demand of RPGs in contrast to NPGs and GPGs.

These collective action impediments present a dilemma because subsidiarity would dictate that if scale and scope economies are not too great, then action by a regional institution is desirable. A case can thus be made for building up regional institutions starting with the regional development banks, which can raise funding for the RPGs. The rise of regionalism and the growth of more capable regional common markets can overcome some of the collective action concerns associated with RPGs. The EU serves as a role model in its efforts to supply a wide range of RPGs in the form of pollution control, financial standards, scientific research, common defense, traffic control, and infrastructure provision.

In those instances where more than one region confronts a common RPG concern, but the spillover range is clearly not global, strengthened regional institutions can serve as links in a network that spans multiple regions (Arce and Sandler, 2002; Held and McGrew, 2003; Reinicke, 1998; Sandler, forthcoming). For health, knowledge, the environment, and security, these interregional public goods are growing in importance. Multilateral institutions can facilitate these linkages.

Institutions: Some Design Principles

Simple changes to institutional structure can promote cooperation as a dominant strategy, where payoffs are highest no matter what other players do. To demonstrate some helpful design principles, I start with a most unfavorable strategic scenario where a Prisoners' Dilemma applies. Suppose that each of *six* nations must decide whether to contribute a unit of a pure public good at a per-unit cost of 8. Further suppose that every unit provided gives 6 in benefits to each and every nation – contributor and noncontributor alike. Because the net difference between per-unit benefits and per-unit costs is -2 ($= 6 - 8$), a Prisoners' Dilemma results for this summation scenario where *gross benefits* equal the number of contributors times the per-unit benefits of 6. Matrix *a* in Figure 4.1 indicates the associated payoffs for a representative nation *i* for alternative

a. Prisoners' Dilemma

	Number of contributors other than nation i					
	0	1	2	3	4	5
i Does Not Contribute	0 Nash	6	12	18	24	30
i Contributes	−2	4	10	16	22	28

b. Minimal threshold: no refunds, no cost-sharing

	Number of contributors other than nation i					
	0	1	2	3	4	5
i Does Not Contribute	0 Nash	0	0	18	24	30
i Contributes	−8	−8	10 Nash	16	22	28

c. Minimal threshold: refunds, no cost-sharing

	Number of contributors other than nation i					
	0	1	2	3	4	5
i Does Not Contribute	0	0	0	18	24	30
i Contributes	0	0	10 Nash	16	22	28

d. Minimal threshold: refunds, cost-sharing

	Number of contributors other than nation i					
	0	1	2	3	4	5
i Does Not Contribute	0	0	0	14	18.5	23.33
i Contributes	0	0	14	18.5	23.33	28 Nash

Figure 4.1. Alternative institutional forms

numbers of other contributing nations, from 0 to 5 corresponding to the matrix's columns. If nation i does not contribute to the public good, then it receives a free-rider benefit of 6 times the number of contributors. Thus, for three contributors, i nets a gain of 18. The other entries in the top row are computed similarly. If, however, nation i contributes and one other nation contributes, then i receives 4 ($= 2 \times 6 - 8$), which equals the benefits from two units of the public good less i's cost of 8. In the bottom row, country i receives payoffs equal to the number of contributors (including itself) times the per-unit benefits of 6 minus the per-unit costs of 8. The payoffs in the top row exceeds the corresponding payoffs in the bottom row by 2 (the difference between per-unit costs and per-unit benefits) so that nation i's and, hence, all six nations' dominant strategy is to not contribute, leaving zero all-around contributions as the Nash equilibrium. The social optimum is for every nation to contribute for a gain of $6 \times 28 = 168$.

The standard remedy to make contributing the dominant strategy is to either punish noncontributors by something greater than the *net difference* between per-unit costs and per-unit benefits, or to reward contributors by something more than this amount. In either case, the contributor strategy then becomes dominant. There are some difficulties with the use of punishment or rewards. First, and perhaps foremost, punishment requires a "second-order" collective action that is more difficult to accomplish in practice than providing the public good (Heckathorn, 1989). Second, rewarding also requires collective action on the part of the entire group, and faces no less difficulty than contributing. Third, rewards and punishments divert funds and this diversion can reduce social welfare. For rewards, a central authority must raise the money from membership fees or some other mechanism and this reduces the members' resources. Fourth, both schemes have transaction costs. Neither the use of rewards nor punishments represents a panacea for collective action.

A more practical and efficient means to make contributing a dominant strategy is to institute cost-sharing, so that each of n nations agrees through a treaty or arrangement to pay $8/n$ for each and every unit contributed regardless of the contributor. Unlike rewards, no inducement pool must be collected, and, unlike punishments, no authority needs to dole out fines. For matrix a, if $n > 8/6$, then the dominant strategy for cost-sharing is to contribute.[8] Thus, for two other contributors, i nets 14 $\{= 3[6 - (8/6)]\}$, which exceeds 12. Similarly, the payoffs in the bottom row for cost-sharing

---

[8] This cost-sharing matrix is not displayed.

exceed those in the top row, provided that someone contributes. Nations may agree because each must only cover a tiny portion of the cost of each unit when group size is large. In contrast to general principles, group size works in favor of collective action for cost-sharing. The Nash equilibrium of everyone contributing is the social optimum. Cost-sharing gives the participants a social awareness of their actions that fosters good outcomes.

Next, consider the use of cost-sharing and refundability for a threshold technology, where benefits of 6 per unit are only realized once *three* or more units are contributed. As before, each nation can contribute one or no units. To put things in perspective, I display the influence of thresholds in matrix *b* of Figure 4.1 *without* cost-sharing or refunds for failing to meet the threshold. Per-unit costs are still 8. When less than three units are contributed or less than three nations contribute, the threshold has not been obtained and there are no benefits. So in matrix *b* in the top row, free-rider payoffs are zero until three or more nations contribute, at which point the payoffs match those in the top row of matrix *a*. In the bottom row of matrix *b*, *i* pays 8 if the threshold of three units is not obtained; thereafter, *i*'s payoffs match those in the bottom row of matrix *a*. There are now many Nash equilibriums: the one where no one contributes and those where exactly three nations contribute. If more than three nations contribute, then the payoffs in the top row again dominate those in the bottom row. For more than three contributors, another unit contributed adds two less in benefits than in costs for a new contributor. A threshold technology improves the situation because there are now positive contribution equilibriums unlike the Prisoners' Dilemma. All environmental treaties build a threshold technology into their ratification process; that is, unless a certain number of nations sign the treaty, it does not go into effect. This number depends on the ability of the nonsigners to undo through greater pollution the collective action of the signers and varies among problems.[9] When assembling peacekeepers for a mission, the United Nations Security Council does not deploy the peacekeepers unless a threshold is reached depending upon the troop strength required to keep the opposing sides separated. The use of thresholds is a common ploy to induce collective action; this ploy can be made even more effective through the use of refunds and cost-sharing.

---

[9] See, especially, Buchholz, Haslbeck, and Sandler (1998) on the problems of partial cooperation.

The role of institutional design is evident in matrices c and d in Figure 4.1. In matrix c, a full refund of contributions is given if the threshold is not attained. For example, nations offering firefighting assets to a conflagration are not required to fulfill their promise until a sufficient level of assets are pledged to ensure success of the mission and reasonable safety for deployed teams. The sole payoff difference between matrices b and c concerns the bottom row where 0 replaces –8 in the first two columns of matrix c. As a consequence, the bottom row now weakly dominates the top row until the threshold is reached. Focal Nash equilibriums correspond to precisely three contributors. An equilibrium with less than the threshold number of contributors is less interesting because a nation has nothing to lose by contributing if the threshold is not attained and much to gain from meeting the threshold (Bagnoli and McKee, 1991). After the threshold of three contributors is attained, the payoffs in the top row from being a noncontributor are higher than the corresponding payoffs from being a contributor. Thus the social optimum of everyone contributing is not achieved; nevertheless, the Nash equilibrium is pushed toward contributing as compared with the scenarios in matrices a and b. As the minimal threshold increases, the Nash equilibrium moves nearer to the social optimum whenever refunds are given for failing to achieve the threshold. Refundability can play an important role in promoting transnational collective action for some aggregation technologies.

In matrix d, both refundability and cost-sharing exist among the group's members. In the bottom row, the payoff is 14 when nation i and two others contribute. This follows because nation i receives 18 ($= 6 \times 3$) in gross benefits and must then pay its cost share of 4 ($= 3 \times 8/6$). The other payoffs are computed similarly. Now the bottom row weakly dominates the top row, so that the dominant strategy is for nation i and, thus, all other nations to contribute. With refundability and cost-sharing, the Nash equilibrium may become the social optimum, so that the invisbile hand returns. Any institutional design that provides players a "collective view" of their decision – as in the case of cost-sharing – has the virtue of promoting collective action through incentive-compatible influences.

Other design principles can have similar influences in promoting collective action. For example, a supranational institution can collect a small amount from each nation that is then used to subsidize contributions to ensure that $b_i - c_i > 0$ from the contributor's viewpoint. If the collection is small, then nations may agree to such payments. Another helpful device is to tie contributor-specific benefits to contributions so that joint products are encouraged, not unlike the way that charities and governments provide special inducements to donors – for example, special recognitions, rewards, or tax deductions. In a supranational organization, these inducements may take the form of votes or other privileges. The IMF allocates votes to members based, in large part, on their share of the capital stock that they put into these organizations. The United States possesses almost 18% of IMF votes in 2001 (Buira, 2003) based on its basic voting allocation (250 per member) and large quota contribution. Recent suggestions to reduce the votes of the large contributors (see, for example, Buira, 2003) will surely limit their support of the organization.

Another favorable principle of institutional design involves engendering an air of permanency in the structure so that members view the interaction as ongoing and long-lived. This aspect of supranational structures transforms the interaction among members into a repeated game where the institution's rules determine the available strategies and payoffs rather than the nations' governmental representatives, who may change with elections or other circumstances. This air of permanency may be bolstered by institutional rules that make exit difficult and require advanced notice. For example, NATO members could not exit for 20 years after the treaty was initially approved and, once permitted, exit requires giving a year's advance notice (Article 13 of NATO treaty). Permanent bureaucracies that carry on the routine activities of supranational organizations also add to the perception of longevity.

All supranational structures must overcome the inertia of initial formation. Various tricks are employed to surmount this barrier in practice (Sandler, 1992, 1997). To guarantee formation, supranational structures begin negotiations with a minimal number of essential members. In the case of the Montreal Protocol, only eleven countries, which comprised two-thirds of CFC use, were required to sign for the treaty to be ratified (Barrett, 2003a, pp. 226–7). The first negotiations of the NATO treaty only included a small number of key allies (United States, United Kingdom, France, Belgium, Canada, Luxembourg, and the Netherlands) with others – Denmark, Iceland, Italy, Norway, and Portugal – asked to ratify the treaty after its drafting (Sandler and Hartley, 1999). As the years passed, new allies – Greece, Turkey, West Germany, Spain, unified Germany, Hungary, Poland, and the Czech Republic – joined the alliance. If the treaty had required ratification by more allies from the outset, then the negotiations would have taken longer and the treaty may have never been consummated. Another formation device is to include fairly homogeneous nations when setting up the organization. Homogeneity may involve not only income but also the level of the relevant activity covered by the supranational structure – for example, many of the major CFC users were involved with the Montreal Protocol. Yet another device to ensure formation is to start with a very loose structure that is tightened over time if warranted. Looseness shows up with very inclusive decision rules – unanimity or veto-rights voting – so that members do not have to go along with unfavorable decisions, thereby preserving potential members' autonomy. Looseness can also be reflected by infrequent meetings, nonbinding decisions, small common-funding budgets, and limited infrastructure. Once formation takes place, the net benefits from cooperating can be reevaluated and this can lead to greater tightness if cooperative gains become viewed more favorably over time.

Supranational Institutions in Practice

The United Nations takes advantage of economies of scope and scale by providing a wide variety of GPGs and TPGs through its regular membership fees and donors' voluntary contributions. Many donors contribute to the United Nations, using it as a brand name or monitoring device to ensure that the money gets to its intended purpose. Reliance on multilaterals to support TPGs is an attempt for donors to address the asymmetric information problem where the agent (the organization) is better informed than the donors. That is, the agent knows better than the donor how much effort it puts forward to supply the TPGs. By establishing a reputation for providing TPGs, the United Nations limits information costs among supporters who channel money through it rather than giving directly and then having to do its own monitoring. The World Bank is in the same position. The downside, however, is mission creep in which the United Nations and the World Bank take on more and more public good chores; hence, the growing need for regional entities and development banks to provide some RPGs. The United Nations is supported in large part by regular membership fees that reflect vertical equity and ability to pay in terms of income and development status.

To address specific public good issues, the United Nations created specialized agencies. For example, WHO pursues the maintenance of world health by monitoring disease outbreaks, coordinating medical research, immunizing populations, assessing health risks, and disseminating information. WHO is financed by donated trusts and membership assessments. WHO also provides information and data, from which they charge fees to support its research activities. Other UN agencies – for example, the IMO and ITU – also finance themselves from membership fees and other service charges. The latter charges are based on benefits received. Nations sacrifice some autonomy to achieve coordination benefits from standards and regulations in shipping and telecommunications.

The World Bank is a multilateral agency that supplies TPGs in the form of developmental assistance, technical advice, and research findings. In recent years, this institution views itself as a "knowledge bank," but it provides much more than knowledge to the developing world. The Bank coordinates development assistance from myriad donors including charitable foundations and member countries. In this capacity, the Bank serves as an intermediary between donors and recipients, not unlike the role assumed by charitable organizations within a nation. The Bank's TPG activities vary in their public characteristics with many giving rise to joint products that have both public and donor-specific benefits. The latter helps to motivate donor generosity.

The Bank is supported by member countries' subscriptions to its capital stock, used for loans and grants to finance the Bank's operations. As mentioned earlier, donor-specific benefits stem from assigning a member country's votes in the Bank based on the size of its subscriptions (World Bank, 1999). In return, a larger subscriber gains greater influence over the World Bank's policy decisions and direction. When providing TPGs to recipient countries, the World Bank relies on grants when a significant portion of the public benefits go to the world community, whereas it utilizes loans when primarily the recipient country's NPGs are being funded (World Bank, 2001). With NPGs, there may be few benefit spillovers to the world community. This distinction may be difficult to apply in practice because some NPGs are necessary for a developing country to be able to supply or absorb TPGs. By supplying numerous public goods, the World Bank is exploiting economies of scope.

Concluding Remarks

This chapter reviews institutional and financial concerns associated with the provision of TPGs in practice. If one subscribes to the standard view of public goods as being purely public with per-unit costs exceeding per-unit benefits, then there would be few, if any, TPGs supplied. In fact, many

TPGs are provided by individual nations and supranational organizations; thus, the question arises as to why the true situation is so different from predicted scenarios. The answer hinges on a few key insights. First, essential properties of public goods vary along three dimensions that influence incentives for nations and collectives to circumvent the provision problem. If TPG benefits are impurely public and excludable and if individual contributions abide by certain aggregation technologies (for example, weakest link and threshold), then the prognosis for provision at either the individual or collective level is more hopeful. At times, the institutional design may itself change the underlying properties of the TPGs to bolster provision. Second, institutions have developed design innovations conducive to fostering the proper incentives for individual contributions to the public good. Third, favorable institutional innovations have been rapidly adopted by other organizations; thus, the promotion of jointly produced agent-specific benefits characterizes activities of national, regional, and global institutions that supply public goods. It is no accident that multilateral institutions share many of the same institutional features as successful national charitable institutions. Fourth, institutional structures differ based on the underlying publicness characteristics of the TPGs supplied because these properties determine the incentive structure and, hence, the form that the institution should assume to promote efficiency. With sufficient excludability of benefits, club arrangements can be used. Fifth, successful supranational institutions have devised means for getting around the initial formation dilemma by starting with a limited number of fairly homogeneous participants and a deliberately loose structure. If circumstances warrant, then more participants with greater diversity can be included later. Additionally, the tightness of the organization can later be increased when sufficient cooperative benefits appear likely. Sixth, the application of the subsidiarity principle can address mission creep of the multilaterals, thereby devolving more authority to regional institutions. Greater reliance on these organizations will give rise to greater provision of RPGs. My basic message is that practical means for providing TPGs are being discovered.

5

Global Health

In March 2003, the world learned about Severe Acute Respiratory Syndrome (SARS) and the threat that it poses to infected individuals. The international transmission of SARS to other countries far beyond China was caused by infected airline passengers, thus highlighting how a virulent disease can disperse rapidly worldwide.[1] Therefore, SARS represents a global public bad and its containment is a global public good (GPG). Criticism has been leveled at Chinese officials for not fully reporting the extent of the outbreak to the World Health Organization (WHO). Intelligence on diseases also represents a GPG that can allow for swift efforts at containment and control that can save lives. Quarantine of diseased persons is both a GPG and a regional public good (RPG) that provides benefit spillovers to recipients depending on their likelihood of coming into contact with those infected. As such, the public good associated with quarantines abides by a weighted-sum aggregation technology where weights relate to some spatial transmission process.

Globalization creates an increased health interdependency worldwide that stems from enhanced transmission pathways for infectious diseases through greater mobility and transfrontier exchanges. Despite the high stakes, there is no overall strategy for promoting worldwide health owing to collective action problems stemming from the need for global participation, lack of awareness, and national protection of autonomy. To date, WHO tries with limited resources to coordinate efforts worldwide. Its actions are bolstered in an ad hoc fashion by the US Centers

---

[1] The factual information in this paragraph comes from the Centers for Disease Control (CDC) (2003) website at http://www.cdc.gov/od/oc/media/transcripts/t030414.htm and *The Economist* (2003a, pp. 18–19).

for Disease Control and Prevention (CDC), US National Institutes of Health (NIH), the multilateral institutions, nongovernmental organizations (NGOs), and a variety of other institutions. The various institutions reflect concerned rich nations and special interests taking a leadership role and, in other instances, multilaterals coordinating a collective response. The current pattern of institutions displays wasteful overlapping efforts, inadequate and delayed responses, and innovation following exigencies. Understandably, nations will not sacrifice their autonomy with respect to health policy unless the threat is especially dire or they do not have the means to address the challenge alone. Thus, developing countries solicited assistance from the international community to address Ebola, human immunodeficiency/acquired immune deficiency syndrome (HIV/AIDS), and other deadly diseases despite the consequent loss in autonomy, while developed countries try to handle disease outbreaks on their own until a more coordinated response becomes imperative.

The twenty-first century is confronted with three plagues: HIV/AIDS, tuberculosis (TB), and malaria. Since 1982, more than 40 million people have been infected with HIV and over half of them have died (*The Economist*, 2002b, p. 65). In 2001, there were 5 million new HIV infections and some 3 million deaths (WHO, 2002, p. 4). New cases of TB are growing at about 2% per year with 80% of them concentrated in just 20 poor countries.[2] Annually, about 2 million TB patients die. At least 1 million people die from malaria each year, with 70% of the deaths concentrated in sub-Saharan Africa. Every year, the three plagues of the twenty-first century cause a half a billion illnesses and kill at least 6 million people. With these diseases posing the greatest threat to the developing world, there is much less concern about them in the developed countries, where efforts are focused on treating HIV/AIDS, keeping new diseases out, and preventing noninfectious diseases (for example, cancer and heart disease).

There is a fascinating – and easy to comprehend – mix of global collective action successes and failures with respect to transnational responses to promoting health. A notable success is the world's eradication of smallpox in 1977 with the financial and technical assistance of rich countries and the coordination role of WHO. If vials of the smallpox virus had not

---

[2] The facts in the rest of this paragraph come from WHO (2002, pp. 1–6).

been kept by the rival superpowers owing to their mutual distrust, small-pox would not present the terrorist threat that it does today.[3] For measles, poliomyelitis, and dracunculiasis (guinea worm), eradication efforts have failed to date. Effective leadership by the United States and other rich nations has not adequately materialized for those infectious and noninfectious diseases that pose little threat to them because of climate, location, or other risk factors not shared by these wealthy nations. Leadership has, however, characterized rich countries' efforts to isolate, track, and evaluate new diseases that present a clear danger to all countries. In recent years, the world has become aware of the state of health in less-fortunate countries whose incomes have fallen farther behind during the current era of globalization. This awareness of a growing inequality and a worsening health situation has mobilized new participants to bring money and know-how to improve global health. In the process, new institutional arrangements emerged in the form of partnerships and networks that draw on the diverse comparative advantage of the participants in geographically separated regions. These latter efforts are driven by altruism and an understanding that good health is absolutely essential if poor countries are to develop.

The Bush Administration's initiative to spend $15 billion over five years (announced on 29 April 2003) to address the AIDS epidemic in Africa appears motivated by the realization that African development and stability is hindered by this disease. Whatever its true motivation, this initiative serves a leadership role heretofore absent in fighting AIDS in developing countries. An essential question is how much of the proposed money will materialize. Debates in the US Congress during July 2003 have already slashed the first-year funds of $3 billion by one-third and conditions are being attached to their disbursement. A second question is whether US leadership will merely lead to free riding by other developed countries as predicted for similar Prisoners' Dilemma situations. If others do not follow the US lead, the United States is unlikely to carry through with subsequent year funds.

---

[3] The holding back of these vials is a classic Prisoners' Dilemma, where each superpower feared that the other would maintain its vial if it destroyed its own vial, thus giving the rival the highest payoff and itself the lowest payoff. When both rivals kept the vials, each ended up in the Nash equilibrium with the next-to-lowest payoffs. Mutual destruction would have given each superpower the next-to-highest payoffs.

The purpose of this chapter is to investigate the need and prognosis for collective action with respect to global health. There is a rich array of collective outcomes because global health embraces many activities that vary along the three dimensions of publicness. This variety has caused some (for example, Terrell, 2002) to dismiss the usefulness of the public good representation of global health. Quite to the contrary, the presence of numerous health activities with varying publicness properties means that different policy prescriptions apply depending on the action investigated; universal conclusions are difficult to draw. In very few instances do health public goods satisfy the three classic properties of pure public goods – complete nonrivalry, nonexclusion, and a summation technology of aggregation. Consequently, many health needs may result in some collective action, leaving less call for corrective policy; nevertheless, there still remain many market failures involving the current and future generations. Another purpose is to distinguish standard market failures from intergenerational ones involving the current and future generations. Because a disease is passed from one generation to the next, positive action today – say, eradicating a disease – has consequences for generations in perpetuity. A final purpose is to examine the role of institutions in promoting collective action and addressing health-related market failures. Varied institutional forms have evolved owing to the many public health activities and their diverse requirements for intervention. If health activities had presented a more homogeneous degree of publicness, then fewer institutional forms would have evolved. For some health issues, further institutional innovations are required, especially for intergenerational collective action concerns.

Taking Stock

In the introduction, the morbidity figures for the three plagues do not really capture the true impact of these diseases. A better measure is the Lost Healthy Years of Life (Lost HLYs), which account for the victim's age at the onset of the disease and the duration of the disease – that is, a child who dies from malaria loses more HLYs than a middle-aged adult. Since these diseases impact the young so greatly, there is a large number of HLYs: 90.4 million years, AIDS; 40.2 million years, malaria; and 35.8 million years, TB (WHO, 2002, p. 3). The impact of these diseases differs greatly between the developed and developing countries. For HIV/AIDS, deaths from AIDS is on the decline in the developed world where the main focus is on treating infected patients with antiretroviral therapies that extend their lifetimes. The vast majority of new HIV cases are in sub-Saharan Africa, eastern Europe, and central Asia (WHO, 2002, p. 4). Thus, the developing world would gain much if a vaccine could be developed to immunize the population against the disease that is passed from those infected in heterosexual activities, the sharing of needles, and from mother to unborn child. Commercial pharmaceutical companies earn more profit from treatment therapies than from a vaccine, thereby leading to a market failure that requires subsidization of vaccine development from governments and other outside interests (for example, charitable foundations). Bush's African initiative on AIDS is primarily directed at promoting abstinence and safe sex and supplying antiretroviral therapies. Only the small portion that goes to the Global Fund may eventually support vaccine development.

The rise of TB is certainly related to the HIV/AIDS epidemic because an impaired immune system is less able to cope with the TB bacillus, which in most healthy people will not result in the disease. The developed world continues to experience a decline in TB cases since 1980; most new cases are found in Africa, Southeast Asia, and Eastern Europe (WHO, 2002, p. 5). Effective TB treatments exist and are inexpensive. Of course, the patient must seek treatment and there must be sufficient capacity in disease hot spots for doctors to diagnose and treat the ill. A prime worry is the administering of incomplete treatments that can aid the bacteria to acquire drug resistance, which then presents a risk to the world and future generations. The drug-resistant form of TB is on the rise and provides a motivation for developed countries to become involved in augmenting the health infrastructure in TB hot spots. That is, clear benefit spillovers motivate developed countries to become involved. Thus, during 1980–82, only 4.1% of aid spent on transnational public goods (TPGs) went to the health sector; but during 1996–98, this percentage rose to 11.4% (Willem te Velde, Morrissey, and Hewitt, 2002, Tables 5.4, 5.6). Given the trends in the three plagues, this expenditure percentage will continue to grow.

Malaria's impact on developed and developing countries could not be more different. Unless global warming changes climate drastically, the developed world has little direct interest in malaria because there are few cases and those that enter with travelers are easily treated. Moreover, the disease is not passed from person to person. In sub-Saharan Africa, which has 90% of the world's cases, malaria is a killer with its greatest influence on young children among the 300–500 million individuals infected worldwide each year (WHO, 2002, pp. 5–6). Death is due to misdiagnosis or lack of timely treatment. Malaria control involves four critical interventions: the distribution of insecticide-treated bed nets (at a cost of $3–$5 a year); prompt diagnosis and treatment; antimalaria therapy for pregnant women; and effective monitoring and response to epidemics (*The Lancet*, 2000; Sandler and Arce, 2002). As with the other two plagues, the at-risk developing countries require added capacity to prevent and treat malaria. A further concern is the need for new antimalaria therapies as existing ones lose their effectiveness over time.

The three plagues share some commonality. First, each can be prevented: safe sexual practices, sterilized needles, and education for HIV/AIDS; treated bed nets and insecticide for malaria; and vaccination for TB. Second, prevention is the most cost-effective action in all three cases. Third, the developed countries have only modest direct interests in these diseases. Fourth, these illnesses have their greatest impact in parts of the developing world, especially in sub-Saharan Africa for HIV/AIDS and malaria, where money for prevention and treatment are very limited. Fifth, commercial interests do not view the healthcare needs of plague-ridden developing countries as highly profitable areas for investment. Sixth, at-risk countries do not have sufficient healthcare capacity to address these plagues and require help from elsewhere. Since aid-associated direct benefit spillovers to donor countries are limited, this aid requires new participants beyond the standard donor countries. The Commission on Macroeconomics and Health (CMH) (2001) provides restrained estimates of the annual expenditures needed to curtail the three plagues: $0.4 billion for TB treatment; $1.2 billion for malaria prevention and another $0.3 billion for treatment; and $3.6 billion for HIV/AIDS prevention and another $2.6 billion for treatment. In total, CMH calls for $27 billion annually to bolster healthcare in the developing world (see Kremer, 2002; WHO, 2001). Despite the world's growing awareness of the health blight in the developing countries, the inflow of money from old and new donors will come nowhere near this goal.

An important concern in the development of new medicines, vaccines, and treatments is the "90/10" gap, in which less than 10% of the US annual spending on health-related research and development addresses the health concerns of 90% of the planet's population (WHO, 2002, p. 23). Given differences in life expectancy, life styles, immunization programs, healthcare infrastructure, education, and wealth, people in high-income countries primarily suffer from noncommunicable diseases, whereas those in low-income countries suffer greatly from infectious and parasitic diseases (Kremer, 2002, p. 71; WHO, 2001). Diseases such as measles, syphilis, and pertussis kill relatively few individuals in high-income countries but cause hundreds of thousands of deaths in poor countries (WHO, 2001). These differences imply that developed countries have difficulty in fathoming the healthcare needs of poor countries. Most important, healthcare breakthroughs in developed countries are geared toward diseases of less concern to the developing world. This bias is exacerbated by the profit motive; the high income elasticity and low price responsiveness for some medicines and treatment regimes motivate pharmaceutical companies to concentrate on maladies most germane to high-income countries. Even when high- and low-income countries share the same healthcare concerns, medical breakthroughs may be ill suited to low-income countries where medical technology and training are primitive. Moreover, these countries may not be able to afford the medicines, even when sold at marginal costs.

Market Failures and Healthcare

Market failures result when individuals' optimization decisions do not achieve a social optimum. For health decisions, market failures involve externalities, public goods, and asymmetric information and have consequences for the current and future generations. When a person decides whether or not to be immunized, the individual focuses on his or her benefits and costs, while ignoring positive externalities conferred on strangers. Herd immunity, which varies by disease, means that less than 100% of the population needs to be immunized to eradicate the disease – for example, in the case of smallpox, herd immunity is estimated at 70–80%, so that immunization levels as high as 80% can eradicate the disease (Anderson and May, 1991, p. 88). Given the costs and risks, a person is best off if he or she can free ride on the immunization of others. As individuals attempt to free ride, immunization levels are undersupplied, leaving society at inefficiently high-risk levels. This market failure can be reduced if the costs and risks of immunization are reduced (for example, with additional vaccination sites and safer vaccines) or if immunization is made compulsory. The latter action may, however, result in too much immunization, especially if the vaccine carries relatively high risks as in the case of smallpox.

Another market failure concerns the insufficient efforts applied to outbreak surveillance and intelligence. The WHO, NIH, and the CDC have sought to redress this underprovision. Underprovision may also involve excludable health public goods which have little, if any, rivalry (see Chap. 3, Fig. 3.2). For example, health intelligence should be made widely available, especially today when the Internet makes transmission virtually costless.

Market failures may also arise from monopoly and oligopoly interests that may sell at prices above marginal costs so as to maximize profits. At times, this monopoly situation is granted by government patents, so that there are sufficient incentives for companies to invest the high fixed costs for developing new drugs. Patent-protected monopoly profits compensate, in part, for high risks associated with discovering new medicines, since many discovery attempts end in failure. Thus, patents present a trade-off between greater discoveries today and reduced provision owing to higher prices during the patent period. This issue may be somewhat attenuated with greater government subsidies of pharmaceutical research and development (R&D). I emphasize *greater* subsidies because such support is already given. Asymmetric information limits the effectiveness of these additional subsidies because the drug companies are better informed on the development costs of new medicines and have little incentive to reveal this information truthfully to government sponsors. A situation of moral hazard thus arises, not unlike government-subsidized development of weapons where defense contractors have little incentive to control R&D costs.[4]

Another market failure concerns a developing country's promise of future patent protection or guaranteed sales to entice a pharmaceutical company to develop a medicine. Once the medicine is discovered and brought to market, the promising government may renege on its pledges (Kremer, 2002, p. 75). This is a time-inconsistency problem where an agent's optimizing choice changes at a later point once an action is taken by the agent or someone else. This problem may be controlled by repeated interactions. If, for example, a government reneges on its pledge to one drug company, then other companies will take note and not enter into similar arrangements; thus, reputation consequences can help limit this particular time-inconsistency market failure.

---

[4] This is a moral-hazard problem where asymmetric information leads to a change in behavior (Sandler, 2001, Chap. 7).

Global Health and Publicness

A distinguishing feature of health public goods is the diversity in terms of activities and their associated publicness characteristics. Of all of the problems studied in this book, health public goods are the most diverse and can be purely public, impurely public, club goods, or private and marketable. In some instances, a health activity may give rise to joint products, whose outputs vary in their degree of publicness.[5] Discovering a cure is purely public, while monitoring disease outbreaks is impurely public. Once uncovered, a cure can be used in a nonrival fashion by everyone who suffers the disease. Monitoring is, however, partially nonrival because focusing attention in one area detracts from surveillance elsewhere. Moreover, monitoring is excludable to some extent because monitors can be withheld from some areas. If a health-promoting public good that serves people internationally is partially rival in terms of crowding, but nonpayers can be completely excluded at a negligible cost, then the activity is a transnational club good. Examples are the Mayo Clinic or M.D. Anderson Cancer Center where patients worldwide come for these institutions' expertise. Patients are charged according to treatments received and the fees collected support the hospital and its staff. A technical consultation network via the Internet is also a transnational club good, whose use can be monitored and charged accordingly. As use increases, crowding takes the form of slower replies and longer queues. Club principles can be applied to determine the level of provision, supported by tolls based on crowding costs.

Joint products are prevalent among health-related activities. For example, immunization provides the recipient with agent-specific benefits, while giving purely public benefits to the larger population from a reduced risk of contracting the disease. Research hospitals not only supply patient-specific private benefits but also generate purely public benefits from research findings stemming from patient care. Health activities also involve marketable private goods in terms of prescriptions of medicines, doctor visits, or diagnostic tests.

Equity issues arise when fees for health-promoting club goods, excludable nonrival goods, and private goods are beyond the means of some sick individuals, a real worry in developing countries. These equity concerns

---

[5] On the nature of health public goods, see Arhin-Tenkorang and Conceição (2003), Chen, Evans, and Cash (1999), Sandler and Arce (2002), and Zacher (1999).

may also have allocational consequences. If the healthcare infrastructure is sufficiently primitive in some poor countries, then the country's population is vulnerable to diseases that can gain a foothold there before spreading globally. Diseases, like other invaders, seek out the weakest link. The SARS epidemic, which established a foothold in China in November 2002, is an excellent example (*The Economist*, 2003a). The recognition of these negative spillovers, when countries possess insufficient financial and technical capacity to supply their own public and private health needs, has enhanced interests in providing GPGs and RPGs in health. Thus, the existence of markets and club-like structures does not eliminate the need for actions to bring others up to acceptable standards to avoid disease-creating transnational externalities.

The most interesting dimension of publicness for health activities is the aggregation technology. For many health public goods, this third dimension has important implications for the form of the corrective policy. These health goods rarely abide by a summation technology, where the level of the good available for consumption equals the sum of the individual contributions. More often, health activities display weakest-link or best-shot properties.

A summation technology characterizes educating the public about transmission of infectious diseases and about screening for noninfectious diseases. The overall level of awareness is the sum of the educators' cumulative efforts. Summation health public goods are anticipated to be undersupplied, leading to the need for intervention by the international community (see Chaps. 3 and 4). This assistance is sure to come when the public goods involve infectious diseases that pose a threat to developed countries, but is less apt to materialize for public goods associated with infectious diseases that do not present such a danger. Public goods associated with noninfectious diseases are also likely to be underprovided, so that assistance may be justified on equity grounds.

For weakest-link health public goods, nations with similar income and tastes will maintain roughly equivalent provision levels, so that no corrective policy is needed. Contributing nations will want to match the smallest provision level because doing more will achieve nothing. Weakest-link examples include prophylactic measures to stem the spread of an infectious disease and information-sharing networks for noninfectious diseases. When stemming the dispersion of a disease, the most-porous barrier determines the success of the efforts. In a network, the least-reliable information influences the level of intelligence for all participants.

Weakest-link health activities are more problematic when contributors have different tastes and capacities. In this scenario, the provision level achieved by the smallest supply amount is apt to be an inadequate standard for those who can afford to do more. Either the poor countries' capacities must be bolstered, or else the rich must raise the poor's contribution level. This can be accomplished directly by providing the good in these countries (for example, immunizing their populations) or funding others (for example, the multilaterals) to supply an adequate level. In either case, incentives are there to provide this capacity because the safety of everyone is at stake.

Weaker-link public goods are a more subdued form of weakest-link public good, in which efforts beyond the least add some benefits, thus matching behavior is not a necessary outcome as shown in Chapter 4. Examples include maintaining sterilization in hospitals and curbing the spread of a pest. With less need to accomplish matching behavior, there is a reduced need to augment the capacity of the poor countries as greater efforts at home by the rich countries can partly offset the inadequate capacity abroad. When doing more at home becomes more costly than improving provision levels abroad, assistance of lower-capacity countries is then advisable.

Best-shot health public goods present a different sort of capacity challenge where the most-capable research team or country must acquire the requisite means to accomplish the breakthrough – for example, isolating a virus for an infectious disease or finding a cure to a noninfectious disease. Best-shot health public goods justify the establishment of premier research institutions when discovery is likely to result from the greatest efforts. In these cases, *coordination* is needed to concentrate resources and to prevent duplication of efforts. If the breakthrough is more random and based on good luck, then multiple providers are necessary to increase success. Multiple suppliers are also advisable for better-shot health public goods, where smaller effort levels can still achieve benefits. When discovering new vaccines or treatment regimes, second-best alternatives may be beneficial for patients who cannot tolerate the best vaccine or treatment. For these better-shot goods, less coordination is required. The provision of best-shot and better-shot health public goods gives spillover benefits to poor countries. The worry for tropical diseases is that the premier research institutions are not motivated to make the discovery unless there is a push based on altruistic concerns. With such altruism, the richest countries will determine the best-shot health agenda of the entire world. Thus,

Table 5.1. *Alternative Aggregation Technologies for Health-Promoting TPGs*

Aggregation Technology	Infectious Diseases	Noninfectious Diseases	Public Policy Implications
Summation: public good levels equal the sum of individual contributions	Educating the public about transmission	Educating the public about screening	Need for international cooperation for infectious diseases. Some international assistance is required for noninfectious disease if country is poor.
Weakest link: only the smallest provision level determines the public good level	Providing prophylactic measures	Sharing information in a network	When the countries have similar income, little intervention is required. If, however, standards for infectious diseases cannot be met by poor countries, rich ones will have to bolster the poor's capacity to contribute. This is more of a concern for infectious diseases.
Weaker link: the smallest contribution has the greatest marginal influence, followed by the next smallest, and so on	Maintaining sterilization	Curbing the spread of a pest	The need for matching behavior is less pronounced. Rich may assist poor countries if infectious or noninfectious diseases pose a danger.
Best shot: only the largest provision determines the overall public good level	Isolating a virus	Finding a cure	Effort must be concentrated where talent is the greatest with discoveries benefiting everyone. Coordination in the form of directing resources to those most likely to succeed is desirable.
Better-shot: the largest provision has the greatest marginal influence, followed by the next largest, and so on	Discovering new vaccines	Developing treatment regimes	Less need for concentrated effort, but some coordination still required.
Threshold: cumulative contribution must surpass threshold for benefits to be received	Eradicating a disease with herd immunity less than 99 percent	Assessing risks	Coordination is needed so that threshold is met. Cost sharing and refundability promote action. Public coordination can be helpful.
Weighted sum: each contribution can have a different additive impact	Curbing spread of AIDS	Reducing sulfur pollution	Need for intervention must be on a case-by-case basis. Localized benefits may limit policy intervention.

there is a real role for the push for TB, malaria, and HIV/AIDS research by the charitable foundations, NGOs, and partnerships involving diverse participants.

Threshold health public goods also highlight the needs for coordination among providers. Consider the case of eradicating an infectious disease with vaccinations when herd immunity is less than 99%, so that, say, an 80% vaccination level can achieve full population protection.[6] Coordination is essential because it is in a person's interest to be among the 20% who do not get inoculated but free ride on those who do. Efforts expended to assess health risks can also abide by a threshold aggregation technology that requires a certain level of intelligence for a reasonable safety level. From the analysis in Chapter 4, we see that some institutional innovations – cost-sharing and refundability – can promote the required coordination. Of course, refundability is not feasible for vaccinations because the inoculation cannot be undone, nor would people want to give up their private protection once acquired.

A final aggregation technology for health public goods is weighted sum, where contributions have different impacts and so are not perfectly substitutable. Because of differences in education and sexual practices between regions, a weighted-sum technology applies to public good actions to curb the spread of AIDS. That is, identical measures taken in west and sub-Saharan Africa do not have the same effectiveness as when applied in North America or Europe where there is a greater understanding of the disease and its transmission. In addition, reducing transnational air pollution – for example, sulfur emission – is a weighted-sum technology because depositions downwind depend on an emitter's size and position along with the prevailing winds. The percentage of an emitter's pollutant that falls on others depends on these considerations. Since weighted-sum public goods are associated with so many different game forms, general conclusions about policy are difficult to draw. For example, incentives are favorable to reduce sulfur emissions because countries often receive a relatively high percentage of their own pollutants (see further discussion in Chap. 10).

Table 5.1 provides a summary of the discussion on alternative aggregation technologies for health-promoting TPGs, along with examples for infectious and noninfectious diseases. Certain insights require emphasis. First, there is a concern that developing countries do not have the technical

---

[6] See the interesting theoretical analysis of this situation in Barrett (2003b).

and financial capacity for weakest-link health public goods. This inadequate capacity will only drive collective action when infectious diseases present a risk to rich nations. Second, the prevalence of best-shot public goods in the health sector implies that one or more rich countries will privilege the rest of the world with discoveries. Third, new institutions and multilaterals must compensate for capacity deficiency regarding weakest-link and best-shot activities for diseases of little concern to the rich countries. The need for these new players is particularly acute because pharmaceutical companies focus on accomplishing breakthroughs where profits are the greatest in the treatment of noninfectious diseases in the rich countries.[7] There is, consequently, too little development of vaccines and insufficient prevention for diseases plaguing developing countries. Fourth, the prognosis for collective action is varied owing to a plethora of aggregation technologies and other publicness properties that characterize health public goods. Some aggregators promote sufficient collective action, while others do not.

Institutional Considerations

In Table 5.2, the six essential institutional forms in the global health sector are indicated along with some examples of each category. Multilateral institutions are arguably the most important participants that not only augment the provision of undersupplied health public goods, especially for the developing world, but also provide funds for emerging public–private partnerships. The WHO generates knowledge and serves an essential coordination role to address inadequate provision of weakest-link health public goods and to limit duplication for best-shot health public goods. A similar role is served by the World Bank which coordinates donations for the health sectors of developing countries and then oversees the disbursement and accounting of these donations. When health activities are RPGs that are best addressed at the regional level, the World Bank can increase the funds of the regional development banks.

In recent years, public–private partnerships that draw on the comparative advantage of diverse participants have become an important institutional arrangement (Sandler and Arce, 2002). Some partnerships focus on specific diseases that affect developing countries – for example, the Onchocerciasis Control Partnership (OCP) and the Medicines for

---

[7] New participants also bring a net inflow of income that is helpful in overcoming the neutrality problem for pure public goods.

Table 5.2. *Key Institutions in the Global Health Sector*

Institutional Categories	Purposes/Functions
Multilaterals: WHO, World Bank, UNDP	Pool funds for best-shot and summation public goods and bolster capacity for weakest-link public goods. Participate in partnerships. Coordinate aid inflows into the health sector of developing countries. Provide knowledge and statistics. Oversee funds disbursement and accounting.
Partnerships: Global Fund, Medicines for Malaria Venture, Onchocerciasis Control Partnership	Draw on the comparative advantage of diverse participants. Target tropical diseases and other plagues in developing countries. Include diverse participants that include firms, nations, NGOs, multilaterals, and charitable foundations.
Networks: Global Environment Facility (GEF), Consultative Group for International Agricultural Research (CGIAR)	Link together interests within and among regions in providing TPGs. Support sustainable development. Limit air and other forms of pollution. Bolster food supplies for better health. Networks can be used to join places with similar health problems. Contain diverse participants.
Charitable Foundations: Wellcome Trust, Gates Foundation, Open Society Institute, Rockefeller	Inflow of new funds for addressing orphan diseases and plagues affecting the developing world. Bolster capacity for weakest-link public goods and pool resources for best-shot public goods. Support diseases where there are little commercial interests. Provide leadership.
Nongovernmental Organizations (NGOs): Médecins Sans Frontières (MSF), Red Cross, Save the Children, CARE	Champion specific health public goods and complementary activities (e.g., providing food) including disaster relief, immunization, and charity. Treat the ill.
Nation-Based Institutions: CDC, NIH, Pasteur Institute	Supply health public goods in the form of performing outbreak surveillance, collecting data, isolating new diseases, and coordinating efforts to develop treatments and vaccines. Address diseases that pose or might present a risk to rich nations. Concerns in host country create a privileged group.

Malaria Venture (MMV). OCP consists of a partnership between Merck, WHO, host countries to the disease, and donors to control river blindness, endemic to 34 countries in Africa, Latin America, and the Arabian Peninsula. Under OCP, Merck contributes Ivermectin to treat the disease (a single dose is effective for a year), while the other participants facilitate Ivermectin's distribution. MMV arose from the Roll Back Malaria initiative of the WHO and consists of a nonprofit institution that provides funding incentives for partnerships among pharmaceutical companies, academic entities, and public agencies for the purpose of developing new medicines, treatments, and prevention regimes. As such, MMV promotes best-shot and weakest-link public goods for curbing malaria and its consequences. Some future commercial interests are preserved by MMV so that some discoveries can have marketing and profit potential. The Global Fund is a partnership with interests in the three plagues afflicting the developing world. This nonprofit foundation raises money and disburses it in a public–private foundational arrangement on prevention, treatment, and discovery that limits the impact of HIV/AIDS, TB, and malaria in developing countries. Financial resources are raised from NGOs, charitable foundations, nations, and the private sector.[8] The Bush initiative on AIDS can result in $1 billion of funding for the Global Fund.

In practice, these public–private partnerships represent a useful institutional innovation that draws on the varied expertise of the participants and enhances the capacity required for supplying weakest-link and best-shot public goods in the health sector. Partnerships coordinate the institutional players that now perform a role in supporting health TPGs. Such partnerships can spring up wherever action is inadequate and can adopt institutional rules tailored to further an intended outcome. Thus, a variety of institutional designs can characterize these partnerships with each partner deriving some specific benefit along with the purely public good outcome. A pharmaceutical company can derive useful advertising and goodwill from its altruistic efforts in partnerships, thereby reducing criticisms of high-profit margins in its lucrative markets in developed countries. Multilaterals are seen to be promoting world health and curbing poverty, while donor countries may be protecting their own citizens from negative spillovers by reducing the number of infected immigrants.

Networks are becoming an important institutional participant because health public goods may possess benefit spillovers that *transverse regions.*

---

[8]   For the purposes and structure of the Global Fund (2003), see http://www.globalfundatm. org. The Fund's bylaws and disbursement charts are available at this website.

Examples of these networks include the Global Environment Facility (GEF), whose donors include the World Bank, UN Development Program (UNDP), UN Environmental Program (UNEP), NGOs, and others, and the Consultative Group for International Agricultural Research (CGIAR), whose donors include the World Bank, UNDP, and donor countries (World Bank, 2001). GEF is primarily intended to promote sustainable development through environmentally friendly program assistance. In accomplishing its mandate, GEF supports improved health by limiting pollutants in air, in water, and elsewhere in the environment. Given the transport of these pollutants, donor countries, even some distance away from the aid-recipient countries, have a direct interest in supporting GEF's activities. By preserving species and their habitats, GEF also conserves biodiversity, which benefits the global community. GEF leverages its fund through some loans to provide additional support to environmental-based programs in diverse regions of the developing world (World Bank, 2001, p. 115). Client countries are motivated to borrow to augment GEF grants based on borrower-specific benefits derived from ecotourism, reduced erosion, and watershed preservation. Networks tying together regions are especially germane for addressing environmental issues, since economic activities in neighboring and even more-distant regions can have interregional impacts. The network structure is particularly suited for addressing weakest-link and weaker-link public goods where some reasonable standard of performance is required of all vulnerable countries. By pooling resources across countries or regions, networks can assist efforts to surpass critical thresholds or achieve best-shot breakthroughs.

This resource-pooling activity also applies to CGIAR, which is a network that fosters agricultural-based technological advances to augment food supplies in poor countries. Better nutrition and more ample food stocks are a building block to improved health. CGIAR promotes knowledge-based public goods that are often geoclimatic specific, so that only nearby regions may benefit. As with GEF, CGIAR can focus funds and coordinate efforts within regions facing similar problems. Like partnerships, networks can draw on the comparative advantage of diverse participants while bringing in new sources of funds.

In recent years, charitable foundations have grown greatly in importance in furthering global health because of their large budgets. Prominent foundations include the Wellcome Trust, the Gates Foundation, the Rockefeller Foundation, and the Open Society Institute (part of the Soros Foundation Network). These foundations bring an inflow of new funds that do not crowd out other sources of contributions to global health. Some of these funds arise from high profits on commercial activities (for example, Wellcome Trust and Gates Foundation) or from earnings from endowments. Crowding out is minimized because these contributors are funding research and assistance for the third-world plagues where there is little public good provision or commercial interest. These funds can support best-shot research efforts and provide much-needed capacity for weakest-link actions to stem the spread of diseases. These institutions also assume a leadership role that can generate and coordinate support from other kinds of participants. For partnerships, these foundations are an important player with unique expertise.

NGOs – Médecins Sans Frontières (MSF), Red Cross, Save the Children, CARE, and others – champion specific health public goods such as the provision of medical care in conflict zones or disaster relief. Such organizations offer not only funds but also labor to distribute the public goods. In this capacity, providers receive a joint product from the training they acquire in the field. Also, these NGOs participate in partnerships. For both NGOs and charitable foundations, there is a worry that these institutions will pursue their own agenda by optimizing the proportion of donor-specific benefits in the activities that they support. If, for example, a charitable foundation is interested in the publicity that it receives from its good deeds, then diseases that have lower newsworthiness may be ignored in deference to a disease with greater public interest, even though the suffering may be nearly identical for the two diseases. For some foundations, monopoly pricing created the available funds so that the true supporters are the consumers of drugs in the case of Wellcome Trust or the buyers of computer software in the case of Gates. These "supporters" have, however, no say in what the foundations support.

A final class of key institutions is the nation-based and nation-supported institutions such as CDC, NIH, and Pasteur Institutes that supply myriad public goods: surveying disease outbreaks, collecting statistical data, isolating new viruses and bacteria, developing vaccines, and uncovering new treatments. These institutes create a *privileged group* where a single nation is so concerned about these activities that they single-handedly underwrite them for all nations. This altruistic behavior is driven by their own interest to stop new diseases at their origin rather than waiting until they arrive on their soil (Arce and Sandler, 2003). Nation-based institutions are primarily supplying weakest-link and best-shot public goods.

Intergenerational Considerations

Many global health public goods yield benefit spillovers both spatially among countries and intertemporally over generations. When a disease is cured, it is cured for the present and all future generations (Sandler, 1978, 1999). If a vaccine is discovered for HIV/AIDS or SARS, it generates benefits for the present and subsequent generations. The overuse of antibiotics or antiretroviral therapies reduces their effectiveness over time, thereby causing an intergenerational public bad. When patients take an antibiotic, they do not consider the harmful consequences of requesting an antibiotic needlessly (say to address a virus) or consuming the antibiotic improperly by not taking the entire course of pills. As a result, the bacteria can acquire immunity, as in the case of antibiotic-resistant TB. Weakest-link health public goods may also have intergenerational implications. That is, failure to control or eradicate a disease increases the distribution of the virus or bacteria worldwide, which places future generations at greater risk.

Spatial spillovers are easier to take into account than temporal spillovers because all recipients are contemporaries and so can make their preferences known and consummate agreements to bolster public good provision. For intergenerational spillovers, future generations are not present and so must rely on the far-sighted altruism of the current generation. The sequence of generations has an important implication for capacity. If this capacity is insufficient for a weakest-link health public good, then future generations confront an even greater capacity problem as more people become vulnerable owing to past inadequate actions. For a best-shot health public good, any generation that acquires the capacity eliminates the problem for all subsequent generations. Thus, weakest-link intergenerational public goods pose a greater allocative concern than their best-shot counterparts. The presence of intergenerational public benefit spillovers raises an interesting dilemma: greater efforts to account for transnational spillovers may exacerbate intergenerational externalities. For example, efforts to enhance antibiotic availability in developing countries may hasten the appearance of antibiotic-resistant diseases. Similarly, effective vaccination programs may make for a more vulnerable future generation if the disease is not eradicated and uninoculated individuals are subsequently exposed. Clearly, there is anticipated to be underinvestment in intergenerational public goods that is generally greater than the underinvestment in health public goods with no intertemporal component, since spillover awareness must transcend both space and time.

Underinvestment also involves the patent issue, where monopoly rights are given to investors of new medicines and vaccines, so that they can recover past R&D expenditure. The cost profile of medicines and vaccines involves high fixed costs and relatively low marginal costs per dose (Kremer, 2002, pp. 73–4). Marginal-cost pricing results in large losses, so that some period of competition protection as provided by a patent is necessary if incentives to discover new medicines are to remain. If, however, the patent period is too long, then many patients cannot benefit from the drug or vaccine owing to prohibitive costs. Given the negligible cost of production in some instances, a new medicine is analogous to an excludable public good with virtually zero marginal costs (see Chap. 3, Fig. 3.2), where a welfare loss results from the exclusion of those who possess a positive marginal willingness to pay, less than the market price. The higher the patent-protected price and the lower the marginal costs, the greater the current welfare loss. A trade-off exists because the current welfare loss stemming from a prohibitive price provides the incentives for the discovery. Without these incentives, there would be fewer discoveries and therefore greater welfare losses for current and future generations from not having the medicines. Thus, current welfare losses motivate future welfare gain. Ideal patent protection would account for this trade-off by choosing a length of patent protection that equates the present value of welfare losses with the present value of welfare gains from the discoveries. These latter gains are experienced by those in the current and future generation who can afford the medicine. If monopoly pricing is limited, then a longer patent period is needed to allow drug companies to offset their fixed costs of R&D. Of course, R&D costs can be reduced for the pharmaceutical firms through subsidies; for example, MMV promotes discoveries through public–private subsidization.

One way to limit welfare losses is to institute a multitier pricing system so that people with lower income levels pay a smaller price.[9] This multitier system is being used to increase the availability of antiretroviral medicines for African countries (Kremer, 2002). The problem remains that these countries are still too poor to afford much of the drugs even

---

[9] This price discrimination allows the discoverer to capture more of the area under the demand curve, thereby reducing consumer surplus – the difference between a consumer's derived value and payment.

at the marginal-cost price. Foreign aid can play a huge role in these instances, as recognized by the WHO's Commission on Macroeconomics and Health (2001). There is also the concern that the drugs will be resold at a higher price in developed countries where prices are higher. This is less of a worry for drugs aimed at diseases indigenous to these poor countries.

For some diseases, the *orphan drug* issue arises because *effective* demand is insufficient to cover costs, so that the patients' willingness to pay is less than per-unit costs, inclusive of the fixed costs of R&D (Bruce, 2001). The source of this inability to cover costs is different in developed and developing countries. In developed countries, the orphan drug problem arises when the disease is sufficiently rare that the potential number of patients is too small to support the high fixed development costs associated with discovering new drugs and vaccines. The shortfall of demand in developing countries stems instead from an inability of patients or the host government to afford the medicines. Often the disease is quite prevalent, as in the case of HIV/AIDS, TB, and malaria. Consider the discovery of a vaccine for HIV/AIDS, which generates much less profit opportunities for the pharmaceutical companies as compared with lucrative antiretroviral treatments. To address this nonprofitability, either the *effective* demand must be increased or the per-unit cost of the vaccine must be reduced. From a society's viewpoint, this demand should also include that of unborn future generations who will gain greatly from the vaccine but cannot express their derived benefits at the time that such funds are allocated to the research. Far-sighted institutions can play an essential role in boosting the demand to reflect the needs of the current and ensuing generations. Charitable foundations, public–private partnerships, multilaterals, and donor countries can proxy and support these implicit demands. By drawing on their members' comparative advantage, partnerships can reduce per-unit costs, which helps close the gap between demand and per-unit costs.

In Table 5.3, intergenerational and intragenerational market failures associated with global health are displayed for comparison purposes. Patent protection can lead to either intragenerational market failures by granting monopolies to drug suppliers or intergenerational market failures by not providing sufficient incentives for potential innovators to uncover cures or vaccines with their intergenerational gains. Excessive reliance on antibiotics and antiretrovirals influences future generations, while insufficient outbreak surveillance may only jeopardize the

Table 5.3. *Intergenerational versus Intragenerational Market Failures*

Intergenerational market failures
- Insufficient patent protection
- Overuse of antibiotics or antiretroviral therapies
- Curing a disease
- Discovering new vaccines
- Insufficient investment in research capacity including research hospitals
- Insufficient control of long-lived pollutants

Intragenerational market failures
- Patent protection
- Monopoly/oligopoly supply of medicines and equipment
- Insufficient outbreak surveillance
- Insufficient development of best treatments
- Asymmetric information
- Underprovision of immunization

current generation. For cures and vaccines, the benefit spillovers extend beyond the current generation as the disease is eradicated or potential future victims are protected; in the case of best treatments, the benefit spillovers are unlikely to extend beyond the current generation as new insights are realized and better treatments engineered over time. Insufficient investment in research capacity limits new findings that may benefit future generations. In contrast, asymmetric information where, say, medical providers are more informed about risks and success rates than patients, may result in overprovision of some medicines and procedures to the present generation. For the environment, long-lived pollutants (for example, plutonium, lead, mercury, and cadmium) pose risks for many generations so that their cleanup or containment generates intergenerational spillovers. In contrast, undersupplied immunization short of herd immunity has a current generation influence because future generations can acquire immunization.

Concluding Remarks

Of the five primary categories of GPGs and RPGs, global health public goods have increased in importance. As a consequence, the share of public good funds devoted to supplying these goods will continue to grow because wealthy countries are becoming increasingly aware of the risks that inadequate healthcare in one country means for them. In 2003, SARS made this abundantly clear. Even diseases that do not directly threaten developed countries present global concerns by inhibiting the ability of many poor countries to utilize foreign aid effectively – that is, healthy populations make for more productive workers. If poverty in these nations is to be effectively addressed, improving healthcare is likely the best place to start. The spatial and temporal mix of benefit spillovers makes these global health public goods especially fascinating to study and tricky to develop effective policy for.

6

What to Try Next? Foreign Aid Quagmire

Past demonstrations in Seattle, Washington, DC, Genoa, Stockholm, and elsewhere against the World Bank, the International Monetary Fund (IMF), ánd the World Trade Organization (WTO) have highlighted criticisms not only of globalization[1] but also of foreign assistance practices. It is ironic that well-intended actions to improve the welfare of those less fortunate can lead to such outbursts of rage and indignation that even resulted in the death of one demonstrator in Genoa in June 2001. James D. Wolfensohn, the President of the World Bank, must now have bodyguards to protect him. These multilateral institutions have had to deploy greater security and brace themselves for demonstrations and violence during their major meetings. Such rage comes from a belief by some that these institutions have either failed in their mission or their policies have harmed some constituents by promoting an agenda of the rich. The proof is circumstantial but powerful: the growing inequality worldwide and a developing world mired in misery, poverty, and conflict.

---

[1] Some scholars view globalization as "the removal of barriers to free trade and the closer integration of national economies" (Stiglitz, 2002b, p. ix). My view differs because globalization involves myriad and varied cross-border flows that need not involve trade – e.g., the exchange of ideas, microbes, pollutants, terrorists, computer files, and viruses. Such exchanges limit the protection once afforded by borders and, in so doing, reduce a country's sovereignty. Furthermore, increased economic integration is neither necessary nor sufficient for globalization. An earlier era of globalization at the end of the nineteenth and start of the twentieth centuries involved many cross-border flows, including unprecedented movements of labor, but it was associated with very little economic integration. For alternative definitions of globalization, see Reinicke (1998), Rodrik (1997), and Sandler (1997).

Despite hundreds of billions of dollars of foreign aid given to developing countries since the end of World War II,[2] many recipient countries are still poor with heavy debt burdens and apparently little to show for past loans and grants. Foreign assistance in the form of the Marshall Plan was, nevertheless, instrumental in helping war-ravished economies recover following World War II. In the latter case, these countries had a well-educated population, entrepreneurial skills, a development vision, and market-promoting institutions (for example, contract laws and a central banking system). In recent years, some Asian economies – for example, South Korea, Singapore, Thailand, and Taiwan – have effectively used foreign aid in underwriting their development. Why has foreign assistance been so successfully employed by some recipients but not by many others? These unsuccessful countries face myriad problems such as corruption, ill-conceived development strategies, ennui for Western-style development projects, limited absorptive capacity, officials' incompetence, or aid-related roadblocks. In his recent condemnation of IMF practices, Stiglitz (2002b) characterizes one such blockage as IMF-imposed contractionary monetary policy when a developing country experiences an imbalance in the form of a trade deficit. Such IMF-ordered hikes in the interest rate typically do not achieve the sought-after foreign capital inflow owing to the imbalance-induced heightened perceived risks in the minds of potential investors; instead, the higher interest rates may bankrupt leveraged firms (those with heavy debt) and inhibit the economy from investing and growing.

The lack of development results has led to "aid fatigue" as developed countries have decreased their support. In the case of the United States, the share of federal spending devoted to foreign aid has fallen from about 9% in the early 1950s to well under 1% in 1997 (US Congressional Budget Office, 1997, p. xii). During 1990–2000 – a period of reduced foreign aid compared with earlier decades – official development assistance (ODA) worldwide either declined or remained the same, depending on which ODA measure is consulted. For example, the share of donor gross national product (GNP) devoted to foreign assistance was 0.24% in 1999, down from 0.33% in 1990 (World Bank, 2001, pp. 87–9, Table 4.2). During the 1990s, nongovernmental organizations (NGOs) and charitable

---

[2] The United States alone has given $1 trillion in foreign aid (in 1997 dollars) from 1945 to 1997 (United States Congressional Budget Office, 1997, p. 1).

foundations (for example, Wellcome Trust and Gates Foundation) augmented their foreign assistance; this increase somewhat countered the decline in ODA. There has also been a large increase in private foreign direct investment in developing and transition economies during some of the 1990s (US Congressional Budget Office, 1997, p. 19). The problem with private capital inflows is that they can be quite volatile and can decline during crises or economic downturns, which are the times when support is most needed.

The purpose of this chapter is to present the collective action aspects of foreign aid as a paradigm for understanding the behavior of both donors and recipients. This collective action analysis not only addresses why some aid practices work and others do not but also indicates why public goods are playing a larger role in foreign assistance. Individual and collective incentives are key to understanding which development policies succeed and which go awry. Has the global community learned from its past mistakes and is it now pursuing a more promising path? These questions are examined in light of recent changes in the process of aid delivery under such names as the Comprehensive Development Framework (CDF). The only constant in foreign aid is that some "new" philosophy will emerge and give rise to novel procedures and emphasis. Every decade or so the process of doling out foreign aid is revamped. These "fixes" then direct the disbursement of foreign assistance until the next epiphany.

My treatment of foreign aid differs from Easterly's (2002) provocative book on aid ineffectiveness with its mantra, "it is all about incentives." Easterly is correct that foreign aid has failed during the last 50 years because the incentive implications of well-intentioned policies have been ignored. Unfortunately, Easterly does not enlighten the reader on how better policies can be designed. In contrast, I apply insights from collective action theory to propose some incentive-compatible aid policies.

Foreign Assistance: A Retrospective

Over the past five or six decades, the thinking about foreign assistance has gone through many transitions, which have been driven by external events (for example, the rapid industrialization of the Soviet Union following World War II, Cold War rivalries, the eventual collapse of the Soviet Union, and the East Asia miracle), ideologies, economic conditions, and

periodic assessments of aid effectiveness.[3] In the late 1940s and throughout the 1950s, the emphasis was on achieving growth in GNP rather than
development, the thinking being that growth would bring development,
which involves structural, economic, and institutional maturation beyond
income growth. Development economists looked to the Harrod–Domar
growth model to underscore the importance of savings and investment.
Foreign assistance could provide the needed savings. By the 1960s, this
fixation on income growth took on the new focus of trying to achieve
the preconditions for the *takeoff* to sustained growth through an infusion
of money for projects, especially social overhead capital (for example,
roads, schools, hydroelectric dams, and other infrastructure). This interest in takeoff was spurred by Rostow's (1960) *The Stages of Economic
Growth*, which emphasized the need for sufficiently high levels of investment to sustain growth.

This focus on growth was due for a reckoning because income growth
need not lead to poverty reduction if growth favors the rich. Even Kuznets'
(1955) analysis indicated that income distribution is expected to worsen
before improving with industrialization. A larger gross domestic product (GDP) may not translate into less poverty, a true development of
the economy, and associated institutional transformations. In addition,
Solow's (1957) seminal work on growth demonstrated that technological
progress, and not investment per se, explained the largest proportion of
growth. As such, technological improvement could overcome diminishing
returns associated with raising capital without augmenting other inputs
such as labor and land. The promotion of technological progress requires
more than just an increase in capital, insofar as an economy needs the
prerequisites to absorb technological progress. There was also a greater
interest in distributional concerns and the need to provide the "basic
needs" of the people in less-developed countries (LDCs). With this new
focus, the social dimension of development grew in importance – that
is, there was recognition that social and economic transformations are
complementary for development.

During the 1970s, development policy was guided by a belief that state-
led sectors could promote growth. Certain sectors were viewed as catalysts

---

[3] This retrospective view on the drivers of development assistance draws from Arce and
Sandler (2002), Carlsson (1998), Easterly (2002), Kanbur, Sandler, and Morrison (1999),
Kuznets (1955), and World Bank (1998).

to the development process – it was just a matter of bolstering the right sector. By the 1980s, the viewpoint changed, primarily because of a lack of results and debt crises. The once-held belief that export-led growth could bolster development through a spillover of this sector's more advanced technology to other sectors was losing favor. Two ideologies then gained prominence over development thinking. The first stressed market-led growth through trade liberalization and privatization, while the second emphasized accountability with the help of conditionality – that is, the placement of conditions on receiving grants and loans for development.

Trade liberalization and increased openness did not necessarily lead to high per-capita GDP growth. Rodrik (1999) demonstrates that rapid growth may be associated with openness, but openness need not be associated with rapid growth unless complementary policies and institutions are present. If an economy does not appear attractive to investors, then privatization of state-owned enterprises need not result in greater development. Host-country infrastructure and entrepreneurial skills may be insufficient to sustain large-scale privatization efforts. Moreover, money gained from the sale may be usurped by corrupt officials, thus leaving the public sector even more impoverished.

In recent years, the use of conditionality to enhance accountability of aid recipients has also lost favor for a number of reasons. First, aid in exchange for policy reform may have no lasting effect, since a recipient government's policy is influenced by a host of political factors that remain despite a pledge to reform. These factors may then return a changed policy to its previous form. Expediency would induce an aid recipient to agree to conditions in the short run that they later choose to ignore – that is, a time-inconsistency problem arises (Collier, 1997, p. 60). Given all of the contingencies that can intervene, time-inconsistent behavior regarding conditionality is probably the rule. Second, funds are fungible so that a recipient can rearrange revenue flows to bypass the conditions. Third, the threat to withhold future aid unless conditions are met is not credible to the recipient, especially if past violations did not result in punishment. Fourth, conditionality allows donors to impose their ideologies or put their own interests above those of the developing countries. For example, conditions that the recipient must use the donor's technical advisors not only increase the cost of this advice but also limit the recipient's acquisition of its own experts. Conditions may be especially disturbing to recipients when driven by a donor country's moral agenda – for example, AIDS assistance if the recipient stresses abstinence rather than safe sex before marriage. Fifth, policing conditions entail high transaction costs that are likely to have no development payback.

In the 1990s, interest shifted to building the right institutions and minimizing transaction costs. As such, the establishment of property rights became a primary driver of aid. Institutions to provide the necessary environment for emerging markets (for example, sound financial practices, courts, and central banking system) were essential. The concern over institutions extended to regional collectives that promote trade and public goods.

A current concern is whether aid really alleviates poverty while setting the foundations for sustainable development. Some consensus is forming with respect to aid effectiveness. Development assistance appears to succeed in recipient countries with stable macroeconomic environments, where governments engage in sensible policies that stabilize prices, protect property rights, and curtail corruption (World Bank, 1998; Burnside and Dollar, 2000). Furthermore, recipient countries must become integrally involved in their own development process so that a feeling of ownership is fostered (van de Walle and Johnston, 1996). Aid must be channeled to bolster economic, physical (for example, social overhead capital), structural (financial and judicial institutions), and human aspects of development. In addition, aid delivery must economize on transaction costs by harmonizing donor–recipient practices and limiting aid conditionality. Finally, capacity in recipient countries must be enhanced so that they become more capable partners. The design of CDF is intended to foster the principles of development held by this new consensus.

Collective Action and Foreign Aid

Foreign aid poses collective action problems for the international community that are analogous to charitable giving within a nation. Donor countries contribute to an LDC in order to improve the well-being of its people. As such, foreign aid is intended to produce an outcome of reduced poverty that is both nonexcludable and nonrival to all nations with an interest in the recipient's welfare. If all of the derived benefits of foreign aid are purely public, then only the wealthiest nations will contribute and the others will free ride so that the large nations are exploited by the small. Unlike this prediction, both large and small nations are notable contributors to foreign assistance: Denmark, Sweden, and Norway give a higher share of their GDP to foreign aid than large, rich countries such as the United States. This suggests that foreign aid is not purely public.

Foreign aid typically yields both purely public benefits to the world community and donor-specific private benefits that may arise from a donor's relative location or relationship to the recipient. If, say, a recipient country is positioned strategically vis-à-vis a donor nation, aid-assisted growth may augment the recipient's political stability, which, in turn, fosters the donor's own security. Certainly, US generosity to Israel and Egypt over the last couple of decades is partly motivated by strategic concerns. Forgiveness of billions in aid-related debt for Middle Eastern countries by the United States prior to the Gulf War of 1991 was tied to their joining the alliance against Iraq. Thus, the United States extracted a donor-specific benefit. Donor-specific benefits may also stem from tying foreign aid to certain stipulations (conditions) advantageous to the donor that include political concessions, strategic concessions (for example, military bases in Uzbekistan), or tied technical assistance. Additionally, donor-specific benefits may arise from trade opportunities in terms of resources or final products. Following World War II, the rebuilding of Europe by the Marshall Plan led to market opportunities that later paid back some of the US generosity once the economies had recovered. Finally, donor-associated benefits may come from how a country's generosity is perceived in the world community; for example, prestige may be afforded a donor country.

NGOs also direct their aid to causes and projects that provide them with the greatest organization-specific benefits; thus, environmental NGOs contribute to environment-supporting projects. Similarly, charitable foundations champion aid projects that bolster the foundation's particular agenda. For example, the Gates Foundation has helped fund the search for a malaria vaccine and better treatment regimes for the disease. A breakthrough in the treatment of malaria, which kills over a million annually, would confer significant prestige and goodwill on the Gates Foundation and other supporters of these efforts. Even before the breakthrough, supporters can publicize their efforts – as they do – to gain recognition and the respect of the world community.

The presence of these donor-specific benefits is both a blessing and a curse. As a blessing, these benefits partly circumvent the free-rider problem by providing gains to donors that they could not obtain from the donations of others. Thus, jointly produced donor-specific benefits augment the level of foreign assistance. The curse arises because the pursuit of these donor benefits creates aid practices that inhibit poverty reduction. For example, the rise of conditionality has been motivated as a means to foster donor-specific benefits. Despite its pitfalls, donors are slow to give up conditionality because they crave the direct benefits that they derive often at the expense of the recipients. Aid-tied political or military concessions may seem to the recipient government to be a payment for services rendered, so the officials might then use the money for their own purposes rather than for the poverty relief for which it is intended. When the conditionality assumes the form of a Western-style norm of development, the recipient may lose any sense of ownership so that if the money later dries up, the program is dropped. Such programs may be alien to the recipient's culture, which also limits the aid's effectiveness.

The multilateral institutions try to address the free-rider problem by being an intermediary between donors and recipients. In this capacity, donors can minimize transaction costs by relying on the Bank to allocate their contributions and later report how effectively they have been used. By collecting and disseminating information, the World Bank limits for donors the asymmetric information surrounding recipients. Donors can then channel some of their aid through the Bank, which identifies worthy recipients. Even when depending on the Bank and not giving in a bilateral arrangement, donors can still obtain donor-specific benefits by supporting the countries and sectors of their choice.

CDF and PRSPs

Since the 1990s, there has been an enhanced interest in rethinking the whole process of foreign assistance to engineer novel delivery mechanisms that will improve not only aid effectiveness but also recipient country involvement (World Bank, 1998; World Bank Partnership Group, 1998). To implement the current consensus to foster ownership among recipient countries and to boost their capacity, the World Bank is relying on some "innovations" in its assistance program. The first concerns *partnerships* where joined agents or partners pursue shared interests. If there is sufficient commonality of purpose, then, as a partner, a recipient country will "own" the outcome. To be effective, partners must possess a common vision and gain benefits *beyond the transaction costs of the association*. Partners must also be prepared to allocate tasks to draw on their comparative advantage. At times, the capacity or ability of a weaker partner must be raised to be effective, especially when partnership involves donor and

Partners	Structural		Human			Physical			Specific Strategies	
	Justice	Financial	Governance	Education	Health	Energy	Roads	Environment	Rural	Urban
National Government										
Provincial Government										
Local Government										
Multilaterals										
Bilateral Institutions										
Civil Society										
Private Sector										
NGOs										
Charitable Foundations										
Donor Countries										

Figure 6.1. Sample CDF matrix

recipient in a development context. The forging of partnerships among donors and recipient countries dates back to Pearson (1969). What is new about today's interest in partnerships are the specific institutional mechanisms put forward to capitalize on partners' aligned interests to improve coordination, enhance ownership, and reduce aid dependence.

The CDF was suggested by Wolfensohn (1999) as a framework for improving foreign assistance by embracing the current consensus on making aid effective.[4] The CDF framework rests on four principles. First, the CDF promotes a long-term holistic view by stressing the interdependence of the structural, physical, human, and economic facets of development. Earlier fixation on short-run macroeconomic stability is eschewed for long-run development goals where poverty is reduced. Second, the CDF emphasizes ownership on the part of recipient countries by having them draw up their own development plan, which usually takes the form of a medium-term Poverty Reduction Strategy Paper (PRSP). Ownership ideally involves participation by both the recipient's civil society and its government in drawing up the development plans. Third, the CDF fosters partnerships among diverse donors, between donors and recipient countries, among a recipient country's sectors, and between donors and the recipient country's sectors. The recipient is envisioned to be a dominant partner or in the driver's seat in these partnerships. Fourth, the CDF is "results oriented" so that development achievements are monitored and evaluated.

The CDF principles are not new – for example, the holistic view dates back to the early 1970s when broader social and development goals took precedence over growth. If anything is new with CDF, it is CDF's *simultaneous embracing* of these four principles in a single framework. The CDF was first put forward by Wolfensohn (1999) as an accounting matrix that delineates the structural, human, and physical sectors along with specific strategies in the columns, and the various participants (partners) in the rows, in which each cell ties participants to sector assistance or development strategy pursued. Figure 6.1 presents a sample CDF matrix. Each of the primary sectors can have additional subsections. For example, I have listed only justice, financial, and governance as subsectors for structural programs, and education and health under human programs. Additional sectors can also be included in the matrix, whose columns keep track of which partners are participating in any subsector. Of course,

---

[4] This paragraph draws from the analysis of CDF in Wolfensohn (1999) and World Bank CDF Secretariat (2000, 2001, 2003).

both the number of partners and the number of specific strategies can be expanded. Under the CDF, the so-called donor partners sign on to support specific sectors to avoid duplication and promote coordination. The CDF matrix represents a holistic approach that is intended to promote balanced policymaking and assistance implementation, in which interdependencies among sectors and participants are tracked. CDF moves away from project-specific conditional aid toward sector-specific assistance that should ease transaction costs and provide recipients with a greater ownership stake. CDF principles, rather than the matrix, are emphasized today.

To receive aid from the World Bank, a developing country must formulate an acceptable PRSP based on CDF principles. Because donors of all types channel their money through the Bank, these PRSPs are now an essential part of current aid practices. An acceptable PRSP must present a fairly detailed and coherent three-to-five-year development plan.

Issues with CDF and PRSPs

On the positive side, CDF principles promote institutional aspects that can circumvent some collective action concerns. The transparency, encouraged by the application of CDF principles and by the associated PRSP, identifies which donors are supporting the various sectors and, in so doing, provides donor-specific benefits. CDF's holistic approach, and its emphasis on individual sectors and the matching of donors to these sectors, facilitates not only coordination among partners but also the avoidance of duplication. Ideally, a reciprocity among aid providers occurs where sector responsibility is assumed by donors so that actions by one donor to support, say, certain requirements in the recipient's health sector are met with other donors' efforts to assist other needs in that sector. By breaking a country's overall development plan into sectors, CDF acts like a federated structure that highlights individual donor's efforts at the lower sector level, where the number of donors is relatively small compared to that of the entire recipient country. This institutional consequence of CDF also assists in circumventing free riding among potential donors. If thresholds of effort must be surpassed to obtain a goal in a sector, then the CDF's focus on sectors can promote coordination among a variety of donors to achieve these thresholds. Another way that the CDF approach reduces perverse incentives is its emphasis on repeated interactions among stable partners so that free riding is curtailed through the recognition of common interests among contributors.

In counterbalance to these favorable factors, there are consequences that inhibit the intent of CDF and PRSPs. The requirement of recipients to draw up detailed PRSPs to the World Bank's specifications as a *pre-condition* for either debt relief or further assistance *limits* the very sense of ownership that CDF and PRSPs are trying to achieve! Ironically, the recipient's "ownership" may be viewed as a new form of conditionality that is more encompassing than that in the past. Some LDCs may view the PRSP itself as a broader *program conditionality*, leading them to put into their development plans what they believe donors want to hear. In addition, the required development blueprint may well be beyond the capacity of many LDCs so that they must rely on donors for assistance in drawing up the plan. Inevitably, the views of those providing assistance will partly shape the plan, thereby further limiting ownership. More atten-tion must be paid to building the capacity of recipients *prior* to drawing up such involved development plans.

To engender true ownership, a partnership must be forged among the civilian sector, the private sector, and the government when drawing up the PRSP. The collective action problem surfaces in regard to synthesizing the diverse development views of the civilian and private sectors into a unified plan. The likely scenario is for the recipient government to take the lead, since the government, unlike its constituency, does not have to overcome a collective action problem, and the time to act is limited for aid to continue. Even if the civilian and private sectors formulate a PRSP, the government must then embrace it or the grass roots PRSP will have no influence and merely add to alienation and frustration. CDF principles envision an ideal of ownership that is likely unobtainable.

Incentive problems that have plagued development assistance since its inception still abound with CDF and PRSP. To qualify for debt relief under the heavily indebted poor country (HIPC) initiative, a country must acquire a certain level of indebtedness. Countries that have been fiscally responsible in the past may now be enticed by HIPC to become more leveraged and less responsible to have debts forgiven. Because the World Bank and its donors are interested in showing greater results, they may pay more attention to large countries' PRSPs even though some small countries' PRSPs are more sound and their past use of assistance more responsible. The use of "basket funding" where CDF encourages multiple donors to contribute to the same sector also presents a free-rider problem, because one donor's contributions are perfectly substitutable for those of another.

Donor-recipient partnerships are inhibited by a host of asymmetries that create market failures. First, there is an informational asymmetry owing to the principal–agent relationship that characterizes these partnerships. Generally, the agent (the recipient government) is in possession of information regarding its true efforts and the disbursement of aid, not directly observable by the principal(s) (donor(s)). The latter can observe the output that may vary owing to intervening unobservable random factors so that effort cannot necessarily be inferred. This information asymmetry can lead to corruption as the recipient government diverts aid away from intended goals to capture a rent or payoff. To align incentives of partners, the donor must provide rewards for observable outputs so that the sought-after action of high effort is a dominant strategy; but these rewards are themselves costly (known as agency costs) and they eliminate first-best solutions, thereby curtailing any net gain from the partnership.

Second, there is a size asymmetry between the recipient country and many of its donor countries. In terms of GDP or GDP per capita, the recipient country is necessarily smaller; otherwise, it would not qualify as a worthy recipient. This size disparity is the source of the capacity problem. Another size asymmetry in terms of area may be in the opposite direction with geographically large recipient countries interacting with some small donors (for example, Denmark and the Netherlands). This difference in size can inhibit donor countries from appreciating the special needs (for example, transportation, communication, and healthcare) of large poor nations. Also, geographically large recipients have difficulty in drawing together civil society countrywide when formulating a PRSP.

Third, there is a technological asymmetry where the donor countries employ technologies that are much more advanced than those familiar to recipient partners. This technology gap is a potential source of friction in terms of donor's expectations regarding recipient's capacity and ability to assimilate new technologies. For instance, blindsided by their own capabilities, donors may request procedures (say monitoring) beyond a recipient's current abilities. When decisions are instituted to augment the capacity of recipients, donors may transfer noninteroperable technologies that are misaligned with recipients' factor endowments.

Fourth, financial and accounting asymmetries also hamper the effectiveness of CDF partnerships. Obviously, the flow of money is asymmetric as it goes from the donors to the developing country. This asymmetry presents a concern when disbursement and accounting practices differ between partners and the unfamiliar practices of the donors are imposed.

Immediately, the recipient is at a decided disadvantage, which limits its sense of ownership and its ability to function as a full-fledged partner. Traditional ex-ante conditional and tranched delivery is apt to be associated with the most extreme case of financial asymmetry as donor's practices are applied. Moreover, the recipient LDC must account to donors, but not the other way around. A greater willingness on the part of donors to adjust procedures to recipient countries' capacities and practices would go a long way to curbing this asymmetry, while putting the partnership on a more equal footing.

Fifth, cultural asymmetries arise when partners differ in their language, norms, standards of contracts, and values. These asymmetries plague all aspects of the development process, including the forging of successful partnerships. Cultural differences not only inhibit understanding among partners, but they also limit partners' ability to accomplish mutual goals. The best procedure for one partner may be culturally ill suited to the other partner. For example, the use of collateral may not be as important as reputation when securing a loan in some cultures. The recognition of cultural asymmetries and the flexibility to accept a partner's culture-based practices would greatly help to address this asymmetry.

These asymmetries indicate that donor–recipient partnerships – a guiding principle of CDF – face many obstacles. If recipients view themselves as an inferior partner to donors, then ownership – a second principle of CDF – will also be compromised. In an initial evaluation of CDF with the help of surveys of recipients and donors, the World Bank CDF Secretariat (2003) notes that asymmetries and tensions among donor–recipient partnerships still exist and inhibit the implementation of CDF and PRSPs. Many donors have resisted changing their practices and continue to impose requirements that are beyond recipients' capabilities. In other instances, donors have altered their practices and have embraced CDF principles. The achievement of a long-run holistic view is, however, inhibited by IMF practices that continue to focus on short-run macroeconomic stability concerns. At this point, it is impossible to know whether CDF and PRSPs will become a permanent part of aid delivery or just another fad adopted by a short-lived consensus.

Public Good Aid

A second major new focus in foreign aid concerns assistance in the form of transnational public goods (TPGs). In my book *Global Challenges*,

Table 6.1. *LDCs' Public Goods by Type and Spillover Range*

Spillover Range	Pure Public	Impure Public	Club	Joint Product
National	• groundwater purification • national defense	• waterways • healthcare infrastructure	• communication network • irrigation system	• education • civil service
Regional	• pest eradication • geoclimatic-specific research findings	• immunization program • acid rain reduction	• extension service • electric grid	• peacekeeping • cleansing a shared river
Global	• curbing global warming • instituting sound financial practices	• curbing organized crime • controlling the spread of diseases	• INTELSAT • transnational parks	• rain forest preservation • bioprospecting

I introduced the notion of public good aid as follows: "A new form of foreign aid – 'free-rider aid' – may come from the provision of transnational public goods and may increasingly replace traditionally tied and untied foreign aid of the post-World War II period. That is, free-riding behavior on the part of the poor may limit even greater worldwide inequality" (Sandler, 1997, p. 183).[5] It is my belief that aid in the form of TPGs will increase as a proportion of development assistance, because donors also receive benefit spillovers (for example, from forestalling the spread of a disease or bringing peace to a war-torn country), thereby making their support more politically acceptable to the donors' constituencies than traditional assistance. My hypotheses about public good aid has generated much interest in recent years.[6]

The World Bank (2001, pp. 110–13) estimates that $5 billion is directly spent annually on aid-assisted TPGs and another $11 billion is spent annually on complementary activities, which permit LDCs to absorb these TPGs. Such complementary activities primarily include the provision of national public goods (NPGs) that improve education, health, and the environment. A study by Willem te Velde, Morrissey, and Hewitt (2002, Tables 5.1–5.2) provides evidence that the financing of both NPGs and TPGs has grown from just over 16% of foreign assistance in the early 1980s to almost 40% in the late 1990s. Estimates by Raffer (1999) indicate that such support varies from 20% to 40% of ODA depending on the definition of public good assistance applied. Although estimates will vary widely until researchers agree on the precise measurement of public good aid, diverse studies find that more aid is either financing TPGs directly or preparing recipients to absorb these goods' benefits, findings in agreement with my 1997 hypothesis. In its recommendation for reforming aid, the UN High-Level Panel (2001) calls for increased support of TPGs in health and other key sectors and cautions that this support must be in addition to traditional assistance to alleviate poverty.

In Table 6.1, public goods of special interest to LDCs are distinguished by geography in terms of spillover range and by type in terms of publicness characteristics. Public goods that benefit a well-defined region

---

[5] The notion of public good aid is also presented in greater detail in Kanbur, Sandler, and Morrison (1999).

[6] Books on the topic include Arce and Sandler (2002), Ferroni and Mody (2002), Kanbur, Sandler, and Morrison (1999), Kaul, Grunberg, and Stern (1999), Kaul et al. (2003), and World Bank (2001).

are regional public goods (RPGs), while those with spillover ranges that involve large portions of the planet are global public goods (GPGs).[7] In the four right-hand columns of Table 6.1, four classes of public goods are considered. Goods may be purely public at the national (groundwater purification and national defense), regional (pest eradication and geoclimatic-specific research findings), or global level (curbing global warming and instituting sound financial practices). Impure public goods include waterways and healthcare infrastructure at the national level, immunization programs and acid rain reduction at the regional level, and curbing organized crime and controlling the dissemination of diseases at the global level. The use of a communication network, irrigation system, extension service, or electric grid can be easily monitored and nonpayers excluded at little expense and so represent club goods. The same is true for INTELSAT and transnational parks. Joint products are associated with varied scenarios. For example, a rain forest provides GPGs by sequestering carbon and supplying oxygen to the planet, while it also yields local public goods in terms of watersheds and ecotourism. At the national level, education benefits the individual while adding to the good of society, while civil service gives recipient-specific benefits and society-wide gains.

The many classes of public goods are germane to understanding when foreign assistance is required to support public good provision in LDCs, because each subcategory may have different collective action implications or prognoses.[8] For example, a number of institutional and collective action factors make support of RPGs more problematic than NPGs or GPGs (see Chap. 4). For example, the absence of a dominant nation in some developing regions may result in the lack of necessary leadership (Arce, 2001). This greater collective action difficulty for RPGs could be countered by building up the regional development banks so that they can take on greater responsibility for funding these goods.

In Table 6.1, pure public goods have the worst prognosis and, in general, need the most development support (see Chaps. 3 and 4). Club goods have the best prognosis because users can be charged a toll that underwrites the good's provision. If a developing country does not have the money

---

[7] In a development context, Arce and Sandler (2002) focus on RPGs, while Kaul, Grunberg, and Stern (1999) and Sandler (1997) study GPGs.

[8] This essential message is discussed in greater detail in Arce and Sandler (2002), Kanbur, Sandler, and Morrison (1999), Sandler (1998, forthcoming), and Sandler and Arce (2002).

to subscribe to a club good, then foreign assistance can give the country the means. Joint products have varied implications for development assistance. If, for example, a large share of jointly produced benefits is donor or recipient specific, then the parties should be able to consummate an efficient agreement on their own.

The basic message is a simple one: generalizations with respect to foreign assistance for public goods must be resisted. Spatial spillovers and the properties of the public goods influence the need to supply such goods for LDCs and, when supplied, they affect the institutional form of the supplier.

Aggregation Technologies and Public Goods for Development

Just as rivalry and exclusion considerations have implications for the choice of an institutional arrangement and financing mechanisms for public goods in developing countries, the underlying aggregation technology of the public goods also impacts these policy choices. For weakest-link and best-shot public goods, the issue is one of inadequate capacity for the developing country. Incentives for supplying weakest-link public goods are generally supportive of collective action, provided that countries have sufficient incomes to finance the good. Because the smallest level of the good determines the overall level of consumption of the public good, there is no reason for a country to exceed this minimum level so that matching of the smallest contribution results. If, however, this smallest level is unacceptable to most developed countries, then they must give assistance to bring the provision levels in developing countries up to a reasonable standard. This aid can take the form of either income transfers in terms of foreign assistance or direct provision of the good on these capacity-poor countries' soil (Vicary and Sandler, 2002). In the case of weaker-link public goods, the extreme of matching behavior is not as relevant and the building of capacity is somewhat attenuated but still relevant.

At the opposite extreme, a best-shot public good requires a single sufficiently endowed supplier who provides the good and a free ride for everyone. Capacity again becomes a concern because the provider must be able to achieve success in supplying the public good. If it is a TPG that benefits the rich and poor countries, then there is less concern insofar as the incentives are there for the rich to act. When the TPGs only benefit the poor countries – for example, a cure for a disease indigenous to the tropics – the rich may have little interest in provision and the impacted countries may have no capacity. In such cases, multilateral institutions, charitable foundations, NGOs, and even private firms must assist.

Once the different aggregation technologies are recognized, some surprising implications for income inequality arise. The contributors of best-shot and better-shot TPGs are often the richest countries, since the demand for most public goods is income normal, implying that the quantity demanded at each price increases with income. If a best-shot technology of public supply applies, then the quantity provided by the best-shot nation is anticipated to increase as income distribution becomes more skewed to the rich. Not only do rich nations have the greater demand for best-shot and better-shot TPGs, but they also have the greater supply capacity. For best-shot goods, globalization-induced income inequality has a silver lining in terms of promoting their provision. Greater income inequality is also conducive to public goods provision for a summation technology (Itaya, de Meza, and Myles, 1997).

Greater inequality is, however, harmful for the provision of weakest-link and weaker-link public goods because enhanced relative poverty means that more countries will lack the necessary capacity to provide these goods to acceptable standards for the world community. As global income inequality increases, the contributions of the poorest nations are expected to fall relative to the desired contributions of the richer countries. Thus, the rich countries will have greater need to subsidize the poorer countries' contributions to weakest-link public goods as a consequence of globalization.

I am not arguing in favor of increased income inequality, which usually has nothing to recommend it. Instead, I am simply pointing out that increased income inequality has important implications for the provision of various classes of TPGs. These implications need to be addressed for intelligent policy. Enhanced inequality may dictate that less attention be paid to some types of TPGs because greater inequality will encourage provision, as in the case of best-shot TPGs, and that more attention be paid to others because greater inequality will discourage adequate provision.

More Radical Proposals

I view the last five decades of foreign assistance as analogous to the storyline of the movie, *Bedazzled* (both the Dudley Moore original and the recent remake). In *Bedazzled*, the devil grants a number of wishes to a luckless hero, whose wishes are each time manipulated by the devil into an even worse outcome. The modern history of foreign assistance is not unlike this storyline. Periodically, a new "foolproof" procedure for foreign aid is uncovered to circumvent the follies of past actions, and each time the outcome turns out even more foolhardy. Although I view CDF and PRSPs as a move in the right direction, they still do not address significant ownership and partnership issues.

I am in favor of an alternative to CDF and PRSPs that goes further by using a *common pool* approach.[9] Such an approach is based on a recipient's national strategy – like a PRSP – that addresses the holistic nature of development. This national blueprint for development would reflect the widest possible consensus of the host-country interests. Like the PRSPs, the recipient is in charge of drawing up its own development strategy, which is then placed before the donor community for its *collective support*. The recipient is permitted to seek technical assistance and advice in drawing up its plans but must determine where assistance is needed and the form that it should take. Allowance for the recipient's initial incapacity and inexperience must be made by the donor community. Interested donors then transfer assistance to the recipient's central budget in an amount determined by their evaluation of the proposed development strategy and the perceived competency of the recipient government's ability to execute it. Unlike CDF or PRSPs, donors support a common pool, *not just* parts of the program or its sectors that they deem promising. This commitment for funds is on a two- to three-year basis to give time for results.

Donors can track the development program's progress, but the main accounting is done by the recipient country, who determines its timing and nature. Unlike business as usual, the recipient is not plagued by separate reports and different accounting practices for each of its many donors. Moreover, the donors cannot impose conditionality. Transaction costs are greatly limited because the recipients must only report the overall results in the hope of attracting further funding in subsequent rounds. Recipients report outcomes first to their own constituent interests, who

[9] The common pool approach is proposed in Kanbur, Sandler, and Morrison (1999), which should be consulted for greater detail. Common pool is different than the Marshall Plan, which relied solely on US funding. Both common pool funding and the Marshall Plan put the recipient nation in charge of drawing up its own development plans.

helped draw up the plans, and only second to the donors who financed these plans. The intent of the common pool approach is to go all the way to fostering recipient ownership and partnerships among diverse donor and recipient entities. Results are needed if the development strategy is to be successful. Obviously, the common pool approach greatly limits the need for donor coordination, even in the context of an absence of consensus on development strategy. Under common pool, conditionality only exists in the sense that future aid is dependent on a blueprint that yields results along development metrics, especially that of curbing poverty.

If the common pool approach achieves its stated goal of greater aid effectiveness, then it may reverse any short-run aid declines owing to its radical nature. This greater effectiveness can counter the anticipated collective action problem that arises from donors' contributions to a common pool being perfectly substitutable, which leads to free-riding worries. To the extent that greater prestige or similar donor-specific benefits are related to *relative* contributions to the common pool, this could set up a positive competition among donors. The common pool may allow for a sorting of donors in which a small number of donors will contribute the bulk of the resources for a given country, thereby reducing the free-rider problem.

Concluding Remarks

As globalization widens the income gap between rich and poor nations, the interest in foreign assistance will grow in importance. With the consequent rise in cross-border flows, concern regarding harmful externalities (for example, pollution, contagion of diseases, and the spread of political instability) is also going to increase, thereby heightening the interest in the provision of public good aid in LDCs to curb these negative spillovers. Because foreign assistance benefits not only donors but also nondonors, there is a collective action issue where publicness of this assistance keeps it undersupplied. This chapter has investigated the collective action aspects of traditional foreign assistance and assistance-based provision of TPGs in developing countries.

The new consensus on foreign aid that promotes ownership, partnerships, a holistic long-term view, and a results orientation has led to institutional innovations for disbursement of foreign aid in the form of the CDF and PRSPs. These innovations are still plagued by some of the same concerns that they aimed to correct. Although it is too early to evaluate the success of these programs, they have many obstacles to overcome. I have suggested an even more radical common pool approach as an alternative aid program to further recipient ownership and poverty reduction. Finally, many aspects of TPGs for development have been considered. Given the myriad forms that these TPGs can assume, general provision principles are difficult to formulate. Nevertheless, I have tried to establish some insight where possible.

7

Rogues and Bandits: Who Bells the Cat?

Once upon a time, there lived an agile cat, whose favorite treats were tender mice from a colony that lived in constant fear of becoming the cat's dinner. One day, one of the mice had a brilliant idea: why not place a bell on a rope around the cat's neck while he was asleep? With such an early-warning device, the mice could avoid the cat's silent stealth. When the clever mouse looked to the others for a volunteer, there were just blank stares and a deafening silence as each mouse weighed the great personal risk that "belling the cat" would spell for a brave volunteer. Of course, once the bell was secured on the cat, every mouse in the colony would benefit greatly. This children's fable and the collective action problem that it embodies is analogous to the social dilemmas posed by bullies, bandits, tyrants, kleptocrats, or rogue states that have plagued humankind from the beginning of time and the rise of nation states.

With the advent of weapons of mass destruction (WMD), the stakes have increased greatly so that nations are even more concerned about rogue states that operate outside of accepted norms of behavior. Such states may use WMD to threaten other countries, a region, or even the global community. North Korea and Iraq (prior to the US-led March 2003 invasion) are often characterized as rogue nations that seek WMD to invade neighboring countries, to influence the global agenda, or to extort concessions.[1] Although their potential arsenals are more threatening, rogue states have been around throughout recorded history. Examples include Athenian imperialism to maintain the Delian League around

---

[1] On rogue states, see Klare (1995). Revelations following the Iraqi war strongly suggest that US characterization of Iraq's WMD threat was misrepresented or, at best, greatly exaggerated.

400 B.C. following the defeat of the Persians.[2] Other instances include Nazi Germany or Japan before and during World War II. As in the story of the mice, countries that opposed the rogue imperialists faced great peril at the potential collective benefit of all. Often, the slowness to confront the collective threat, as the perils of action are weighed, means that the rogue can accumulate military power and become a more formidable adversary. At a regional level, action may be problematic if there is no sufficiently strong challenger; at the global level, action is difficult since there is no recognized transnational enforcer. Despite the inertia to challenging the rogue, history is replete with examples where either the strongest acted or else a coalition emerged that was sufficiently equipped to defeat the rogue state.

Within a country, society can be tyrannized by bandits whose appropriative acts weaken the workings of markets by diluting property rights and, in so doing, create allocative inefficiencies.[3] Rogues may also take the form of drug cartels, organized crime, or despots, who exploit people individually powerless to respond, thus highlighting the need for collective action. Analogously, a rebel group or terrorists can present dangers for a society whose officials may be too weak to counter the threat.

The purpose of this chapter is to investigate collective action means for dealing with rogues and bandits at the national or transnational level, where there is often a need for actor-specific benefits in the form of joint products to motivate action. To successfully counter the menacing might of a rogue nation or bandits, a challenger must possess its own prowess or must combine sufficient support from others. Thus, an agent with asymmetric endowments or payoffs, including agent-specific gains, is more likely to meet the challenge because this agent may then be sufficiently equipped and/or motivated to provide the best-shot neutralizing attack that benefits everyone. For more homogeneous or symmetric groups, cooperative pooling of efforts is required if the threat is to be confronted. Group asymmetries may, therefore, be more conducive for actions against rogues or bandits, since cooperation may not be necessary. Of course, there are many other scenarios – for example, confronting a deadly plague, diverting an asteroid on a collision course with the earth,

---

[2] A description of Athenian imperialism is provided in Sandler (1992, pp. 96–7).

[3] On appropriative behavior and its consequences, see Anderton (2000), Anderton, Anderton, and Carter (1999), Grossman (1991, 1994, 1995, 1999), and Skaperdas (1991).

recovering a leaking nuclear submarine from the ocean floor, eliminating a terrorist network, or monitoring the planet – that represent nearly identical collective action concerns. As such, the underlying aggregation technology of publicness is best shot, or some near variant such as better shot, and actor-specific asymmetries may be absolutely essential for action.

The chapter proceeds as follows. First, the facilitators of collective action are presented by highlighting the best-shot or better-shot nature of the underlying public goods associated with removing rogues and bandits. The importance of joint products is also studied. Second, banditry and the rise of governments are analyzed. Third, collective action aspects of revolutions against tyrants at the national and transnational level are addressed. Fourth, rogue states and the collective threat that they pose are investigated. Fifth, the collective action implications of organized crime at the global level are investigated. Finally, concluding remarks are presented.

Facilitators: In Praise of Asymmetry

Typically, mounting a sufficient counterattack to a rogue nation, bandits, or other such challenge is a best-shot public good in the sense that the *greatest* action determines the overall level of damage to the adversary, and hence the level of benefits to those who are threatened. Smaller responses may have no effectiveness in the presence of the largest effort. In Chapter 3, best-shot public goods have Nash equilibriums where just a single agent's action is required. Thus, an issue posed by best shot is how to coordinate among players when more than one have the requisite endowments to succeed against the challenge. This coordination ensures that agents do not duplicate efforts or work at cross-purposes. If the need to act arises repeatedly, then sufficiently capable agents can alternate in providing the public good. However, a rogue-type threat may be more episodic so that intertemporal-based strategies may not be relevant. When there is only one capable agent, the collective action problem is solved *provided that* this agent derives a *positive net payoff*, even when it foots the entire cost. After 11 September 2001, the United States was prepared to take on al-Qaida and the Taliban single-handedly, as it was also prepared to confront Saddam Hussein in the Iraq War in 2003 over alleged WMD. If, however, the only capable agent receives a negative net payoff from acting alone, then others have to bolster the agent's efforts or share the costs so that a positive net payoff is perceived, and this may involve a difficult collective action problem.

When the consequences of inaction become sufficiently dire, others will join in as was the case in World War II after a protracted period of appeasement and denial of the Nazi threat. Delay means that risks escalate so that even greater effort and costs are later required, thus making a collective response even more difficult. Nevertheless, the consequences of doing nothing may eventually become so great that some kind of resistance is mounted.

Globalization-induced asymmetry assists in the provision of best-shot public goods by eliminating the need for coordinating who must take action. The growing income inequality associated with modern-day globalization fosters the asymmetry favorable for tackling rogue-like threats. But this increasing reliance on a strong nation or alliance to neutralize such threats comes at a cost owing to another asymmetry that involves provider-specific benefits associated with supplying the best-shot challenge. As provider, the agent can determine the timing, the characteristics of the public good (for example, the offensive plan and its likely collateral damage), and provider benefits. For instance, the defeat of Nazi Germany allowed the allies to partition Berlin such that the more essential participants got the best portions. Jointly produced private benefits are essential for addressing the types of exigencies analyzed in this chapter. During the Cold War, the deployment of theater nuclear weapons (low-yield nuclear weapons intended for battlefield use) by the United States required that the latter, and not the host countries, maintained launch control – an agent-specific benefit; thus, US willingness to underwrite European security from Soviet conventional weapon superiority engendered US-specific provider benefits. Setting the rules of engagement and directing the aftermath of a conflict are instances where the best-shot provider engineers the mix of joint products to limit its costs and extract its due deserts. This is certainly true of US action in Iraq to remove Saddam Hussein and to rebuild Iraq. Only after the costs of rebuilding Iraq became much higher than anticipated did the Bush administration turn to the United Nations for help. This assistance has been slow in coming because the United States wanted to maintain control over contributor-specific benefits, thereby reducing incentives for others to help.

There are times when best-shot public goods require action by more than one agent so that coordination and cooperation cannot be circumvented. If the requisite action requires a greater capacity than that possessed by the most-capable agent, then efforts must be pooled so that the necessary provision threshold is achieved. Threshold public goods have a reasonable prognosis (see Chaps. 3–4).[4] If the achievement of the best-shot public good is a random event, there is then a need for multiple potential providers to expend efforts to maximize success. Having many different (asymmetric) approaches results in a greater likelihood of success. Coordination is still needed to ensure that *different* approaches are tried by potential suppliers. When the world community tries to neutralize the danger of a rogue state, alternative approaches may be diplomatic, intelligence gathering, economic, and military.

Better-Shot Public Goods

A better-shot public good represents a less extreme example of a best-shot public good, because contribution levels less than the highest also add to aggregate benefits received.[5] For a better-shot public good, the greatest marginal gain stems from enhanced efforts by the provider already making the greatest overall level of contribution. Better-shot public goods are prevalent in the global community. Consider the development of a medicine or a vaccine against a disease. For the Salk (inactivated) and Sabin (oral) polio vaccines, the second-best effort generated beneficial spillovers, since the less effective Sabin vaccine could be tolerated by people who could not take the Salk vaccine. In the same way, efforts below the largest, to monitor a rogue state, may still provide some intelligence gains, although at a smaller level than the best.

In Table 7.1, possible payoffs for a better-shot public good are displayed, where payoffs are indicated in the left-hand column and agent i's (j's) contribution is given under q_i (q_j) in the right-hand columns. If no one contributes, then the payoff to each agent is zero. When just one agent supplies a unit, the payoff is 4. If the second unit comes from the same contributor as the first unit, then each agent receives 7; if, however, the second unit comes from a different contributor (that is, each agent contributes a unit), then each agent receives just 6. Hence, additional contributions by others add less to aggregate benefits than additions to the largest overall effort. The rest of the entries in Table 7.1 are self-explanatory.

---

[4] On threshold public goods, see Palfrey and Rosenthal (1984) and Sandler (1992).

[5] This subsection draws heavily from my works with Daniel Arce; see Arce and Sandler (2001) for further details.

Table 7.1. *Payoffs for a Better-Shot Public Good*

Payoffs	Agent Contribution	
	q_i	q_j
0	0	0
4	1	0
4	0	1
6	1	1
7	2	0
7	0	2
9	2	1
9	1	2
10	2	2

		q_2		
		0	1	2
	0	0, 0	4, 2	Nash 7, 3
q_1	1	2, 4	4, 4	Nash 7, 5
	2	Nash 3, 7	Nash 5, 7	6, 6

Figure 7.1. Better-shot game derived from Table 7.1

These gross payoffs for alternative contribution patterns are used to display the underlying game in normal form in Figure 7.1 where a 3×3 matrix is displayed. To derive these *net* payoffs, unit costs of provision are assumed to be 2. The two agents are now denoted by 1 and 2. Each has three pure strategies: provide 0, 1, or 2 units of the public good. To illustrate the matrix construction, consider what happens when individual 1 provides nothing and individual 2 supplies two units. According to Table 7.1, each agent receives 7 in gross benefits. Since agent 1 can free ride, he or she keeps the whole 7. Individual 2 only nets 3 because he or she must cover the 4 in costs from providing 2 units at a per-unit cost of

2 apiece. Next, suppose that individual 1 provides one unit and individual 2 supplies two units. Each individual gains 9 in benefits. Individual 1 nets 7 (= 9 − 2), while 2 nets 5 (= 9 − 4) as provision costs of one and two units, respectively, are deducted. The other entries are computed similarly. There are now four Nash equilibriums: two involve a single agent contributing two units and two involve one agent contributing two units and the other giving one unit. These latter equilibriums represent a greater social welfare than the best-shot (associated) equilibriums of a single contributor.[6]

There is a curse of symmetry[7] because these agents must still find a way of coordinating their actions in order to decide who gives 2 and who contributes 1. Without this coordination, lower payoffs will be hit – for example, where both contribute a single unit. Thus, a coordination device is needed to achieve the sought-after asymmetry. This coordination could be achieved by a supranational institution that transmits costless signals that allow the participants to condition and anticipate strategic choices to avoid low-paying outcomes. Such a correlation mechanism is self-enforcing in the sense that everyone gains from its operation. The formulation of conventions governing shipping lanes – for example, procedures for ships to avoid collision at sea – is a correlating mechanism to limit accidents. Such conventions are a means for addressing truly random encounters at sea. Many institutions correlate by agreeing to simple rules of thumb, not unlike rules to limit accidents. When addressing a rogue nation or other exigency, a correlation mechanism can achieve the proper asymmetric response by signaling whose turn it is to put forward the greater effort – this correlation may be based on relative location to the threat (for example, Australia leading peacekeeping efforts in East Timor) or some scheme for taking turns.

Bandits and the Rise of Government

In Chapter 2, I made the case that governments evolved from the natural state of anarchy as a bunch of thugs provided protection in return for tribute. With this protection, citizens' resources could be redirected from guarding their property to more productive activities. If the protectors extract less in taxes (tribute) than what these citizens would have

---

[6] That is, these equilibriums Pareto dominate those in which a single agent contributes.
[7] Skyrms (1996) coined the phrase "curse of symmetry." Also see the extensive discussion in Arce and Sandler (2001).

used for their own security, then everyone gains from the arrangement. By specializing in the protection business, the evolving thug-based government could acquire more formidable weapons while honing its skills. Essentially, the government evolved from bandits whose services became welfare improving. This ability to augment social welfare grew as the government provided other public goods – schools, justice system, and infrastructure. The promotion of laws that enforced property rights meant that less of the government's arsenal had to be deployed to address internal threats, thus leaving its armies to secure the country's borders.

The banditry analogy is particularly apt in Olson (1993), who makes a fascinating distinction between roving and stationary bandits in terms of the origin of governments. Stationary bandits have greater interests in the prosperity of their subjects (prey), and therefore provide public goods so as to enhance their tax base. Roving bandits have little concern about their prey's well-being because they move on to pillage a new community. I am reminded of the opening scene of Akira Kurosawa's cinema masterpiece, *The Seven Samurai*, where a band of roving bandits eyes a village's crops from a nearby hilltop and decides to return in a few weeks once the harvest is complete to maximize the pillaging. Following such a raid, this same band would not return for many years, so that the bandits' interest in leaving many villagers alive or anything for the survivors to subsist on was very limited. Faced with this dire prospect, the village hired its samurai protectors who trained the villagers to fight beside them. Drastic consequences require drastic measures!

A government's legitimacy rests on its citizens favorably viewing the net gains from security and other government-provided public goods, after accounting for taxes. A government that extracts much more in taxes than what it returns in services may become the "tyrant" that must be overthrown. Thus, the power of the government to tax is limited if its goodwill with the people is to be maintained. This power is enhanced when the government effectively uses some of the taxes to provide public goods. By the same token, the tyranny of the majority, which may stem from unfair tax burdens placed on the minority, is also held in check if a government is not to be overthrown (McGuire and Olson, 1996).

At the supranational level, no global government exists to tax the constituent countries to provide security and other global public goods; rather, some weak international institutions perform a few of these functions, but on a more ad hoc basis. For example, transnational treaties possess no automatic enforcement mechanism. Thus, North Korea's decision on 10 January 2003 to pull out of the Nuclear Nonproliferation Treaty leaves the world community with no automatic sanction. Given the grave consequences of a preemptive attack on North Korea, the world is confronted with a collective action dilemma. Some nine years prior, US unilateral action resulted in the 1994 Agreed Framework where P'yongyang promised to abandon its nuclear weapons program in return for energy aid from the United States, Japan, and South Korea. Clearly, earlier US action represented the best-shot response, whose effect has now dissipated. Any creation of greater global governance on selective exigencies would require a much greater anarchic cost to the world community than it currently faces. Thus far, the world has adopted conventions to control the anarchy; such conventions apply to the open seas, air transportation, the postal services, and the electromagnetic spectrum. In the face of real crises, such as Nazi Germany, alliances have been forged to pool power.

Revolutions

In a 1991 opinion editorial, Mancur Olson asked why the people of Iraq had not assassinated Saddam Hussein. To answer this question, Olson offered a collective action explanation:

> The gains from the removal of a calamitous leader go to the population as a whole, including those who have done nothing to get rid of him. But the terrible costs of opposing a dictator – which can include life itself – are borne entirely by those who take action against him. Thus, everyone could gain if a totalitarian leader were overthrown, yet each individual could at the same time lose from acting to get rid of him (Olson, *Wall Street Journal*, February 22, 1991).

Olson is surely correct that the overthrowing of a repressive regime represents a collective good with the potential for inactivity due to free riding. The real puzzle is why assassinations and political revolutions ever occur. In Iraq, the Kurds tried to topple Saddam Hussein from power during Iraq's defeat in the 1991 Gulf War, and they may have succeeded with some outside help. In May 1991, a woman, believed to be a Tamil revolutionary, assassinated Rajiv Gandhi in a suicide bombing. People Power brought down the Marcos government. Other instances include the American Revolution, the French Revolution in 1789, the Russian Revolution in 1917, the Iranian Revolution in 1978–79, the Czechoslovakian Velvet Revolution in 1989, the Romanian Revolution in 1989, and other revolutions in Eastern Europe. There is also the Northern Alliance's participation with the United States in the overthrow of the Taliban in Afghanistan in 2001.

Clearly, the rebels face a collective action problem identical to that of the mice who contemplated belling the cat. Individual action must be motivated by either significant expected private benefits or a strong sense of altruism to the group. When weighing the alternatives to rebelling, a potential revolutionary looks at the opportunity costs from work and other nonrebel activities.[8] The greater these opportunities, the less motivation there is to rebel. Moreover, the potential rebel weighs the expected benefits of rebelling – that is, the probability of success times the private and public gains from overthrowing the government – against the expected costs of rebelling. These expected costs include not only the lost opportunity costs from other activities but also the expected personal costs from being caught by the authorities. The latter depends on the probability of being apprehended times the penalties imposed. If there is strength in numbers so that the likelihood of being captured decreases as the revolutionary fervor grows, then revolutions can generate their own momentum once a participation threshold is surpassed. That is, participation snowballs as the expected costs of participation fall off drastically (Kuran, 1989, 1991a, 1991b; Tullock, 1974). This phenomenon applied to People Power in the Philippines that overthrew Marcos and the Velvet Revolution in Czechoslovakia. Greater numbers also raise the success probability, which fosters still further participation.

On the other side, the despot must allocate resources among at least three activities: arming to stay in power, providing public goods to raise social welfare, and stealing from the people (Grossman, 1991). The more resources put into raising social welfare, the less needed to arm. The more resources stolen from the people and the less used to raise social welfare, the more arming that is necessary. Both arming and stealing require some form of taxation.

A number of ironies stem from the interplay of the rebels' and the despot's choices. First, the more oppressive the regime, the more likely that the people will resort to revolution as their opportunity costs from nonrebellious activities drop to zero. Quite simply, they have nothing to lose. Thus, there is a clear upper limit to oppression and "kleptocracy." Second, arming is needed to stay in power, but with less arming, there

---

[8] On these calculations, see Grossman (1991, 1992), Lichbach (1996), Sandler (1992), and Tullock (1974).

are less taxes and less need for arming. The arming/rebelling interplay has an embedded Prisoners' Dilemma. Third, despots, who appear invincible, may cross an invisible threshold with their stealing and repression, whereby the tide of revolution can rise up quickly and sweep them from power. Fourth, private gains given to the rebels to promote participation may lead to sequential despots. That is, rebel gains often involve acquiring the power once held by the overthrown tyrant, which was true of the Taliban's rise to power. Once in power, the "liberators" may become the new tyrant as they arm and tax to maintain their newly acquired power. Finally, there is a paradox of power as the technology of conflict may favor the weak, who can attack with surprise and can hide easily. Small forces may provide relatively great marginal gains owing to stealth, mobility, and surprise against far superior forces that are difficult to protect from random attacks (Hirshleifer, 1991). This paradox of power encourages revolution by raising the success probabilities. It also favors terrorism.

Rogue States

A great deal of concern has been expressed regarding so-called "rogue states" that operate outside of accepted norms of international behavior.[9] The worry is that these states will acquire WMD and the means (for example, ballistic missiles) to deliver them. In some instances, rogue states – some of which were characterized by George W. Bush as the "axis of evil" – are said to sponsor or condone terrorism as a legitimate means of bringing about political change in other countries.

In the past, the United States has branded five states as rogues: Iran, Iraq, Libya, North Korea, and Syria (Klare, 1995). In the upper portion of Table 7.2, these five alleged rogues are listed along with educated guesses (see sources listed) as of 2001 about their acquisition of WMD (nuclear, chemical, or biological weapons), ballistic missiles, active armed forces, heavy tanks, combat aircraft, and their percentage of GDP devoted to defense (Def/GDP). In the bottom portion of Table 7.2, the same information is provided for three "possible rogues" that according to Klare (1995) have nuclear weapon capabilities. In terms of nuclear weapons, North Korea and Iran pose the greatest future threat; however, four of the five alleged rogues represent a real concern in terms of chemical and

---

[9] Sources on these concerns include Gompert and Larrabee (1997) and Klare (1995).

Table 7.2. *Rogue and Possible Rogue States: Selective Military Indicators, 2001*

Country	Nuclear Weapons[a]	Chemical Weapons[a]	Biological Weapons[b]	Ballistic Missiles	Active Armed Forces[c]	Heavy Tanks	Combat Aircraft	Def/GDP (%)
Rogues								
Iran	u.d.	yes	prob	yes	513	1,565	306	5.8
Iraq	no	?	?	no	424	2,600	316	9.3
Libya	no	yes	prob	yes	76	2,210	400	4.1
North Korea	prob	yes	yes	yes	1,055	3,500	621	11.6
Syria	no	yes	prob	yes	321	4,700	611	10.9
Possible Rogues								
China	yes	prob	prob	yes	2,310	7,010	1,900+	4.0
India	yes	prob	prob	yes	1,263	3,898	701	2.9
Pakistan	yes	prob	poss	yes	620	2,337	366	4.4

[a] From Klare (1995, Table 5.1, p. 134), Stockholm International Peace Research Institute (2000, Chap. 9), and recent news events.
[b] From Dando (1994, p. 181) and Stockholm International Peace Research Institute (SIRRI) (2000, pp. 526–7).
[c] In thousands. Does not include reserves or paramilitary.

u.d. = under development
prob = probably
poss = possibly

Source: International Institute for Strategic Studies (2002) for active armed forces, heavy tanks, combat aircraft, and Def/GDP.

biological weapons. Prior to the Iraq war, there had been circumstantial evidence, but no proof, that Iraq possessed chemical and biological weapons. During the 1980–88 Iran–Iraq War, both countries used battlefield chemical weapons on opponent troops, which prompted the 1993 Chemical Weapons Convention. This Convention had been signed by 130 countries by 19 January 2003, but it had not been signed by Iraq, Libya, North Korea, or Syria. Saddam Hussein used chemical weapons attacks against Kurdish citizens in Northern Iraq during 1987–88, with the most devastating attack on Halabja where mustard gas and hydrogen cyanide killed 5,000 persons and injured 65,000. Possession of biological weapons is still not as important as a country's ability to "weaponize these assets" – the latter ability is not known for the so-called rogues. With the exception of Iraq, whose missiles had a limited range of 200–300 km following the Gulf War of 1991, the rogues have ballistic missile delivery systems with varying ranges of flight. All five rogues have sizable heavy tank forces and air forces. During the Iraq War of 2003, Iraqi ground forces were annihilated by US smart bombs and superior forces, while Iraqi combat planes never played a role. Thus, the military assets in Table 7.2 are not so formidable.

For 2001, Table 7.3 rank orders countries according to the size of their active armed forces, excluding reserves and paramilitary forces. Just the top sixteen armies are listed. Four of the so-called rogues and the three possible rogues possess armies among the top sixteen. The size of a country's army may not reveal very much about its true military prowess, because large armies may be poorly equipped, poorly trained, and no match to superior technology. This is especially clear when comparing China with the United States. China's army ranks first in size, but its military expenditure is about one-seventh that of the United States, so Chinese spending per soldier is dwarfed by that of the United States, leading one to severely discount Chinese forces when compared with those of the United States. By the same reasoning, North Korean forces pale in comparison with US forces. The real concern must be the signal sent by these large forces: such large militaries may indicate that the country is more interested in offense than defense. This is also reflected in the large percentage of GDP devoted to defense by the rogue nations.

The real worry of countries outside of the rogue's immediate region comes from threats to their friends and strategic resource supplies. In addition, WMD and their delivery capabilities can be used for extortion purposes to force the world either to assist the rogues or to change policies.

Table 7.3. *Sixteen Largest Armies in the World, 2001*

Country	Rank	Numbers in Armed Forces (000)[a]	Military Expenditures[b] in Millions of US Dollars
China	1	2,310.0	46,049
United States	2	1,367.7	322,365
India	3	1,263.0	14,167
North Korea	4	1,082.0	2,049
Russia	5	977.1	63,684
S. Korea	6	683.0	11,165
Pakistan	7	620.0	2,395
Turkey	8	515.1	7,219
Iran	9	513.0	4,698
Vietnam	10	484.0	2,351
Egypt	11	443.0	4,318
Iraq	12	424.0	1,372
Syria	13	321.0	1,884
Germany	14	308.4	26,924
Ukraine	15	303.8	4,899
France	16	273.7	32,909

[a] Does not include reserves or paramilitary.
[b] In 2000 constant prices.
Source: International Institute for Strategic Studies (2002, Table 26, pp. 332–7).

These weapons and capabilities also pose the threat that they may be acquired by terrorists.

The threats associated with rogue nations create numerous collective action failures. To keep the rogues in check, the world community needs intelligence, which is a best-shot public good that is likely to be undersupplied as the world relies on superior US capabilities. When deciding its level of surveillance, the United States will place little if any weight on the safety of other countries, unless their safety impacts US security. Because preemption benefits are purely public to all countries at risk from the rogue, preemption will also be undersupplied as the community relies on the best shooter to secure everyone's safety. This reliance on a single nation or alliance is inevitable as nations do not initiate the investment required for preemption prior to when it is needed. This earlier inactivity means that their assistance when needed is limited. Such global inaction may even be strategic to save on resources at the best shooter's expense. Timing underlies another collective failure. As countries maneuver to limit their responses, the rogue gains time to develop its WMD. Once nations wake up to the risks, the size of the required collective response has grown, and this inhibits action still further. This timing failure has been exploited by North Korea in recent years, as the United States tries to convince the world that North Korean intentions are not benign. Commercial interests represent yet another collective failure as countries' firms create the risks in the first place by supplying these alleged rogues with the requisite equipment, technology, materials, and know-how. Each individual transaction might appear harmless, especially for dual-use technologies that have defense and civilian applications. Because there is no collective monitoring of transactions to judge their aggregate strategic implications, countries are able to acquire WMD.

Unfortunately, I am not sanguine about the control of rogue nations or the risks that they present, now or into the future. Incentives are perverse for effective collective action; rather, incentives favor the global community to rely on either the strongest or the most-threatened nation to preempt the threats posed by rogue nations. An example of the latter scenario is the Israeli air raid on 7 June 1981 on the Osiraq reactor at Tuwaitha, located twenty miles south of Baghdad.[10] Although this reactor was allegedly intended for peaceful research, Israel and others felt that its capability to produce weapon-grade plutonium made it too much of a risk. Ironically, France had assisted Iraq with building the Osiraq reactor.

The Iraq War of 2003 highlights the dilemma posed by rogue nations. After failing to convince the world community that Iraq possessed WMD, the Bush administration invaded Iraq with significant help from the United Kingdom and token assistance from some other allies. If WMD had been found, then the world would have received a free ride. To date, no such weapons have been uncovered or are likely to be discovered and this reduces both American and British credibility now and into the future. The world's perception that these two countries deliberately exaggerated the threat makes action against future threats, if they were to arise, more difficult. Currently, the United States must try to keep order in Iraq which is costing almost $1 billion per week and greatly limiting US abilities to keep peace elsewhere. The best shooter will be more cautious in future deployments.

The North Korean threat was a prime motivator in the US decision on 14 December 2002 to abrogate the 1972 Anti-Ballistic Missile Treaty

---

[10] On Osiraq, see Klare (1995, pp. 45, 199).

(ABM) in order to allow for the development of a ballistic missile defense system. Under ABM, the United States could not deploy such a system. Once the United States has an effective ballistic missile defense system, it will have much less interest in preempting future exigencies. Before this becomes a reality, hundreds of billions of dollars must be spent by the United States to perfect this shield, which involves overcoming many technological difficulties (see Chap. 11).

Organized Crime at the Global Level

Not all cross-border flows associated with globalization are desirable. A prime example of an undesirable flow is organized crime at the global level. Some of the criminal players in the international arena are the Russian mafia and the drug cartels of South America. Transnational criminal activity exploits modern information technology to control a disperse network of operatives and support personnel (for example, money launderers). Even international treaties can create profit opportunities to unscrupulous individuals. To phase in the mandated reductions in ozone-depleting chlorofluorocarbons (CFCs), the Montreal Protocol (see Chap. 10) instituted high taxes on CFCs to raise their prices so that consumers have incentives to switch to non-CFC-using technologies. These high taxes provide profits for illegally traded CFCs by individuals who sell these substances below market, tax-inclusive prices. Some estimates put the black market in CFCs at five to ten kilotons in the United States and 2.5 kilotons in the European Economic Community during the mid-1990s.[11] In 2001, arrests of major smugglers of CFCs suggest that the problem has not disappeared. This illegal trade curtails the effectiveness of the treaty; thus, successful collective action among countries may be inhibited by actions by subnational agents.

Some transnational criminal activities infringe on copyrights and patents, while others involve trade in counterfeit inferior products. These criminal acts reduce the importance of property rights, which, in turn, curtails innovation and investment incentives as innovators or investors retain less of the return from their action. Counterfeit goods present an asymmetric information problem, where consumers are less certain whether they are buying the real product or not. The price on the

---

[11] See, for example, Fridtjof Nansen Institute (1996, p. 26).

real goods therefore falls and this reduces suppliers' incentives.[12] The increased volume of global trade means that an ever smaller proportion of containers are checked so that the ability to catch counterfeit or illegal goods decreases. This reduced enforcement encourages even greater criminal activity and augments consumer uncertainty. The rise in such criminal activities provides a positive externality among criminals owing to the thinning or dilution of law enforcement; that is, limited police resources are stretched when there are more criminals to pursue.

Faced with differing standards of enforcement in countries, organized crime will locate operations in those places with the lowest enforcement standards, while posing a threat to host-country citizens as well as foreigners. If the organized criminals wisely target the property of foreigners, leaving the country's citizens alone, there is apt to be underenforcement by local authorities owing to the absence of citizens' complaints and the positive economic stimulant derived from criminal activity. If, however, the crime network poses a significant threat to the host country's interest (for example, tourism or foreign direct investment), there may result an overenforcement that causes the criminals to move elsewhere – to a neighboring country. In this case, neighbors can engage in an "enforcement race" as each tries to transfer the criminals abroad. Little may come from this resource expenditure if the criminals still target the same prey no matter their location of operation. Criminal activities on the Internet certainly fit this pattern.

In a globalized economy, the pattern of externalities favors the criminals at the expense of victims. Global crime networks can exploit weakest-link aspects of law enforcement, analogous to actions by international terrorists (see Chap. 8). Moreover, authorities in different countries may work at cross-purposes when they do not coordinate enforcement decisions, because they view the consequent loss of autonomy and increased transaction costs as outweighing the coordination benefits. Unfortunately, this calculus does not include the benefits conferred on others so that an optimal outcome is not achieved. The real solution involves greater reliance on international police forces that not only share intelligence but also coordinate enforcement for such transnational criminal activity. More progress has been made through Interpol in terms of sharing information

---

[12] This "hidden-type" problem is analogous to the so-called lemons problem made famous by Akerlof (1970).

than in coordinating enforcement. In fact, this partial cooperation may make matters worse, since the shared intelligence can provide countries with better insight as to how to deflect the criminals abroad. The enforcement race consequently worsens with more resources expended without anything to show for them.

The globalization of crime also requires that laws are harmonized among targeted countries. Harmonization of criminal penalties is especially important because venues with more lenient penalties will attract criminal activities that can target people worldwide. There is little progress on this harmonization: autonomy has great sway over nation-states, particularly when it comes to law enforcement.

The post-9/11 increased threat of transnational terrorism has a negative implication for other global criminal activities. Since 9/11, more police assets are being allocated to thwarting terrorism. For example, a significant portion of Federal Bureau of Investigation (FBI) resources has been redirected from crime prevention to antiterrorism. This reallocation weakens the FBI's ability to fight crime. The same is true for policing agencies elsewhere.

Concluding Remarks

Efforts to address a rogue state or organized crime at the global level are typically best-shot or better-shot public goods where the greatest or greater responses have the most impact. Historically, the world has relied on either the richest nation or the strongest coalition of nations to take on such exigencies. Throughout this chapter, a common theme is that asymmetry, in the form of countries with diverse endowments (capabilities) and/or privately derived benefits, is essential for action. A proper response is more likely when there is sufficient inequality in means so that one nation can counter the threat single-handedly. In other scenarios, countries must pool resources, and this necessitates a level of coordination and consequent loss of autonomy that is only seen during dire times. Nations' reluctance to sacrifice their autonomy over security or law enforcement to a collective implies that time is required to understand the gravity of the circumstances before acting collectively. As time elapses, a rogue can gain a greater foothold [for example, overrun more countries (Nazi Germany and the Soviet Union) or acquire WMD], which then makes the task more difficult and dangerous. Given that rogues and bandits can exploit the weakest link of a defensive perimeter, they have a distinct advantage. Moreover, a weakest link will always be present until the prey of these pariahs unite and accept a loss of autonomy.

A worrying development is the United States' unilateral intent to shield its people from rogue nations' missiles, because the most capable country will thus become less interested in preempting rogue nations' threats in the future, thereby leaving the rest of the global community to find a new savior. The rise of a new savior is highly unlikely given current defense spending levels and defense research and development budgets in European allies (Hartley and Sandler, 2003; Stockholm International Peace Research Institute, 2000, Chap. 7, Table 6.5, pp. 316–7).

8

Terrorism: 9/11 and Its Aftermath*

On a clear, crisp morning, the peace and security of the United States was forever shattered by four hijackings on 11 September 2001 (henceforth, 9/11) that resulted in the collapse of the World Trade Center (WTC) towers, the destruction of a section of the Pentagon, and the passenger-induced plane crash on a rural Pennsylvania field. Within a mere 90 minutes, the potential threat of terrorism and the vulnerabilities of America became understood by a traumatized public. In today's technology-based society, an everyday object could be transformed into a weapon of mass destruction (WMD). Apparently, al-Qaida terrorists surpassed their wildest dreams of robbing Americans of their serenity and security. Their heinous attack captured headlines for months and will continue to do so for years to come. By broadcasting much of the disaster live, including the toppling of the north and south WTC towers, the media unwittingly assisted in magnifying the potential risks that modern-day terrorism poses. This heightened state of anxiety probably induced the anthrax terrorist to capitalize on the insecurity and hysteria that had already gripped the nation. That is, the mailing of anthrax letters was a complementary incident to the 9/11 hijackings, thereby allowing the two incidents to have a greater influence than either would have had on its own. Although those responsible for the two sets of events surely differed, the timing of the anthrax letters was not coincidental.

The events of 9/11 marked the largest ever terror attack on US soil – or anywhere – and resulted in the death of just over 3,000 people. The second largest terrorist attack on US soil had been the bombing of the

*   An *abbreviated version* of this chapter appeared in the June 2003 issue of *World Economy* (Vol. 26, No. 6, pp. 779–802) and is being published here with the kind permission of Blackwell Publishing.

Alfred P. Murrah Building in Oklahoma City on 19 April 1995, where 168 people died, while the third largest attack had been the bombing of Wall Street on 16 September 1920, where 34 people died and 200 were injured. The Wall Street time bomb left in a horse-drawn carriage had been technologically unsophisticated, similar to the Murrah building bomb and the 26 February 1993 bomb at the north tower of the WTC. The 1993 WTC bombing resulted in a 100×100 foot crater in the underground parking garage (US Department of State, 1994); a slightly different placement of a larger bomb could have imploded the building with much greater loss of life than 9/11. Based on these last two US incidents, we see that terrorism has been a threat for some time, while mass-casualty terrorism has been tried well before 9/11.[1]

Terrorists bent on mass destruction only have to be "fortunate" once, while society must be fortunate daily to avoid such catastrophes.[2] Another asymmetry between terrorists and the targeted society involves resources: society must protect everywhere to be secure, so that homeland security is very expensive, while terrorists can concentrate their best effort at a single vulnerable point, so that terrorism is a cost-effective activity. This is well illustrated by the 1993 bomb of fertilizer, diesel fuel, and icing sugar at the WTC. Even though this bomb cost just $400, it caused $550 million in damages (Hoffman, 1998). Yet another asymmetry involves information in which the terrorists know their own capabilities, unlike the targeted government, which is not fully informed about the terrorists' resources.

Terrorism is the premeditated use, or threat of use, of extranormal violence or brutality to gain a political objective through intimidation or fear of a targeted audience. To qualify as terrorism, an act must be politically motivated; that is, the act must attempt to influence government policy at home or abroad. Incidents that are solely motivated for profit and do not directly or indirectly support a political objective are not considered to be terrorism. The political motives of terrorism are varied and may include Marxism, nihilism, religious freedom, racism, separatism, anti-capitalism, anti-US dominance, or other goals. Since the 1979 November takeover

---

[1] On mass casualty bombings since 1946, see Quillen (2002a, 2002b). For Quillen, a bomb causes mass casualties if more than 24 people die.

[2] This asymmetry paraphrases what the IRA terrorists said in a letter after they learned that their 12 October 1984 bombing of the Grand Hotel in Brighton had narrowly missed killing Prime Minister Margaret Thatcher. Their letter said, "Today, we were unlucky. But remember we have only to be lucky once. You will have to be lucky always." (Mickolus, Sandler, and Murdock, 1989, Vol. 2, p. 115.)

of the US Embassy in Tehran, some terrorism has been motivated by the establishment of an Islamic state.[3] To create an atmosphere of fear where everyone feels vulnerable, terrorists *simulate randomness* when choosing targets. As the authorities focus on a likely venue, the terrorists often strike elsewhere at less watched targets. Terrorists often direct their violence against a large audience not directly involved with the political decision that they seek to influence. On 9/11, the plane that crashed into the Pentagon and the one that was intended for the US Capitol marked departures from this pattern by targeting decision makers. Extranormal violence is employed not only to grab headlines but also to elevate anxiety levels, so that the general population overreacts to these low-probability but high-cost events. As the public becomes desensitized to the violence, terrorists escalate the lethality of their attacks.

Terrorism falls into two essential categories: domestic and transnational. Domestic terrorism is home grown and has consequences for only the host country, its institutions, people, property, and policies. In a domestic terrorist incident, the perpetrators and targets are from the host country. Through its victims, targets, institutions, supporters, or terrorists, *transnational terrorism* involves more than one country. If an incident begins in one country but terminates in another, then it is transnational terrorism, which would be the case for a hijacking of a plane in country *A* that is made to fly to country *B*. The toppling of the WTC towers was transnational because victims came from many different countries, the mission was planned abroad, and the terrorists were foreigners. An incident may also be transnational if its implications transcend the host nation's borders. Transnational terrorist incidents represent *transboundary externalities* insofar as actions conducted by terrorists or authorities in one country may impose uncompensated costs or benefits on people or property of another country. In a globalized world of augmented cross-border flows, the distinction blurs between domestic and transnational terrorism.

When terrorist events have significant transnational consequences, numerous collective action concerns arise. Targeted countries may either work at cross-purposes or fail to cooperate to address the terrorist threat. For example, deterrence efforts by two or more countries to deflect an attack from the same terrorist network may create a deterrence race as each country tries to outspend the other target(s). In some instances, the

---

[3] The takeover of the US Embassy in Tehran is a watershed event, which marks the rise of religious terrorism in recent decades (Hoffman, 1998; Enders and Sandler, 2000).

deflection may merely result in a country's people or property being hit abroad, where the country has little say over terrorism-thwarting efforts. The absence of cooperation may involve a country's single-handedly mounting a preemption on the terrorists and their bases. The purely public benefits derived from the annihilation of a common terrorist threat lead to free riding, especially when a powerful country is anticipated by other targeted countries to act. A similar retaliator's dilemma characterizes actions to punish a state-sponsor of terrorism. Ironically, terrorists' ability to form global networks not only solves their collective action problem but also exacerbates the collective action problem for the target countries.[4]

The purpose of this chapter is to investigate the nature of transnational terrorism and some of the collective action issues that it poses in the aftermath of 9/11. In particular, rationality is investigated from alternative viewpoints that include the terrorist group's leaders, suicide bombers, and the targeted government. Difficulties associated with the deterrence and preemption dilemmas of targeted governments are also discussed. These governments' cooperative failures are shown to play into the hands of networked terrorists, who utilize their collective strengths to augment these governments' inadequate and noncooperative responses. Other collective action failures on the part of governments that involve intelligence and duplication of efforts are investigated. Another purpose is to identify what works and what does not work against terrorism. Finally the costs of terrorism are addressed for a globalizing society.

A Look at the Past

Table 8.1 provides a perspective on the nature of transnational terrorist incidents from data published by the US Department of State (1988–2003) or else made available by the Office of the Ambassador at Large for Counterterrorism, US Department of State. The coverage is the 1968–2002 period that represents the era of transnational terrorism, which really began after the Arab–Israeli conflict in 1967 and the subsequent Israeli occupation of captured territory. The columns in Table 8.1 indicate the year, the number of transnational terrorist events, the number of deaths and wounded caused by these events, and the number that involved attacks on US interests.

---

[4] On terrorist networks, see Arquilla and Ronfeldt (2001).

Table 8.1. *Transnational Terrorism: Events 1968–2002*

Year	Number of Events	Deaths	Wounded	Attacks on US Interests
2002	199	725	2,013	77
2001	355	3,296	2,283	219
2000	426	405	791	200
1999	395	233	706	169
1998	274	741	5,952	111
1997	304	221	693	123
1996	296	314	2,652	73
1995	440	163	6,291	90
1994	322	314	663	66
1993	431	109	1,393	88
1992	363	93	636	142
1991	565	102	233	308
1990	437	200	675	197
1989	375	193	397	193
1988	605	407	1,131	185
1987	665	612	2,272	149
1986	612	604	1,717	204
1985	635	825	1,217	170
1984	565	312	967	133
1983	497	637	1,267	199
1982	487	128	755	208
1981	489	168	804	159
1980	499	507	1,062	169
1979	434	697	542	157
1978	530	435	629	215
1977	419	230	404	158
1976	457	409	806	164
1975	382	266	516	139
1974	394	311	879	151
1973	345	121	199	152
1972	558	151	390	177
1971	264	36	225	190
1970	309	127	209	202
1969	193	56	190	110
1968	125	34	207	57

Source: US Department of State, *Patterns of Global Terrorism* (1988–2002) and tables provided to Todd Sandler in 1988 by the US Department of State, Office of the Ambassador at Large for Counterterrorism.

Several essential insights can be drawn from these numbers. First, with the exception of 2001, transnational terrorism on average results in relatively few deaths, especially when compared with the annual 40,000 people killed on US highways. In fact, the deaths on 9/11 are approximately equal to all transnational terrorist-related deaths recorded during the 1988–2000 period. Second, transnational terrorism follows a cyclical pattern with much of the 1990s being a relatively calm era in terms of the number of incidents.[5] Third, attacks on US interests accounted for almost 40% of events, even though relatively few transnational terrorist incidents took place on US soil. In 1998 and 2000, there were no such events, while in 1999 there was just one such event (US Department of State, 1999–2001). This is especially noteworthy from a transnational externality perspective and underscores that US success in deflecting attacks abroad has *not* secured the safety of US interests. Fourth, some years may represent outliers in terms of deaths, wounded, or attacks on US interests. For example, a single noteworthy event – known in the terrorism literature as a "spectacular" – may account for a spike in the number of dead or injured. Obviously, 9/11 is such an event regarding deaths. In 1998, the simultaneous bombings of the US Embassies in Nairobi, Kenya, and Dar es Salaam, Tanzania, accounted for 291 deaths and almost 5,000 injuries (US Department of State, 1999). The presence of outliers means that statistical analysis must adjust for them. Fifth, except for the casualty figures, transnational terrorism in 2001 does not appear to be different than in other years. This lack of difference would be confirmed by examining other measures not displayed in Table 8.1 – for example, terrorist modes of attacks, venue for attacks, or worldwide distribution of attacks.

Terrorist modes of attacks include bombings, kidnappings, assassinations, skyjackings, threats, and other kinds of events. The data set, *International Terrorism: Attributes of Terrorist Events* (ITERATE), developed by Mickolus, Sandler, Murdock, and Flemming (1989, 1993), tracks 24 categories of terrorist attacks. For instance, suicide car bombings are distinguished from other types for bombings (for example, incendiary devices, other car bombings, letter bombs, and explosive bombs). Figure 8.1 displays ITERATE quarterly data for 1970–2000 for all incidents and bombings. Prior to 1995, ITERATE totals did not differ greatly from State Department data; however, after 1995, ITERATE totals

---

[5] The cyclical nature of transnational terrorism is established with rigorous statistical analysis in Enders, Parise, and Sandler (1992), Enders and Sandler (1995, 1999), and Im, Cauley, and Sandler (1987).

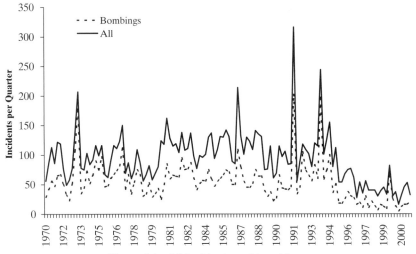

Figure 8.1. All incidents and bombings

departed greatly from the State Department data. This departure is due to a narrowing of ITERATE's source material so that only significant or newsworthy events are being monitored. Figure 8.1 reflects the cyclical pattern of transnational terrorism. In addition, the figure indicates that bombings are the favorite mode of attack of terrorists and account for about half of all incidents on average. The plot of the bombing series influences the shape of the all-incident series.

In Figure 8.2, the quarterly number of assassinations and hostage-taking incidents (that is, skyjackings, kidnappings, barricade and hostage taking, and takeover of a nonaerial mode of transportation) are depicted based on ITERATE data. Although cycles are again evident, the two series do not move together, implying that different underlying determinants influence the shape of these series. Assassinations are relatively low in recent years in sharp contrast to hostage-taking missions, which remain at levels consistent with the peaks and troughs during the last three decades.

Recent analyses show that the underlying motive behind transnational terrorism has become less driven by Marxist left-wing beliefs and more directed by religious fundamentalism.[6] Of course, various motives still justify transnational terrorism, but the dominant drivers have changed.

---

[6] On the changing motives of terrorists, see Hoffman (1997, 1998), Enders and Sandler (2000), and Wilkinson (2001, 2002).

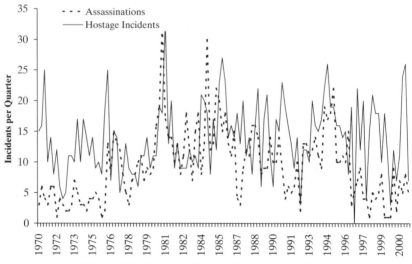

Figure 8.2. Assassinations and hostage incidents

With this shift to more religious-based terrorism has come a greater willingness on the part of terrorists to cause casualties. For example, religious groups that declare a Jihad or holy war against another nation consider its people, not just its officials, as the enemy and thus legitimate targets. Moreover, religious terrorist groups act out of a desire to satisfy their own goals (for example, ascent to heaven) rather than to win favor with an external constituency. Violence may be viewed as a purifying act, justified for its own sake, so that claims of responsibility or a list of demands are not issued. Even though the number of transnational terrorist events is generally lower in the post-Cold War era, the greater violence prediction is borne out by statistical analyses – the likelihood of death or injury for each event is now 17 percentage points greater per incident (Enders and Sandler, 2000).

Suicide Attacks

In recent times, the importance of suicide attacks has increased; 9/11 illustrates the carnage that a suicidal mission can wreak. The presence of suicidal pilots allowed the planes to be guided into the WTC towers and the Pentagon. A bomb placed on board these same flights is unlikely to have caused the same death toll and destruction on the ground. In addition, Hamas's use of suicide bombers against Israeli targets has increased greatly during 2002, thereby augmenting public awareness of such attacks. Suicidal missions are, of course, not new and can be traced back to Japanese kamikaze pilots during World War II. Kamikaze planes were loaded with explosives to create maximum damage to enemy targets such as ships.

One must ponder a rationality argument for suicide bombers. Alternative explanations have, however, been offered to justify suicide missions. Wintrobe (2001) characterizes suicidal terrorists as rational individuals who engage in an extreme trade-off between their autonomy and group solidarity. Wintrobe's analysis hinges on an individual's desperate search for group acceptance and cohesion as driving a suicidal terrorist into an extreme choice, where group solidarity is more valuable than one's very existence.[7] Wintrobe, however, rejects that rewards in heaven can motivate a rational self-sacrifice in a suicide mission.

To show that self-sacrifice is rational, one must demonstrate that the utility associated with the suicidal mission is at least as large as the utility of the status quo. If the utility of the status quo is sufficiently low owing to an absence of economic opportunities or a sense of injustice, or if the utility of the suicide act is sufficiently high because of group approval or other rewards, then a terrorist may rationally choose self-sacrifice.

There is no reason to dismiss heavenly rewards as one, but not the only, factor that can tip the utility comparison in favor of a suicide mission. Compensation paid by Iraq under Saddam Hussein to the families of suicide bombers can also tip the balance, especially when the status quo offers grim economic realities. If heavenly rewards, martyrdom, or family compensation are relevant, then an intertemporal utility comparison is necessary in which the decision maker places value on postmortem utility. Everyday acts of purchasing life insurance or church attendance suggest the relevancy of postmortem utility in an individual's decision calculus. The suicide mission can also be motivated by deceit, where the terrorist is not told the true nature of the mission. There is some evidence that the two terrorists who drove a yellow Mercedes truck full with explosives into the US Marine barracks at Beirut International Airport on

[7] Wintrobe's (2001) argument bears some similarity to Hardin's (1995) *One for All* theory to explain the logic of group conflict, where the collective action problem can be overcome through group identity that bolsters an individual's self-interest when engaging in extreme behavior against members of a hated opponent group. Self-sacrifice is not a necessary outcome in Hardin's theory.

23 October 1983 were not informed about the suicidal nature of their mission (Mickolus, Sandler, and Murdock, 1989, Vol. 1). After setting the bomb to detonate, the bombers jumped from the cab of the truck and tried to run to safety but did not get very far. In some instances, the terrorists may be forced to take the action because of threats made to their family; thus, many considerations can induce a terrorist to make the ultimate trade-off.

While poverty can play a role in limiting the operative's status-quo utility, there is no reason why poverty must be a factor if group identity or heaven's rewards are large enough. In a recent study of Hezbollah martyrs, an inverse relationship between poverty and participation in suicidal missions was found, contrary to media reports (Krueger and Maleckova, 2002). Hezbollah's suicidal terrorists did not tend to be poor nor poorly educated in the sample. The study did not, however, include the employment opportunities of these suicidal terrorists.[8] Education is a necessary, but not a sufficient, condition for obtaining a good job. Nevertheless, this study suggests that the size of the expected utility from carrying out the suicidal mission may have to be large, insofar as the utility of the status quo is not necessarily small.

Important participants in suicidal missions who have been left out of the analysis to date are the terrorist leaders and strategists – for example, Osama bin Laden and Ramzi Binalshibh – who dispatch terrorists to their death. It is noteworthy that the higher echelon of al-Qaida, Hamas, and Hezbollah do not sacrifice themselves. Their calculus is impeccable – they preserve their organization by employing low-cost resources in the form of dispensable young men (and sometimes women) to create maximum anxiety in a targeted audience. The inverse relationship between poverty measures and participation in suicide missions is probably due to these leaders choosing bombers for the mission who possess the requisite intelligence for logistical success. Moreover, the attainment of a level of education is a signal of a person's determination to carry through on commitments. Suicidal missions can create particularly high anxiety in a targeted society because a determined suicide bomber may not only mimic the identity of the target audience (for example, dress like a devout Jew), but also create maximum damage by detonating the bomb at the most

---

[8] In the case of Israeli Jewish settlers, individuals who attacked Palestinians in the West Bank were generally from high-paying jobs. These settlers were not on suicide missions.

opportune moment. Such missions underscore both the determination of the terrorists and the vulnerability of the targeted audiences.

A final participant is the targeted government, charged with protecting the lives of its citizens. Suicide missions present a real dilemma to these governments. In general, deterrence policies work best if they can create price changes associated with terrorist operations that induce terrorists to switch from more harmful activities to less harmful ones. Ultimate trade-off (or "corner solution") for the suicidal terrorist implies that policies that reduce these missions' probabilities of success have no influence whatsoever on these agents' choices (Enders and Sandler, forthcoming). This then implies that the government must either apprehend or kill suicidal terrorists for attacks to stop. The US fear that suicidal missions will come to American cities is well founded because effective terrorist methods get either mimicked or exported worldwide in a globalized society.

Cooperation Failures and Their Costs

Unlike the governments that they target, terrorists have progressed in solving their collective action problem. From the early 1970s, terrorist groups engaged in transnational acts have been tied either explicitly or implicitly to networks consisting of left-wing terrorist groups united in their goal to overthrow democratic governments (Alexander and Pluchinsky, 1992), Palestinian groups united in their aim to establish a homeland or to destroy Israel, and fundamentalist terrorist groups united in their goal to create nations founded on fundamentalist principles (Hoffman, 1998; US Department of State, 2001). Terrorist networks cooperate on many levels including training, financial support, logistical assistance, intelligence, weapon acquisition, pooling resources, and the exchange of operatives – for example, the 21 December 1975 attack on the Organization of Petroleum Exporting Countries ministerial meeting in Vienna, or the 27 June 1976 hijacking of Air France flight 139 (Alexander and Pluchinsky, 1992).[9] The al-Qaida network operates in more than 60 countries and stages their attacks worldwide. This network includes such groups as Abu Sayyaf in the Philippines, Egypt's Islamic Group, Harakat ul-Mujahidin in Pakistan, Islamic Movement of Uzbekistan, Al-Jihan

---

[9] These specific incidents are described in Mickolus (1980) under their specific dates. The hijacking of Air France flight 139 is famous because of the eventual storming of the plane at the Entebbe airport in Uganda by Israeli special forces.

in Egypt, and bin Laden's own group (US Department of State, 2001). Even left-wing groups and Palestinian groups have been known to train together and to have other ties (Hoffman, 1998; Wilkinson, 1986, 2001), so that separate networks have explicit links to one another. These networks have a common hatred of the United States and Israel, which means that heightened attacks by groups in one part of the world can spark increased attacks in other parts of the world. This implicit coordination shows up as distinct cycles of peaks and troughs in transnational terrorist activities.[10]

The ability of terrorists to cooperate heightens the inefficiencies associated with governments' inability to cooperate, except episodically – for example, in building the coalition to defeat the Taliban and to attack al-Qaida camps and bases in Afghanistan. This inability of governments to cooperate is first illustrated for deterrence and preemption.

The Deterrence Race

In the top panel of Figure 8.3, a symmetric deterrence game is displayed for two countries – A and B – that are confronted by a common terrorist threat. Suppose that increased deterrence gives a private, country-specific gain of 6 to the deterring country at a *cost* of 4 to *both* countries. For the deterring country, cost arises from deterrence expense and the increased likelihood of experiencing damages abroad if the attack is deflected there. For the nondeterring country, the cost stems from the damages that it can suffer from attacks diverted to its soil. If there is a host-country disadvantage from damages, then this damage can exceed that of the other country. For simplicity, the damage and deterrence expense of the deterring country is equated to the damage cost of the nondeterring country – hence, the common cost of 4.

Based on country-specific gains of 6 and the public costs of 4 stemming from each country's deterrence, the payoffs in panel a arise, where country A's payoff is on the left and country B's payoff is on the right in each cell. If only one country deters, then it receives 2 ($= 6 - 4$) as a deterrence cost of 4 is subtracted from its private benefit of 6. The nondeterring country loses -4 by becoming the target of opportunity by not acting. When both countries deter, each receives -2 [$= 6 - (4 \times 2)$] as common costs of 8 are deducted from the deterrer-specific benefit of 6. Inaction

---

[10] See the statistical results in Enders, Parise, and Sandler (1992) and Enders and Sandler (1999).

	B	
	Increased Deterrence	Status Quo
Increased Deterrence	Nash -2, -2	2, -4
Status Quo	-4, 2	0, 0

A (row-label to the left)

a. Symmetric deterrence game

	B	
	Do Not Preempt	Preempt
Do Not Preempt	Nash 0, 0	4, -2
Preempt	-2, 4	2, 2

A (row-label to the left)

b. Symmetric preemption game

Figure 8.3. Deterrence and preemption games

on the part of both countries gives zero payoffs. The deterrence game has a dominant strategy since $-2 > -4$ and $2 > 0$, so that the payoffs associated with increased deterrence are larger than the corresponding payoffs associated with the status quo for each of two countries.[11] Each country plays its dominant strategy and augments deterrence, thereby ending up at the Nash equilibrium of mutual action where payoffs are less desirable than mutual inaction. The former is a Nash equilibrium, because neither country would *unilaterally* want to change its strategy and return to the status quo. The deterrence scenario in Figure 8.3 is a Prisoners' Dilemma, analogous to an arms race, where countries spend more but do not necessarily become more secure. With fanatical terrorists who will not be deterred from attacking some country, deterrence will

---

[11] This analysis of deterrence is analogous to models presented in much greater detail in Sandler and Lapan (1988) and Sandler and Siqueira (2003).

not necessarily improve security, especially in a globalized world where a country's citizens can be attacked at home or abroad. Thus far, the deterrence analysis suggests *overdeterrence* in which each country does not account for the external cost that their efforts to deflect the attack generate for another country. For this scenario, the greater the number of countries, the greater the extent of overdeterrence.

Underdeterrence may characterize the deterrence game for an alternative set of payoffs. Suppose that a country's people or property is most vulnerable abroad owing to secure borders at home. Further suppose that the host country experiences little collateral damage from an attack on its soil. In this case (not displayed in Figure 8.3), there will be underdeterrence, because the host country will not account for the external benefit that its deterrence confers on foreign visitors targeted by host-country terrorists.[12]

In the general case, the deterrence scenario has both external cost and external benefit. External cost arises as deterrence deflects an attack abroad, while external benefit stems from either the protection afforded to foreigners or the elimination of an attack altogether. Thus, a wide range of strategic scenarios and results are possible depending on whether external cost or benefit is stronger.

Deterrence may not result in a Prisoners' Dilemma if the actions of the targeted countries are complementary, so that each country's deterrence bolsters the additional benefits associated with the other country's deterrence. If deterrence of both countries is required for any benefits to be realized, as would be the case when deterrence is a weakest-link public good, then an assurance game follows as in Chapters 2 and 3. The same is true if a minimal threshold of cumulative deterrence is required before any benefits are realized.

Preemption Game

In the bottom panel of Figure 8.3, a canonical *preemption game* is displayed, in which each of two targeted countries must decide whether to

---

[12] This scenario characterizes the Greek authority's inability to deter attacks by 17 November terrorists against US, NATO, and other foreign targets in Greece. In the summer of 2002, an accidental explosion – and not clever police work – led to the first arrests of 17 November members. Since 1973, 17 November carried out 146 attacks and murdered 22 people prior to these arrests (Wilkinson, 2001, p. 54).

launch a preemptive attack against a common terrorist or state-sponsored threat. The preemptive strike is intended to weaken the terrorists or their sponsors so that they pose a less significant challenge. For comparison purposes, payoffs analogous to the symmetric deterrence game in Figure 8.3 are chosen. If a sole country preempts, then it confers a public benefit of 4 to itself and the other country at a cost of 6 to just itself. In the off-diagonal cells in the bottom matrix of Figure 8.3, the country doing the preemption nets -2 ($= 4 - 6$), while the free rider receives 4. When neither country preempts, each receives 0, whereas mutual preemption gives 8 ($= 2 \times 4$) in benefit at a cost of 6 for a net payoff of 2, as listed, for both countries. The dominant strategy is not to preempt, since $0 > -2$ and $4 > 2$. Mutual inaction results in the Nash equilibrium of this Prisoners' Dilemma game.

Even though in their most basic form the deterrence and preemption games lead to Prisoners' Dilemma, there are essential collective action differences in these two problems. First, the Nash equilibrium for the deterrence game requires mutual action, while the Nash equilibrium for the preemption game requires mutual inaction. Second, the matrix games are negative transposes of one another, in which the Nash payoffs are more damaging for the deterrence game.[13] Third, whereas the deterrence game has scenarios for both too much and too little deterrence owing to the presence of external cost and benefit as the game is generalized, the preemption game involves too little preemption owing to the presence of just external benefit. Fourth, deterrence efforts may be complementary, while preemption efforts are always substitutable unless a threshold level of action is required. Thus, increased deterrence by one country should augment these efforts by the other country, whereas preemption actions by one country should limit these efforts by the other country.

A Maximal Externality

The deterrence and preemption dilemmas have plagued international efforts at a coordinated response for the last 36 years from the start of the modern era of transnational terrorism. The deterrence and preemption dilemmas are but two manifestations of the unwillingness of nations collectively to confront the terrorist threat. Similar dilemmas involve

---

[13] The deterrence game is analogous to the commons problem, while the preemption game is analogous to the pure public good problem (Sandler and Arce, 2003).

retaliation against a state-sponsor of terrorism or the pooling of intel-ligence. The application of game theory to the study of terrorism shows that there may be a rational basis – for example, the playing of a dominant strategy – for these collective action failures. Nevertheless, one must won-der why terrorists but not governments can solve their collective action dilemma.

Governments place great weight on the importance of their autonomy over national security. Only during times of great threat (such as after 9/11) or war, do nations eschew their autonomy and form tight alliances to present a united front against an adversary. In contrast, terrorists are always at grave risk from a more powerful opponent so that they have little choice but to pool their limited resources and rely upon one another. In addition, terrorists are relatively united in their hatred of a few countries – the United States, Israel, and the United Kingdom. Countries perceive their risks differently – that is, some are worried about being the target of an attack and others are not – and possess economic interests that may be at odds with addressing the terrorist threat. If, for example, country A has lucrative contracts with a country that helps sponsor terrorism, then country A will not support hostile actions against this alleged state-sponsor. Moreover, terrorists take a long-term view of their struggle and consider their interactions with other groups as continual; in contrast, governments take a short-term view (limited by the election period) of the terrorist threat and do not necessarily consider their interaction with other governments as continual. As a consequence, terrorists view the underlying game as infinitely repeated, while the governments do not, so that cooperation becomes a potential solution for terrorists but not for governments.[14]

By forming a global network and exploiting targeted countries' unco-ordinated responses, terrorists not only limit the effectiveness of these countries' efforts to counter terrorism but also maximize the externali-ties (and, hence, inefficiency) that governments impose on one another. Uncoordinated responses on the part of governments mean that there is a weakest-link vulnerability for the terrorists to exploit. For exam-ple, by not maintaining airport security to an agreed-upon global stan-dard, some airports present an easier target than others. Terrorists will probe airport security until these weakest links are uncovered and then direct attacks there. Such terrorist actions are no different than those of

---

[14] On such repeated games and cooperative solutions, see Sandler (1992, Chap. 3).

a virus that seeks out and attacks a more vulnerable host. In a globalized world where a country's citizens can be targeted anywhere, the consequences of terrorist cooperation coupled with government noncooperation is that the true level of protection of targets is very small. The external cost imposed by the most inadequate prophylaxis is further exacerbated because the terrorist network dispatches its *best-shot* response in the form of its best placed and trained squad. Hence, terrorist targets experience the maximal external cost possible, while terrorists gain the maximal external benefit. This nightmarish outcome continues today.

This combination of collective action success and failure on the part of terrorists and governments, respectively, highlights the unusual challenge that transnational terrorism really poses to the world. Today, a country cannot rely on its own efforts to ensure its citizens' safety. As Table 8.1 illustrates, the United States experiences the largest share of transnational attacks even though few occur at home. So what is the solution? The answer is easier said than accomplished. Unlike terrorists, who have global networks, nations must also form a global network to face off against the terrorist networks. Short of terrorists using WMD, governmental networks on par with those of the terrorists will not form; instead, there will be partial cooperation – for example, sharing of select intelligence.

Ironically, partial cooperation can worsen the inefficiency as compared to noncooperation. Suppose that countries are deciding whether or not to coordinate efforts on deterrence and intelligence. Further suppose that countries decide to share intelligence but not deterrence efforts – this is a common outcome. Among other things, the intelligence provides information as to the terrorists' preferred target – that is, which country they want to attack. Knowledge of terrorists' preferences assists the would-be targets to better deflect the attack, so that an even greater level of overdeterrence results.[15] This "second-best" outcome is not uncommon in economics when only one of two choice variables is controlled.

Another Collective Action Failure

To date, nations have relied on their own commando forces to address hostage exigencies at home or abroad involving their citizens. Thus, the

---

[15] This outcome is shown mathematically in Enders and Sandler (1995) and Sandler and Lapan (1988).

United States has Delta Force, while virtually every EU country maintains its own force. This failure to pool resources means that economies of scale are not exploited so that the average cost of these squads is much higher than necessary. Moreover, since each country's force is dispatched less often when compared with a multicountry force, learning economies, which shift down the average cost per deployment, are not captured. The infrequent use of these commandos means that they do not acquire the experience to hone their skills in real deployments. Of course, the presence of parallel forces indicates that efforts are duplicated, which is an additional waste of resources. Because a squad may have to be dispatched some distance away to address a hostage mission abroad (for example, Delta Force was sent to the Mediterranean during the *Archille Lauro* ship hijacking), a country must either maintain a network of bases worldwide or else risk the news media alerting the hostage takers of the commandos' travel progress (as CNN did during the *Archille Lauro* incident). A multicountry squad can establish such a global network at a more reasonable per-country expense than that associated with a single country's effort. Once again, nations cherish their autonomy and balk at such cooperative approaches. Countries do not want to obtain other countries' permission to deploy such forces during a crisis. Consequently, antiterrorist efforts remain expensive and generally independent among nations.

Is the World Different after 9/11?

Following the events of 9/11, the world better understands the threat that transnational terrorism poses. Before 9/11, only 14 transnational terrorist incidents involved more than 100 deaths and none had over 500 deaths (Hoffman, 2002, p. 304). That the authorities had dismissed the use of a commercial airliner as a murderous bomb is rather incomprehensible given some earlier events. On 5 September 1986, hijackers took over Pan American flight 73, a Boeing 747, at the Karachi airport with the aim of crashing it into an Israeli city (Mickolus, Sandler, and Murdock, 1989, Vol. 2, pp. 452–7). This plan was never executed because commandos stormed the plane in Karachi while it was still on the tarmac. The true intentions of the terrorists were revealed during the 1988 trial of those captured. Another unmistakable omen was the 24 December 1994 hijacking of an Air France passenger plane in Algiers by Armed Islamic Group (GIA) terrorists, dressed in Air Algerie uniforms. Their mission was to crash the Algiers–Paris flight into a crowded area of Paris with great loss of life. In a stopover in Marseilles, a French antiterrorist commando squad stormed the plane and killed the four hijackers before they could wreak death and destruction from the sky (Oklahoma City National Memorial Institute for the Prevention of Terrorism, 2002). Another portentous event was the capture of Ramzi Youssef, the mastermind of the 1993 bombing of the WTC and an al-Qaida associate, in the Philippines in 1996. At the time of his capture, he had plans to use a dozen commercial airliners to destroy a variety of targets including the Central Intelligence Agency (CIA) headquarters in Virginia.

These forerunners to 9/11 indicate that the threat of catastrophic incidents with massive casualties has been around since 1986. As such, 9/11 marked the day when the terrorists were very lucky and their target unlucky. Although 9/11 was a watershed event of transnational terror, given its horrible consequences, it is better viewed as a reality check than the start of a new type of terrorism. Annual death tolls will remain like those of Table 8.1 with deaths well below 1000 on average in any given year. There has been little change in the pattern of global terrorism since 9/11, except that the total number of events is temporarily smaller in 2002, owing to the disruption in al-Qaida operations worldwide. Given the massive casualties of 9/11, authorities are quite worried about terrorist use of WMD in the form of chemical, biological, radiological, or nuclear (CBRN) attacks. Nevertheless, many terrorist experts believe that greater vigilance should be directed toward conventional methods rather than CBRN attacks (Hoffman, 2002; Wilkinson, 2002).

Global efforts to thwart terrorism have only changed marginally. The global response is still US-led, which is not surprising because US interests remain the favorite target of international terrorists. As such, the United States gains the most country-specific benefits from its antiterrorism "war." With US actions in Afghanistan, the Philippines, and Iraq, US interests will continue to attract the lion's share of transnational terrorist attacks. Unlike other countries, the United States has the power-projection capabilities to move massive forces to trouble spots quickly; as such, the United States affords free-rider opportunities for others.

Although the US-led retaliation against the Taliban on 7 October 2001 for harboring bin Laden involved other nations as allies, the current fight against terrorist networks is mostly nation driven. Nations still refuse to extradite terrorists and to integrate their antiterrorism efforts, except in terms of the sharing of intelligence. Concern for national autonomy still dominates against efforts to mount a united front against terrorists. Even international actions to freeze terrorist assets have not progressed much after some initial headway immediately following 9/11. International cooperation remains a collective action failure except for a few bright spots – for example, the capture in 2003 of an al-Qaida cell in Spain and US–UK cooperation.

What Works and What Does Not Work Against Terrorism?

One possible recommendation as to what works is to eliminate the causes of terrorism under the presupposition that, with no grievances or perceived injustices, terrorism will not exist. There are some obvious difficulties with this quick fix. If terrorists can extort any political change that they desire by either threatening or performing violent acts, then democratically elected governments would lose their intended purpose, because the voters' choices could be circumvented by well-armed minorities. Obviously, the legitimacy of a liberal democracy, whose mandate rests on the protection of lives and property, would be greatly compromised. Part of these property rights is the ability of duly elected officials to pursue policies that reflect the wishes of the electorate. If governments seek to correct any claimed injustice, then an aggrieved minority can induce sizable redistributions of wealth to themselves by threatening terrorism unless such inequities are redressed. Such extortion-based redistributions undermine property protection. Once terrorists discover a causal link between alleged grievances and government actions, there will be no stemming the growth of terrorism as a tactic. Moreover, social discontent is a dynamic factor that is constantly changing; efforts to rectify one social wrong do not eliminate new injustices tomorrow. In fact, tomorrow's injustice may stem from addressing yesterday's injustice.

Barriers and Fortifications

Given the absence of a simple panacea for transnational terrorism, potential targets have relied on technological barriers to thwart a particular type of attack. The installation of metal detectors to screen airline passengers is, perhaps, the best instance of such barriers. These metal detectors were installed in US airports beginning 5 January 1973. Shortly thereafter, these devices were placed in airports worldwide to monitor passengers and their carry-on luggage on domestic and international flights. Prior to January

1973, skyjackings worldwide averaged over sixteen per quarter or sixty four per year. Shortly after metal detectors were installed, there was an immediate and permanent drop of almost eleven skyjackings per quarter (Enders, Sandler, and Cauley, 1990a). This is a rather dramatic impact that was long-lasting. A similar effectiveness was experienced following the fortification of US embassies and missions in October 1976: prior to the fortification, there were about eight attacks per quarter against US diplomatic targets; after the fortification, there were just over three attacks per quarter.[16]

But this is not the whole story. When one mode of attack is made more difficult or expensive to conduct, terrorists substitute other relatively cheaper events. If, for example, skyjackings are more difficult due to metal detectors, then other hostage-taking events are now relatively cheaper. Similarly, recent efforts to secure commercial airliners from terrorist attempts to use them as massive bombs will induce terrorists to look to the use of cargo planes to accomplish such missions. Therefore, the effectiveness of an antiterrorism policy is to be analyzed properly, its influence on other related modes of attack must be investigated.

When the impact of metal detectors is examined more closely, these detectors are seen to decrease skyjackings *and* threats but to increase other kinds of hostage incidents and assassinations not protected by the detectors. For example, Enders and Sandler (1993, Table 4) show that the installation of metal detectors in 1973 is associated with 14 fewer skyjackings per quarter, almost 12 additional hostage incidents per quarter (not involving planes), and 7 more assassinations per quarter. Enhanced embassy security, while effective at reducing embassy attacks, had the unintended consequence of increasing assassinations of diplomatic and military personnel when they left secured compounds. This substitution is toward events that are more costly to society than those being protected. This outcome suggests that piecemeal policy, in which a single attack mode is considered when designing antiterrorism action, is inadequate. Terrorist substitution among attack modes must be anticipated. Policies that decrease terrorist resources are particularly effective because they should result in an across-the-board decrease in attacks.

Even when barriers and fortifications work and do not cause more costly substitutions, the authorities must be ever vigilant to outguess the

---

[16] See Enders, Sandler, and Cauley (1990b, Table 2) for these statistical results. An even larger long-term decline followed the immediate impact.

next terrorist innovation. There is, thus, a dynamic concern with such barriers and fortification, which are *static inhibitors* that invite the terrorists to invent novel circumventions. Hence, plastic guns replaced metal ones and bottles of inflammable liquids replaced hand grenades because these innovations can pass undetected through metal detectors. Not only have the authorities failed to second guess the terrorists, but they also have been slow to respond to innovations. Media accounts of innovations allow terrorists to rapidly adopt the breakthroughs of others, making such innovations pure public goods. For example, the use of bottles that allegedly contained inflammable liquids spread quickly in the 1980s as homesick Cubans used this method to hijack planes to Cuba (Mickolus, Sandler, and Murdock, 1989, Vol. 1; Enders, Sandler, and Cauley, 1990b).

What Kinds of Substitutions Are There?

Thus far, substitutions among attack modes have been stressed. Another type of substitution is across countries. As discussed earlier, better-secured borders deflect attacks elsewhere. Terrorist attacks aimed at foreign direct investment influence the flow of capital and cause investors to transfer their capital to countries where terrorist risks are smaller (Enders and Sandler, 1996). Thus, substitutions may characterize different agents associated with the terrorism problem. If, analogously, terrorist attacks put tourists at risk, then tourism may be negatively impacted (Enders, Sandler, and Parise, 1992), as in the case of the hijacking on TWA flight 847 on 14 June 1985. This flight departed Athens enroute for Rome with 145 passengers and 8 crew before it was first diverted to Beirut. This protracted hijacking was not resolved until 30 June 1985, with the release of the remaining 39 hostages.[17] Greek tourism suffered greatly as tourists chose alternative holiday venues, because this hijacking and others exposed security weaknesses at the Athens airport.

An intertemporal substitution may involve terrorists' timing of incidents. For example, a retaliatory raid by a targeted government may unleash a wave of terrorist incidents against the retaliator(s) as terrorists move events planned for the future into the present to protest the raid (Enders and Sandler, 1993). Later, terrorism may temporarily decline as

---

[17] This infamous incident is described in detail by Mickolus, Sandler, and Murdock (1989, Vol. 2, pp. 221–5).

terrorists replace expended resources. The news media may mistakenly view the temporary lull as a positive result from the raid. These and other substitutions (for example, terrorists changing their target of opportunity from business people to tourists, as the former acquire bodyguards) highlight the interdependency of decisions of terrorists and authorities. If the analysis or policy is too focused, then important consequences and trade-offs will be missed.

Evaluation of Other Policies: Domestic Laws, International Conventions, and Retaliation

When dealing with domestic crime, nations have instituted laws with stiff punishments in the hopes of deterring crime by making would-be criminals weigh the consequences of their contemplated actions. If the society has the police force to bring criminals to justice and courts to impose harsh sentences, then offenses may be reduced. Similar reasoning may persuade governments to rely on domestic laws and international conventions to curb transnational terrorism. Unfortunately, the antiterrorism effectiveness of such laws and conventions are very disappointing, as shown by past empirical investigations. For example, the so-called Reagan get-tough-with-terrorism laws [Public Law (PL) 98-473 and PL 98-553 signed by President Reagan in October 1984] have had no statistical effect whatsoever against US-directed terrorist acts.[18]

PL 98-473 requires up to life imprisonment for individuals taking US hostages either within or outside of the United States. This law also raised penalties for destroying aircraft or placing a bomb aboard an aircraft. PL 98-553 authorizes the US Attorney General to pay rewards for information leading to the apprehension or conviction, inside or outside the United States, of terrorists who targeted US interests (Pearl, 1987, p. 141; Mickolus, Sandler, and Murdock, 1989, Vol. 2). These laws failed to deter terrorism for a number of reasons. First, because most terrorist acts against US people or property occur abroad, the United States must rely on foreign governments to extradite criminals, which for capital offenses is highly unlikely. Second, by staging their events abroad, terrorists greatly discount the ability to be brought to justice. US successes in capturing

---

[18] The underlying statistical analyses can be found in Enders, Sandler, and Cauley (1990a, 1990b).

terrorists abroad have been sufficiently few in number prior to 9/11 that there has been little influence on terrorists' anticipated probabilities of being brought to US justice. Third, fundamentalist terrorists, who are prepared to make the supreme sacrifice, are undeterred by policy-induced *marginal* changes in risks.

Over the years, nations have formed international conventions and resolutions to thwart terrorist acts. Two early instances include the 1971 Montreal Convention on the Suppression of Unlawful Acts against the Safety of Civil Aviation (Sabotage) and the 1977 UN General Assembly Resolution 3218 on the Safety of International Civil Aviation.[19] Although well intended, neither of these treaties appeared to have much effect on aviation's safety from terrorism. Other significant antiterrorism treaties include the following: the UN Convention on the Prevention and Punishment of Crimes against Internationally Protected Persons, Including Diplomatic Agents (adopted by the United Nations on 14 December 1973), the UN Security Council Resolution against Taking Hostages (adopted by a 15–0 vote on 18 December 1985), the UN General Assembly Resolution 2551 on the Forcible Diversion of Civil Aircraft in Flight (12 December 1969), the Hague Convention on the Suppression of Unlawful Seizure of Aircraft (16 December 1970), and the UN General Assembly Resolution 2645 on Aerial Hijacking (25 November 1970). Conventions are more binding than resolutions, since resolutions are merely agreements in principle and do not imply any real commitment on the part of the adopters. Conventions, in contrast, require that the nations rely on their *own* judicial systems to implement and enforce the agreement. But in neither case is there a central enforcement agency that can force the nations to comply. Without such an enforcement mechanism, signatories will do what is convenient from their viewpoints – a Prisoners' Dilemma is apt to underlie the pattern of payoffs, not unlike the preemption or deterrence games.

When the average number of attacks is examined both before and after the adoption of these conventions and resolutions, there is *no* statistically significant reduction in the post-treaty number of attacks for the relevant attack modes (crimes against protected persons or skyjackings).[20] This is convincing evidence that these UN conventions and resolutions really had

---

[19] See Alexander, Browne, and Nanes (1979) for the text of the treaties on the suppression of terrorist acts.

[20] The statistical analysis is presented in Enders, Sandler, and Cauley (1990a, 1990b).

no impact. To acquire the requisite support from the world community, these antiterrorism treaties were drafted to permit too many loopholes and too much autonomy on the part of the signatories. A more effective treaty-making process involves neighboring nations agreeing to control a common terrorism problem that presents significant and localized effects. Thus, Spain and France have made progress in concerted efforts to control Basque terrorism.

Prior to the US "war on terrorism," retaliatory raids had very little long-run impact on terrorism. One study examines the impact that Israeli retaliatory raids had following significant terrorist incidents (Brophy-Baermann and Conybeare, 1994). Retaliations investigated included the raid on Palestine Liberation Organization (PLO) bases in Syria following the Black September massacre of Israeli athletes during the 1972 Olympic Games; the attack on Palestinian guerrilla bases in Lebanon following a March 1978 Haifa bus hijacking; and the bombing of Palestinian bases in Lebanon following a June 1982 assassination attempt against the Israeli ambassador in London. This study finds that such raids only temporarily suppressed terrorism: within three quarters, terrorism had returned to its old mean values.

The long-run effectiveness of the US-led retaliation against al-Qaida will not be known for years to come. Nevertheless, some conclusions seem self-evident. Given the sustained level of attack against al-Qaida and the unprecedented (but still modest) international cooperation, US-led actions to suppress international terrorism will be longer lived than in the past. Not only has the al-Qaida network lost significant assets (for example, training camps, safe and inaccessible havens, and known strategists), but also linkages within the network have been disrupted. Grievances against America will surely worsen because of US actions, so that attacks will return as the network reconfigures itself. A spate of terrorist attacks in 2003 appears to be signaling al-Qaida's resurrection, but the true success of US-led measures against al-Qaida depends on the number of attacks that would have occurred had this action not been taken. No one can know this magnitude for sure, but it is likely to have been much greater than what occurred in 2002 and 2003 owing to a weakened al-Qaida.

No-Negotiation Strategy

One of the four pillars of US antiterrorism policy is to never negotiate with hostage-taking terrorists or capitulate to their demands. The logic behind this policy is that if a nation adheres to this stated no-negotiation policy, then would-be hostage takers have little to gain. For the policy to work, the nation must preserve its reputation.[21] Virtually every nation that confronts terrorism has, at times, violated its pledge to never negotiate with hostage takers. The Reagan administration's barter of arms for the release of Rev. Benjamin Weir, Rev. Lawrence Jenco, and David Jacobsen during 1985–6 is a violation of this pledge that resulted in the "Irangate" scandal (Mickolus, Sandler, and Murdock, 1989, Vol. 2). Even Israel, the staunchest supporter of the no-negotiation strategy, has made notable exceptions as in the case of the school children taken hostage at Maalot in May 1974 and during the hijacking of TWA flight 847.[22] The effectiveness of the conventional policy to never negotiate with terrorists hinges on a number of crucial implicit assumptions. First, the government's pledge is completely credible to would-be hostage takers. Second, there is no uncertainty concerning payoffs. Third, the terrorists' gains from hostage taking only derive from ransoms received. Fourth, the government's expenditures on deterrence are sufficient to deter all attacks. Each of these assumptions is tenuous in practice.

If the terrorist group realizes a net gain from a negotiation failure, as it may if it values media exposure or martyrdom, then the government's proclamations and its level of deterrence cannot necessarily forestall an attack, so hostages are abducted. Once hostages are taken, the government must weigh the expected costs of not capitulating against those of capitulating. Conceivably, the government may view the cost of not capitulating as too high for the right hostage, even when accounting for lost reputation. In such situations, the government reneges on its pledge. If would-be hostage takers believe that they can impose costs sufficient for a targeted government to renege on its stated policy, then they will abduct hostages because the credibility of the government's pledge depends on an uncertain outcome. Each time a government caves in, the terrorists will update or raise their beliefs about future capitulations. That is, learning based on past actions allows terrorists (and the government) to update or raise their beliefs in an interactive fashion. When a government reneges

---

[21] On reputation and terrorism policy, see Lapan and Sandler (1988). The discussion of the no-negotiation policy follows from their model.

[22] These events are described in Mickolus (1980, pp. 453–4) and Mickolus, Sandler, and Murdock (1989, Vol. 2, pp. 219–25).

and negotiates, it emboldens terrorists to take additional hostages. In so doing, a capitulating government imposes a public bad on future domestic governments and on governments worldwide. Constitutional constraints or congressional hearings, which impose huge costs on officeholders who capitulate, may be the only means of raising the cost of capitulation sufficiently to make a precommitment to never negotiate a policy without regrets, once hostages are captured. Such actions would severely restrict discretionary action for the good of the world community.

What Are the Economic Costs of Terrorism?

Given the annual number of people murdered by international terrorism, the associated security spending may appear excessive. President Bush's proposed budget for 2003 earmarks $37.7 billion to homeland security, which represents an $18.2 billion increase over 2002.[23] This expenditure does not include the tens of billions spent to bring down the Taliban in Afghanistan and smash al-Qaida's operations there. One must wonder how many of the 40,000 lives lost each year on US highways would be saved if some of this money went to making US highways safer. If lives lost are the only consideration, then clearly margins have not been equated and more lives can be saved by a reallocation of spending. The security outlay has, however, the all-important political benefit that the government appears to be in control. When this security perception is achieved, there is the psychological benefit of the traumatized public feeling safer. This security benefit is difficult to evaluate but is certainly very high. The perception of security is arguably more important than the reality for such a political benefit.

Homeland security is expensive because terrorists force governments to protect myriad targets, insofar as an attack can take place almost anywhere. High-profile events, bridges, monuments, government buildings, and public places receive the most security. Deterrence expenditure is an *insurance* payment that must be paid regardless of the outcome – that is, it is not refunded when no terrorist attack ensues. Unfortunately, the enhanced security may not be all that effective despite great efforts, because the terrorists will merely look for a less-watched alternative

---

[23] All data used in this section are obtained from the official website of the President of the United States (2003) located at http://www.whitehouse.gov.

target. If the attack is diverted to where both the symbolic value and lives lost are more limited, then there is a return on the deterrence investment. Of course, the alternative of doing nothing would just mean that the terrorists would succeed with the most damaging attack as they did on 9/11.

In deciding deterrence – both its expenditure and its nature – a liberal democracy walks a thin line.[24] If it overreacts and spends huge amounts while eliminating personal freedoms, the government may lose legitimacy, as citizens view the government as resorting to terrorist tactics. If, however, it underreacts and spends too little, then the government may be perceived as ineffective and not sufficiently protecting its people's lives and property. This negative perception also reduces government legitimacy. In the case of the United States, significant security is needed outside of its borders, where the lion's share of the attacks occur and the US government has no sovereignty.

After 9/11, the stock markets took a precipitous drop owing to the initial shock, associated uncertainty, and dire consequences to select industries. Many people viewed this tremendous loss in equity values as a new cost of terrorism. Prior to 9/11, the economic cost from terrorism was documented in two areas: reduced foreign direct investment for *small* countries and reduced tourism.[25] The attacks on 9/11 suggest that equity cost may be great. While there is no question that some industries (for example, the airline and travel industries) suffered greatly from 9/11, the interesting thing about 9/11 is that the drop in most equity prices was temporary, with most stocks rebounding rather quickly in the ensuing months. A single act of terrorism, or even a sustained campaign, cannot really destroy confidence in an intricate and diversified economy as that of the United States or the global community. A massive attack can, however, temporarily shake confidence and cause stock prices to drop. An instructive exercise is to compare the impact on stock values of corporate fraud, as characterized by Enron and World.com, with the impact on these values of 9/11. With corporate fraud, equity prices have remained depressed for months and months, because corporate fraud strikes at the very confidence needed to hold equity shares.

---

[24] On this trade-off, see the seminal treatment by Wilkinson (1986) and his recent book (Wilkinson, 2001).

[25] These losses are documented in Enders and Sandler (1996) and Enders, Sandler, and Parise (1992), respectively.

Concluding Remarks

Modern-day transnational terrorism taxes the ingenuity of governments worldwide. Countries can limit their exposure at home by relying on barriers, fortification, and intelligence; but this protection comes at a great cost and will never make a society invulnerable. Given the pervasive transnational externalities associated with today's terrorism, the real global challenge relates to the need for greater international cooperation among governments that are loath to sacrifice autonomy. Cooperation is required in terms of deterrence, preemption, intelligence, and punishment of terrorists. Because these decisions are interdependent, partial or piecemeal cooperation may achieve little. Not all of the associated externalities are negative, so governments may engage in too much of some terrorism-thwarting activities and too little of others. Consequently, global collective action *and* inaction may be problematic at times. As long as governments place more weight on their autonomy than on their effectiveness in confronting this common exigency, terrorists will succeed in maximizing their effectiveness while limiting the effectiveness of the targeted governments. The entire dilemma has become worse because terrorists have successfully addressed their collective action problem through the formation of networks, while governments have not.

No matter the ultimate fate of al-Qaida, transnational terrorism will remain a threat. In the 1980s, the Abu Nidal Organization was the most feared group, but now it poses virtually no threat, especially with the death of Abu Nidal in Iraq during 2002. Dangerous groups will come and go, but terrorism will stay. More worrying is the fact that terrorists will continue to innovate and devise ghastly plots that will someday exceed the horrors of 9/11. Over the years, the escalation of the terrorist spectacular in terms of carnage reflects the need of the terrorists to shock to capture headlines. In addition, terrorists will continue to exploit technological innovations, such as the Internet, to their advantage. But the authorities can also exploit these technologies to the terrorists' disadvantage by, for example, tracking their messages and disrupting their websites. Globalization will not only make it more difficult to protect against terrorism but also create more vulnerable "choke" points that terrorists can exploit to adversely affect international commerce.

9

Citizen against Citizen

The end of the Cold War brought hope for a more peaceful world as the risk of war between the United States and the former Soviet Union was no longer a concern. In addition, these superpowers had less motive to support civil wars in the search for client states, so the incidence of civil wars, which was high in the 1980s, was anticipated to decrease. Defense analysts talked of a peace dividend as resources were redirected from the defense sector to other needs of the public sector in terms of education, social overhead capital, and other programs (Kirby and Hooper, 1991; Sandler and Hartley, 1999). In fact, a redistribution did occur: the North Atlantic Treaty Organization (NATO) allies, which allocated 4.5% of gross domestic product (GDP) to defense for the 1985–89 period, assigned just 2.7% of GDP to defense in 2002 (NATO Press Release, 2002, Table 3). For the world at large, most countries' percentages of GDP earmarked for defense similarly have declined since the end of the Cold War [Stockholm International Peace Research Institute (SIPRI), 2002, Table 6A.4, pp. 282–91]. Four notable exceptions to this pattern exist: the United States, some Middle Eastern countries, nations with civil wars, and nations with territorial disputes.

Has the world become a safer place following the end of the superpower confrontation? Clearly, the possibility of an apocalyptic nuclear war where hundreds of millions of people in the superpowers and their allies are annihilated in a matter of minutes is no longer a worry. Yet, a devastating nuclear exchange between India and Pakistan has deepened in concern as has the threat posed by a nuclear-armed North Korea. Since 11 September 2001, the public awareness of deadly attack by terrorists using conventional and nonconventional weapons has also increased in importance. Finally, the prevalence of civil wars presents a collective security concern. Insofar as Chapter 7 deals with rogue states and Chapter 8

192

with terrorism, this chapter focuses on the threat posed by civil wars, pitting citizen against citizen, that dot the globe. Although security worries abound in the post-Cold War world, the true risks to the majority of the world's population is miniscule compared with those associated with the Cold War. This reduced risk is reflected by the smaller percentage of GDP that a representative nation now allocates to defense.

Civil war casualties – though in the tens or hundreds of thousands per year – are typically localized to the conflict-ridden country or its immediate neighbor. Why then do civil wars present a concern for the global community, worthy of global collective action in the form of diplomacy, peacekeeping, or military intervention? Six reasons come to mind. First, these wars are most often in developing countries where they limit development and the effectiveness of foreign assistance, thereby perpetuating the vast inequality between rich and poor countries (Collier and Sambanis, 2002, p. 3; *The Economist*, 2002b; Elbadawi and Ndung'u, 2000). If the world community really wants to make headway in promoting economic development, then the civil war impediment must be removed. Second, the negative economic consequences of a civil war are not contained to the host country but spread to neighbors and neighbors of neighbors and can diffuse up to 500 miles from the conflict venue (Murdoch and Sandler, 2002a, 2002b, 2004). Third, the conflict itself may be contagious and spread to neighbors so that a local instability may grow into a regional instability (Most and Starr, 1980; Siverson and Starr, 1990; Starr and Most, 1983). Fourth, such conflicts can result in trade blockages and price rises in essential raw materials (for example, oil and strategic metals) for the industrial world. Fifth, civil wars can become the breeding grounds for revolutions and diseases that can disperse worldwide. Undernourished populations may have compromised immune systems that can be attacked by microbes looking for an opportune host. Recent research shows that the incidence of malaria and HIV correlates highly with civil wars (*The Economist*, 2002b, p. 24). Sixth, civil wars may spawn terrorist acts in foreign capitals to make known their grievances.

Civil wars in the post-Cold War era have a number of root causes. Collier and Hoeffler (1998, 2002a, 2002b) characterize the essential drivers of civil wars as greed and grievances. In Africa and elsewhere, greed for valuable natural resources (especially oil, diamonds, and gold) motivates civil conflicts. These natural resources not only finance the conflict but also grant the victors vast riches. Since 1998, civil war in the Democratic Republic of the Congo, fueled in great part by neighboring countries' interests in the Congo's natural resources, caused the death of over 3 million people (*The Economist*, 2003b, p. 23). Grievances may be founded on alleged economic, political, or social injustices, which had been the case in the attempted genocide in Burundi in 1993 where Tutsi–Hutu rivalries resulted in the murder of over 200,000 people (SIPRI, 2002, pp. 27–9).[1] From an opportunistic viewpoint, the breakup of the Soviet Union and Eastern Europe unleashed ethnic hatreds that erupted once central power was diminished. Reduced control allowed for a settling of old scores that dated back to atrocities committed before World War II. Both greed and grievances may play a role. At times, the civil wars arise from a power vacuum, where revolutionaries use might to seize governmental control to institute fundamental political and social changes.

The primary purpose of this chapter is to indicate the global collective action issues associated with civil wars. Despite the huge death tolls, collective action regarding civil wars is anticipated to be undersupplied because distant conflicts may not at first be seen as having important global implications. In this regard, short-sightedness may take on a temporal or spatial character; that is, nations do not appreciate that civil wars may have wide-reaching political or economic consequences over time or may spread widely through a sequence of spatial transmissions. Fixed election terms of government officials may nurture this myopia. Even when nations are not short-sighted, their actions may be inadequate because each may wait for others to afford them a free ride. As I show, this potential inefficiency may be attenuated when actions – say, peacekeeping – to address civil wars yield joint products, some of which benefit just the peacekeeper. Thus, the chapter highlights the importance of joint products and their ability sometimes to sidestep a global collective action difficulty. Global efforts to curb civil wars by reducing the profitability of primary commodity exports (through lower prices), limiting inequality, or raising income growth are still far from adequate.

Assessing the Civil War Problem

Table 9.1, taken from SIPRI (2002), provides a stark picture of the civil war problem by region for the 1990–2001 period. Major conflicts are listed in terms of numbers. In some locations, more than one war may

---

[1] For tests of the underlying determinants of civil wars, see Collier and Hoeffler (2002a, 2002b), Elbadawi and Ndung'u (2000), and Elbadawi and Sambanis (2002).

Table 9.1. *Major Conflicts: Regional Distribution, 1990–2001*[a]

Region	1990	1991	1992	1993	1994	1995	1996	1997	1998	1999	2000	2001
Africa[b]	11	11	7	7	6	5	3	4	11	11	9	7
America[c]	4	4	3	3	3	3	3	2	2	2	2	2
Asia[d]	13	11	12	10	10	11	10	9	9	9	9	9
Europe[e]	0	1	3	5	4	3	1	0	1	2	1	1
Middle East[f]	4	6	5	6	6	6	6	4	4	3	4	4
Total	32	33	30	31	29	28	23	19	27	27	25	23

[a] Some locations have two or more wars going on.
[b] In Africa, the only interstate war for the 1990–2001 period involved Eritrea and Ethiopia, 1998–2000.
[c] There were no interstate wars for the 1990–2001 period. America includes North, Central, and South America.
[d] In Asia, the only interstate war for the 1990–2001 period involved India and Pakistan in 1990, 1992, 1996–2001.
[e] There were no interstate wars for the 1990–2001 period.
[f] In the Middle East, the only interstate war for the 1990–2001 period involved US-led coalition and Iraq in 1991.
Source: Stockholm International Peace Research Institute (2002, Table 1A.1, p. 64; pp. 65–6).

be ongoing; for example, during 2001, the Colombian government was in separate conflicts with the Fuerzas Armadas Revolucionarias Colombianas (FARC) and the Ejército Liberación Nacional (ELN). India had two separate conflicts: a civil war between the government and Kashmir insurgents and an interstate war between India and Pakistan. The totals in Table 9.1 record such conflicts as multiple wars. Almost all conflicts listed are civil wars except for three interstate wars that involved Eritrea and Ethiopia (1999–2000), India and Pakistan (1990, 1992, 1996–2001), and the US-led coalition and Iraq (1991). These interstate wars are part of the totals for the relevant years. Thus, for 1993–97, all but one conflict is an intrastate one. Table 9.1 indicates that most of these wars have been centered in Africa and Asia, which have experienced similar numbers of wars. The Middle East endured on average the third greatest number of intrastate conflicts. The totals in the last row of Table 9.1 show no clear trend in civil wars – the totals declined from 1991 to 1997 following the end of the Cold War and then jumped up in 1998, with a subsequent decline in 2000–1.

Figure 9.1 provides a longer-term viewpoint of the incidence of civil wars by displaying the number of country months of civil wars worldwide for the 1951–99 period. Country months consist of the sum of months worldwide that countries suffered a civil war on their own territory during

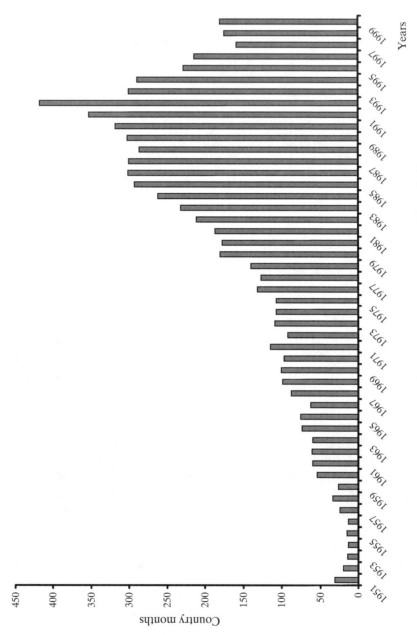

Figure 9.1. Country months of civil war in the world: 1951–99

a calendar year. The data used for Figure 9.1 came from Singer and Small (1993) *Correlates of War Project* and from updates for the 1990s provided by Anke Hoeffler of Oxford University. In Figure 9.1, an upward trend in civil war months is displayed from the mid-1970s until 1993. After a large decline during 1994–97, the incidence of civil wars crept up again during 1997–99, but is now declining (see Table 9.1). Clearly, the era of civil wars started well before the breakup of communist states in 1989 and beyond. Compared with the 1950s, the rise of intrastate wars was already in progress in the 1960s. Starting in about 1980, interstate wars during the Cold War era, fought by surrogate nations for the superpowers, became too expensive and gave way to intrastate wars during the perestroika and the post-Cold War eras.[2]

Table 9.2 provides a very conservative picture of the costs in lives lost from select civil wars that continued to rage in 2001. The countries are grouped according to geographic region. The columns indicate the year that the conflicts ensued, the cumulative deaths (if known), the deaths in 2001, the number of government troops in 2001, and the ratio of government troops to rebel forces in 2001. Civil wars in Algeria, Colombia, Peru, India, the Philippines, Sri Lanka, Chechnya, and Turkey have killed tens of thousands. The same is likely to be true for Angola, Sudan, Afghanistan, and Iraq; millions have died in the Democratic Republic of the Congo. In Burundi, over 200,000 people have died since 1993. The human toll of civil wars is tragic. For 2001, the figures in Table 9.2 merely indicate whether the conflict surpassed certain thresholds rather than provide accurate death totals. Greater than a thousand deaths per year is typically the benchmark used to define a major civil war; hence, its prevalence in the table. As seen in Table 9.2, governments allocate significant manpower to troops in conflict-ridden countries. In the last column, two ratios are often displayed because of ranges given for government troops or rebel fighters or both. The first ratio is the best-case scenario for the government, while the second is the worst-case scenario. For most civil wars during 2001, either the ratio shows a spread or is unknown, thus highlighting the prevalence of asymmetric information where the government is usually ill informed about the true rebel strength. Under these circumstances, the rebels may try to feign greater strength and capability by grouping attacks in an offensive in the hope of getting the government to concede to some

---

[2] On perestroika, see English (2000).

Table 9.2. *Select Civil Wars in 2001*[a]

Country[a]	Conflict Start	Total Deaths	Deaths in 2001	Government Troops in 000s in 2001	Government Troops to Rebel Ratio[b]
Africa					
Algeria	1993	40,000–100,000	>1,000	300	unknown
Angola	1998	unknown	>1,000	130	13:1 to 13:3
Burundi	1998	>5,000[c]	>1,000	40	40:12 to 40:19
Congo, Democratic Republic	1998	unknown	unknown	45–55	55:45 to 45:67
Rwanda	1994	unknown	>1,000	40–60	2:1 to 4:5
Somalia	1991	unknown	unknown	unknown	unknown
Sudan	1983	unknown	>2,000	110–120	4:1 to 11:5
America					
Colombia	1978	>40,000	>1,000	280	140:9 to 280:25
Peru	1981	>28,000	<25	190	950:1 to 950:3
Asia					
Afghanistan	1992	unknown	>1,000	20–40	4:1 to 1:1
India (Kashmir)	1989	>23,000	>3,000	1,300	1300:5
Indonesia	1989	>2,000	100–200	500	250:1 to 100:1
Myanmar	1948	>13,000	50–200	400	200:1 to 100:1
Philippines	1968	>23,000	>100	100	100:21 to 100:28
Sri Lanka	1983	>60,000	>1,000	100–110	50:3 to 100:7
Europe					
Russia (Chechnya)	1999	40,000–70,000	>1,000	1,000	125:1 to 40:1
Middle East					
Iraq	1991	unknown	unknown	430	unknown
Israel	1964	>13,000[d]	>500	160–170	unknown
Turkey	1984	>30,000	100–200	800	800:3 to 800:5

[a] Boldface indicates third-party intervention.
[b] When rebel or troop numbers are known within a range, the best and worst ratio of government troops to rebels are listed.
[c] Since 1993, more than 200,000 deaths.
[d] Since 1948, more than 13,000 deaths.
Source: Stockholm International Peace Research Institute (2002, Table 1A.3, pp. 69–76).

of their political demands rather than endure further attacks.[3] This ratio varies greatly among the nations listed and can be almost 1000 to 1, as in Peru. Clearly, mountains and jungles provide cover for rebels (Collier and Hoeffler, 2002a) and may allow a small force to conduct an effective insurgency for years, especially when the government is unpopular.

During the drafting of this book, a private research institution in one such country asked me to write a report indicating the "efficient size for its country's government troops" to end a long-running civil war. If I had accepted the commission, I would have presented the final report in the capital city to the country's president and select officials. Even though the government troops already outnumbered known rebel forces by nearly 100 to 1, the government was making no headway due, in large part, to its past lack of popularity. I turned down the commission on a couple of grounds. The real question is how to settle long-standing grievances and issues of greed, not how many more troops to deploy to the field. In this instance, the government and rebels seldom ever confronted one another directly, choosing instead to punish alleged civilian supporters of the opposition. More troops could potentially worsen this grievance. Moreover, I never accept an assignment where I would need a bulletproof vest to deliver my final report!

Civil wars have dire economic consequences for the host country. By destroying physical and human capital, an intrastate conflict can reduce per-capita income and its growth at home. Reduced income per capita and lower growth are two key factors that lengthen civil wars, so that negative consequences of civil wars can become an engine that perpetuates the conflict (Collier, Hoeffler, and Soderbom, 2003). These direct adverse consequences may also arise from disruption to trade flows and day-to-day market activities. The risks associated with civil wars divert foreign direct investment (FDI), a crucial source of savings for developing countries, to less risky countries without civil conflicts. This fall in FDI results in less investment and, hence, smaller income growth. Civil wars also redirect government expenditures from productive social overhead capital to less productive defense spending. Income growth is adversely affected from the uprooting of people in rebel-controlled areas. Intrastate wars are also associated with the destruction of infrastructure, including the healthcare system. As crop production is often impacted, resulting

---

[3] This same tactic is used by terrorists (Lapan and Sandler, 1993; Overgaard, 1994).

famines are particularly devastating when healthcare has been compromised; thus, it is not surprising that civil wars and disease are correlated.

The recent literature on civil wars has enlightened us on many issues. The onset of civil war is positively related on the ratio of primary commodity exports to GDP, insofar as these exports can finance the conflict and enrich the rebels (Collier and Hoeffler, 2002a; Collier, Hoeffler, and Soderbom, 2003). Ethnic dominance may also support the onset of civil tension through a tyranny of a minority. Inhibitors of civil wars include the extent of secondary schooling (owing to a higher opportunity cost to rebels), greater growth in per-capita income, longer prior periods of peace, and a greater degree of democratic freedoms (Collier and Hoeffler, 2002b). The duration of civil wars is influenced by similar factors (Elbadawi and Sambanis, 2001, 2002). Most notably, a country heavily dependent on primary commodity exports (say 30%) would on average experience a 12% shortening of its civil war if collective action could reduce these exports' prices by 10% (Collier, Hoeffler, and Soderbom, 2003). Efforts to limit trade in, say, diamonds from a conflict-torn country, such as Sierra Leone, lowered diamond prices and shortened the conflict. In terms of civil war initiation, duration, and prevalence, both greed and grievance play a role. Economic factors (for example, past income growth) and political factors (such as enhanced democracy) can influence the genesis and duration of conflict through greed and grievances. Harmful consequences from civil wars can spread beyond the conflict-ridden nations, thereby motivating the need for collective peacekeeping.

Civil Wars and International Collective Action

The direct effects of civil wars presented thus far have little cost spillovers to warrant international collective action, except in terms of a weakened population becoming vulnerable to diseases that can spread far and wide. A stronger motivation for transnational collective action to quell civil wars is the need to inhibit additional negative influences from spreading to other countries. Thus, one must look beyond the host-country impacts to identify such spillovers and the justification for collective action. An obvious candidate is from the conflict itself spreading to neighbors, thereby destabilizing the region. Propinquity may result in collateral damage to infrastructure and capital from battles fought in neighboring states, especially when conflict is near the border. As neighboring states augment defenses to limit rebel incursions, government resources are directed away from activities that are more income enhancing. Negative spillovers may also stem from refugee migrations that may draw away government resources to care for displaced persons. Another avenue of spillover transmission is economic where fallout from the war reduces income per capita and growth in countries in proximity to those experiencing internal war (Murdoch and Sandler, 2002a, 2002b, 2004). Negative economic consequences may diffuse beyond immediate neighbors owing to regional economic integration and regional multiplier effects (Easterly and Levine, 1998). Regions with greater interregional trade and investment are anticipated to display wider dispersion of these detrimental effects. Thus, economic impacts may extend farther for some civil conflicts as nearby countries reduce trade with others in the region, and potential investors brand even nonneighboring countries as poor investment prospects, thus diverting FDI to safer havens. As countries in a conflict-ridden region contract their economic activities, the multiplier can amplify the civil-war-induced downturn at relatively great distances from the conflict.[4]

Even allowing for a wide dispersion of the negative consequences of a civil war, negative economic impacts are more in the nature of a regional public bad, so that actions to end the conflict are best characterized as a regional public good (RPG). In rare instances, global spillovers may occur if any intrastate war is responsible for the worldwide transmission of diseases, revolutionary ideology, or transnational terrorism. If the civil war impacts key resource supplies for the world community, then global economic consequences may also arise.

Ideally, the principle of subsidiarity (see Chap. 4) dictates that collective action to bring peace to civil-war-torn countries should be instituted at the jurisdictional level nearest to matching the associated reach of spillovers. If, therefore, peacekeeping yields mostly regional spillovers, then a regional institution, such as the European Union or NATO, should intervene to end a nearby conflict. When, instead, peacekeeping curbs a civil war with more far-reaching conflict-induced costs, the United Nations is the more appropriate institution to oversee the operation. This is also the case when a regional organization lacks the capacity or may pursue an inappropriate agenda. The latter occurred when the Nigeria-dominated

---

[4] In a recent article, Murdoch and Sandler (2004) employ spatial econometrics to estimate that the peak effect of these negative spillovers extend up to 800 kilometers (500 miles) from the nearest border of the country experiencing a civil war.

Economic Community of West African States (ECOWAS) intervened for alleged peacekeeping purposes in Sierra Leone and ECOWAS troops ended up looting the country (Dorn, 1998). The United Nations must also be relied upon for curbing civil wars with mainly regional spillovers whenever the requisite local institution does not carry the proper legitimacy with the world community. Additionally, scale economies from peacekeeping may require UN interventions to keep costs down.

Until the rise of peacekeeping in the 1990s, the world community had turned to the United Nations to intervene in civil wars; however, the large increase of civil wars over the last decade and a half has stretched the UN's logistical and financial capacities. As a consequence, NATO has taken on some important peacekeeping roles in Bosnia, Kosovo, Macedonia, Albania, and elsewhere (Shimizu and Sandler, 2002). In other cases, the United States intervened to promote peace, sometimes unsuccessfully (for example, Somalia). The United States and NATO had assumed so many missions by mid-2003 that there will be greater reliance on the United Nations in the next few years, thus necessitating enhanced UN capacity for peacekeeping.

Publicness of Peacekeeping

To end a civil war, the world community has limited options. If the sides are willing to negotiate, the community can bring together the two sides and serve as an impartial mediator. The United Nations is the logical party to assume this role, but at times the mediator role has been performed by a nation – for example, the US efforts in the Dayton peace agreement in 1995 ending the Bosnian war, or the Norwegian actions to broker an Israeli–Palestinian accord. At other times, a regional institution may try to facilitate a peace agreement to "privilege" the rest of the world with less conflict and more stability. When diplomacy is not an option, the world community may have to apply pressure through trade boycotts or other sanctions to get the sides to agree to diplomacy. As mentioned earlier, countries that boycott trade in looted natural resources can reduce their prices and limit the length of the conflict. Another avenue is to cut off arms supplies to the warring factions. This latter action faces collective action difficulties as a country or firm that profits in this arms trade may clandestinely continue to sell weapons. Ironically, as the global community acts in unison to end arms supplies, a supplier's profit opportunities rise and these enhanced gains motivate greater defection.

Once diplomacy finally works and the sides agree to separate, then peacekeeping becomes an option. In its traditional form, peacekeeping involves the deployment of lightly armed military personnel to monitor or observe a ceasefire between hostile forces when the opposing sides agree to accept the monitors. Traditional peacekeepers may also serve as a buffer between hostile factions. Given their light armaments, such peacekeepers can do little to maintain peace if hostilities erupt. During the post-Cold War period, peacekeeping has taken on a more active role in promoting peace during some deployments. Thus, peacekeeping has assisted in the transition to democracy by training police, establishing legislative and other democratic institutions, and providing humanitarian relief (for example, Bosnia since 1995, Haiti since 1996, and East Timor since 2002). This fuller role is known as *peacebuilding*. The most logistically demanding form of mission is peace enforcement where uninvited forces are deployed to separate warring sides in order to impose peace on at least one combatant.

By eliminating negative spillovers to other countries stemming from a civil war, peacekeeping has been characterized as either a pure public good or a joint product activity.[5] In the former characterization, peacekeeping is viewed as providing nonrival and nonexcludable benefits to all those countries receiving negative consequences from the conflict. These benefits may derive from the greater peace and stability achieved or from the knowledge of the improved well-being of those at risk in the conflict-ridden country. For the joint product characterization, peacekeeping activities are seen as yielding both purely public benefits for the world community and contributor-specific benefits. These latter benefits may arise from status enhancement by being recognized as a major promoter of world peace (Kammler, 1997). If a contributor is near the region of instability where peacekeeping forces are deployed, then contributor-specific benefits may stem from the reduced risks that the conflict will spread to it. Certainly, Bosnia and Kosovo posed these risks to nearby NATO allies, while Haiti presented refugee costs to the United States. Additionally, nation-specific benefits may derive from the political value of doing more than one's fair share for peacekeeping. Contributor-specific benefits may also stem from providing humanitarian aid if the donor uses its efforts to gain favorable world opinion or if the donor's citizens take

---

[5] This distinction is discussed in greater detail in Khanna and Sandler (1997), Khanna, Sandler, and Shimizu (1998, 1999), and Sandler and Hartley (1999, Chap. 4).

pleasure in their nation's generosity. Further nation-specific benefits may come from increased trade arising from enhanced regional security.

The prognosis for collective action differs greatly depending on whether peacekeeping is purely public or a joint product activity. If peacekeeping is a joint product activity with a relatively large share of contributor-specific benefits, then action is motivated because a nation can only obtain such benefits by contributing. Although pure publicness is anticipated to lead to disproportionate burden sharing where the rich carry the peacekeeping burden for the poor, this disproportionality need not result if jointly produced contributor-specific benefits are not correlated to income. One potential test to distinguish between the two underlying theoretical explanations is to determine whether contributors' incomes are highly correlated with peacekeeping burdens as predicted by the purely public good representation (Shimizu and Sandler, 2002). Another test is to identify peacekeeping benefit proxies that are correlated with peacekeeping burdens, consistent with the joint product explanation (Khanna and Sandler, 1997). Furthermore, suboptimality will be attenuated as the share of country-specific benefits increases in the case of joint products. The presence of joint products means that there is less need for corrective policy to promote peacekeeping, since those nations that gain country-specific benefits will push for action. If, for instance, all derived benefits are contributor specific, then an efficient allocation toward peacekeeping may ensue as benefits match costs at the margin. Additionally, increases in the size of the group supporting peacekeeping need not affect either free riding or suboptimality if a significant portion of contributor-specific benefits is tied to peacekeeping.

Peacekeeping in Practice

Peacekeeping has had a checkered past after the United Nations subsumed operations in 1947 (Hill and Malik, 1996; Ratner, 1995). During 1947–56, four peacekeeping operations were initiated that involved either monitoring a ceasefire or providing a buffer between hostile forces. A more active period occurred during 1957–74, when there were nine new missions, most of the observer type. One notable exception was the early 1960s peace enforcement mission in the Congo where the United Nations appeared unprepared for the mission's complexity and the subsequent loss of 250 peacekeepers to hostile action. At its height, the Congo operation deployed over 20,000 peacekeepers and put strains on the UN regular budgets, which underscored that the United Nations needed to locate alternative sources of funding for its peacekeeping activities. Actions by the United Nations to obtain financing through voluntary donations were unsuccessful, which was not surprising given the dearth of nations that viewed the Congo as a clear and present danger. The Congo experience curbed UN interest in peacekeeping for some time so that a dormant phase characterized 1975–87, during which a single mission in Lebanon was started. The final period of 1988–2002 was highly active, with 41 missions of varying complexity. Many recent operations involved peacebuilding and peace enforcement. Obviously, UN resources and capabilities have been severely taxed during the post-Cold War era (Palin, 1995). This overextension has meant that non-UN-financed missions have grown in number and importance since 1991 (see Shimizu and Sandler, 2002, Table 3). These missions have been led by NATO, the United States, Australia, the Commonwealth of Independent States, and others. Complex and expensive missions have involved NATO-led operations in Bosnia (since 1995) and Kosovo (since 1998).

Owing to the Congo experience, UN peacekeeping operations have been primarily financed by *assessment accounts* that assign a fixed share of the annual costs for each peacekeeping mission to each UN member. UN Resolution 3101 of the General Assembly established these assessment accounts to create a more permanent funding source to cover the annual expense of peacekeeping. Payments to these accounts are in addition to the annual membership fee that funds the regular UN budget. Payments in arrears to the assessment accounts may be made up from the regular UN budget or voluntary contributions and often result in delays in reimbursing troop-contributing nations. Assessment schedules change slightly every three years and are based on a nation's ability to pay and status. The five permanent members of the Security Council are assigned about 22% more than their regular budget assessment scale;[6] a Council member that pays 20% of the UN regular budget must cover 24.4% of annual peacekeeping cost. Just over twenty developed countries, not permanent members of the Council, pay their regular budgetary shares to the assessment account for peacekeeping. Wealthy developing countries are charged a mere one-fifth of their regular budget-assigned shares so that a country in this category that covers 1% of the UN regular budget

---

[6] For further details on assessment accounts, see Durch (1993) and Mills (1990).

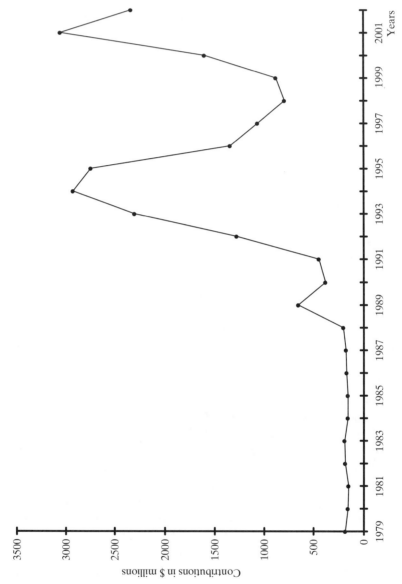

Figure 9.2. UN members' paid assessments to peacekeeping: 1979–2002

must pay just 0.2% of annual peacekeeping expense. Finally, other developing countries pay only a tenth of their regular budgetary share. The outcome of this scheme is predictable: about 27 countries cover over 98% (on average) of annual UN peacekeeping costs. Of course, those countries with the greatest say in peacekeeping operations – the permanent Council members – will likely approve missions where they have the most to gain. Thus, payment shares partly reflect contributor-derived benefits.

In Figure 9.2, UN members' paid assessments to peacekeeping are displayed in millions of US dollars for the 1979–2002 period. Clearly, these payments were flat for 1979–87 during the dormant era of peacekeeping. Since 1987, these peacekeeping payments track the incidence of civil wars, displayed earlier in Figure 9.1, so that peacekeeping is primarily motivated by civil wars. As the Cold War ended, peacekeeping missions and assessments shot up reaching well over $3 billion in 1993. The decline in these paid assessments for 1994–98 is explained by the decline in civil wars and NATO's assumption of peacekeeping in Bosnia, which was over half of the UN peacekeeping expense at the time. In addition, the United Nations became temporarily reluctant to take on costly missions that would again tax its peacekeeping capacity. In recent years, UN peacekeeping missions and expenses have risen again with new civil wars. By 2001, paid assessments for missions totaled just over $3 billion. This payment fell to $2.3 billion in 2002, but should rise in 2003.

In recent studies, tests were performed to ascertain whether the pattern of peacekeeping burden sharing adheres to a pure public good or joint product explanation. The findings of these tests for the 1976–91 period strongly support the joint product representation.[7] This follows because there is *no significant correlation between GDP and peacekeeping burdens*, as measured by paid peacekeeping assessments as a share of GDP. Thus, there is no evidence of disproportionate burden sharing prior to the end of the Cold War, which supports a joint product representation up to 1991. Further evidence follows from deriving two alternative demands for peacekeeping equations – one that applies to the pure public model and one that applies to the joint product representation. After estimating the demand equation for 1975–96 for the primary peacekeeping-contributing nations, the estimated equation is tested to determine which of the two underlying models fits best – the joint product model wins out (Khanna,

---

[7] This evidence is provided in Khanna, Sandler, and Shimizu (1998) and Sandler and Hartley (1999).

Sandler, and Shimizu, 1999). Thus, in the years of low peacekeeping expenditures, contributor-specific benefits are present and motivate action.

The post-Cold War era of high peacekeeping spending tells a different story. Based on correlating GDP and peacekeeping burdens, burden sharing displays behavior consistent with a pure public good explanation, which is especially true when non-UN-financed missions are included (Shimizu and Sandler, 2002). The rise in post-Cold War peacekeeping is placing a greater burden on the rich countries. Despite the high levels of spending, too little appears to be allocated to curbing the negative spillovers of modern-day civil wars that have become more public due to globalization. This is an essential finding that may apply to other GPGs and RPGs. That is, underlying circumstances can change, thereby altering the public character of the associated public good.[8] As the publicness of peacekeeping is transformed, the need for policy changes also becomes relevant. For peacekeeping, its anticipated enhanced publicness and consequent undersupply mean that a greater role for the United Nations is needed at a time when it is stretched thin and limiting new commitments.

For regional disputes, NATO has taken on a greater peacekeeping role in the 1990s, which is now even embodied in changes to its strategic doctrine in the mid-1990s (Sandler and Hartley, 1999). Australia assumed a lead role in East Timor and the United States did so in Haiti. The United Nations took on small missions in recent years, leaving large complex operations as in Afghanistan, Kosovo, and Iraq to NATO and countries with a larger stake in the stability of the region. Although this type of subsidiarity is an understandable course of events, it also implies that the United Nations is not fully performing its intended peacekeeping mission. By leaving peacekeeping operations to those with the greatest gains, the United Nations is allowing the providing countries greater latitude in pursuing their own agendas, which may have little to do with peace and stability. Because these rich nations now have a number of long-term missions, they will again look to the United Nations, as is clearly shown by the Bush administration's call in October 2003 for UN peacekeeping forces in Iraq. Security Council Resolution 1511 calls for an expanded UN role in rebuilding Iraq but falls short of committing the United Nations to a peacekeeping mission.

---

[8] Sandler and Hartley (2001) find that changes in strategy, weapon technology, and threat altered defense publicness for NATO allies.

The era of enhanced UN peacekeeping points to some deficiencies. There was too much of a time lag associated with the procurement of weapons for new missions.[9] With so many missions coming within a short time span, UN logistical capability was stretched too thin. There could also be a considerable delay in approving a new peacekeeping mission. Moreover, the United Nations reimbursed troop-providing countries by just $1000 a month per soldier, which is one-quarter to one-fifth of the costs of troops from NATO countries (Durch, 1993, pp. 39–40, 50). It is therefore not surprising that countries such as India, Pakistan, and Bangladesh, where troops are poorly trained but cheap, were among the largest troop contributors in recent years (United Nations, 2003). This does not bode well for UN peacekeepers' ability to keep warring sides apart.

With the current push to increase the mobility of its forces, NATO will be in a better position than the United Nations to assume complex and distant missions *provided that* allies' economic interests are at stake. Unless the United Nations invests in sufficient transport vehicles, NATO's efforts to bolster its transport capabilities may result in the United Nations habitually relying on NATO's superior power projection. The United Nations may then specialize in humanitarian, observer, and peacebuilding missions, leaving large-scale risky operations for the better-trained and more mobile troops of NATO, the United States, or some other industrial country that perceives sufficient contributor-specific benefits from peacekeeping. When large-scale missions are more generally public to the global community with few contributor-specific benefits, the United Nations will have to act. This action is, unfortunately, anticipated to be delayed, given inadequate UN procurement practices and the politics involved. This is hardly a recipe for the furtherance of world peace in a civil-war-torn world where an eighth of all nations are embroiled in civil wars.

Some Policy Recommendations

Rather than ushering in an era of world peace, the end of the Cold War witnessed a plethora of civil wars in developing countries throughout the world, but particularly in Africa and Asia. With the increased scarcity and enhanced economic importance of oil, strategic metals, and other natural resources, the greed motive for civil conflict will grow in prominence. The

---

[9] Some of the problems raised in this paragraph come from Palin (1995).

large number of conflicts since the late 1980s serves to augment grievances that will ignite new civil conflicts. Ethnic mixtures in some countries combined with past grievances (atrocities) can become the catalyst for new civil wars. Transboundary pollution, terrorist externalities, and the growing scarcity of water may also lead to interstate wars.

With NATO allies' long-term commitments in Bosnia, Kosovo, Albania, and Afghanistan, NATO is unlikely to accept new commitments until some of these old ones are finished or greatly curtailed – neither looks promising. Of course, there is also the long-term commitment in Iraq that is occupying US, UK, and some allies' troops. A need to build up UN peacekeeping capacity appears unavoidable if it is to be a guiding force in global peacekeeping as intended by the framers of the UN Charter. The experience in Liberia in July 2003 portends the future. Given its other commitments, the United States failed to act decisively, leaving the United Nations to take over much of the mission only after many Liberians had died. The increasing public nature of the negative spillovers from civil wars, as reflected in recent empirical tests, underscores the need for a world body to direct these peacekeeping missions as the share of contributor-specific benefits wanes.

For the United Nations to increase its peacekeeping effectiveness, some actions are advisable. The United Nations must streamline its procurement process. It must also raise troop payments if the United Nations is to draw well-trained soldiers for risky and involved missions. There should be different pay grades for troops depending on the mission's risk and potential combat requirements. To address times when the demand for peacekeeping is unusually high, the United Nations must develop a "surge capacity." Moreover, the assignment of missions between the United Nations and regional institutions should be better guided by the nature of spillover benefits – global versus regional benefits – rather than financial considerations or institutional capacity. The ability to transport troops and equipment quickly must also be addressed. Civil wars are likely to be a concern for years to come and the United Nations is still the key body to coordinate diplomacy, relief, and peacekeeping to assuage the human suffering imposed by these conflicts.

The work of Collier and others (referenced earlier) highlight that the duration of civil wars can be foreshortened by other forms of global collective action not involving peacekeeping. A high payoff in terms of shorter conflicts derives from collective efforts to boycott the trade in looted resources. Such boycotts are in the spirit of the successful worldwide boycott of ivory that greatly curbed wildlife poaching by limiting its profitability. The United Nations and other world bodies need to coordinate these necessarily global efforts, which can save many thousands of lives and reduce the amount of subsequent peacekeeping. These researchers also show that efforts to raise per-capita income and its growth through foreign assistance also have a peace dividend by limiting the initiation and duration of conflicts. The recent focus on conflict by the World Bank – though criticized by some – could not have been more appropriate to efforts to curtail poverty and its harmful consequences. Also, collective action to limit corruption and inequality in developing countries can reduce the extent of civil conflicts. Even a few less civil wars and some shorter conflicts can have a huge impact on improving world welfare.

10

Tales of Two Collectives: Atmospheric Pollution*

In a mere forty years, the earth's population grew from 3 billion in 1960 to 6 billion in 1999.[1] This unprecedented growth strains the soils, forests, water supplies, fisheries, oceans, and atmosphere. In short, pressures arising from the need to feed, clothe, and sustain so many people force ecosystems over their "carrying capacity." Prior to this threshold being reached, an ecosystem can withstand pollutants or other influences without noticeable impairment; but once this threshold is surpassed, demands on the ecosystem result in permanent degradation. This damage does not respect political borders; pollutants can travel in air and water currents far from their sources and may even traverse the globe. National borders, once secured by armies and artillery, are now invaded daily by emissions generated by economic activities abroad. Satellites and other modern means of monitoring the planet have shown that transboundary pollutants are ubiquitous and on the rise.

Although this chapter examines a few select cases of atmospheric pollutants, its real purpose is to illustrate how seemingly identical pollution (public goods) problems may have vastly different collective action prognoses. To accomplish this end, I contrast collective action outcomes for providing two global public goods (GPGs): actions to curb stratospheric ozone shield depletion stemming from chlorofluorocarbons (CFCs) and bromide-based substances, and efforts to reduce global warming stemming from greenhouse gases (GHGs). For a second collective

---

* There is a small degree of overlap between this chapter and pp. 99–115 of *Global Challenges: An Approach to Environmental, Political, and Economic Problems* (Cambridge: Cambridge University Press). Permission has been granted by Cambridge University Press to use these pages in an updated and altered form.

[1] On population growth, see UN Population Fund (1994) and recent editions.

action contrast, I examine two acid rain problems – one due to sulfur emissions and one due to nitrogen emissions – to show that two regional public goods (RPGs) problems may have greatly different prognoses. These differences for the acid rain examples are particularly curious because the underlying public goods possess similar nonrivalry and nonexcludability properties as well as identical aggregator technologies. Moreover, both pollutants give rise to virtually identical harmful consequences.

Even though actions to curb ozone shield depletion and global warming are classic instances of purely public GPGs, the global community has made great progress in ameliorating ozone depletion but little headway in addressing global warming. When I was drafting *Global Challenges* in 1996, readers indicated that I should rethink my pessimism with respect to curbing global warming, especially because of the upcoming negotiations on the Kyoto Protocol and the past success on efforts to limit ozone-depleting substances. Nevertheless, I held my ground and my views continue to apply today (Sandler, 1997, pp. 99–106). For these two GPGs, the contrast between global collective action and inaction hinges on factors that go beyond the nonrivalry and nonexcludability of these GPGs' benefits. Thus, knowledge of just the properties of a public good is not always sufficient to provide a prognosis for collective action. In this chapter, other key considerations are identified that play a role in forecasting and fostering global collective action.

This same message holds for the two acid rain problems, where the three underlying properties of publicness are not enough to determine the outcome of collective action because of subtle, but crucial, differences that influence whether nations will act to reduce pollutants. Collective action must be viewed not only at the supranational level as interactions among nations, but also at the national level as interactions among individuals and firms. Thus, nations may agree to do something about a pollutant but then have trouble at the national level owing to adverse collective action considerations.

By identifying the favorable and unfavorable drivers for providing these two GPGs and RPGs, I hope to make the reader aware of considerations that either promote or inhibit provision. This awareness can lead to more informed policymaking. Learning depends on knowing when to generalize and when to differentiate among issues. My primary purpose is to caution against too much generalization when it comes to GPGs and RPGs; an educated differentiation is essential.

Ozone Shield Depletion

The ozone layer stretches from ten to twenty-five miles overhead and if concentrated would be a mere three millimeters thick (de Gruijl, 1995). Despite its small concentration in the earth's atmosphere, representing less than one part per million, ozone absorbs much of the ultraviolet-B radiation of the sun and, thus, shields all living organisms from some of its detrimental effects.[2] A significantly thinned ozone layer presents some grave dangers from the mass extinction of species, disruption of the food chain, inducement of skin cancers, impairment of the immune system, and increased incidence of cataracts. For example, food supplies can be adversely affected through reduced phytoplankton at the base of the marine food chain.

As early as 1974, Mario Molina and Sherwood Rowland theorized that released CFCs could migrate to the stratosphere where they could be broken down by sunlight, thereby releasing chlorine that combines with the ozone. Under the right conditions, this chemical reaction would lead to the destruction of ozone within the shield (Toon and Turco, 1991). This degradation of atmospheric ozone can also result from other halocarbons (known as halons) and bromide-based substances (for example, methyl bromide). The actual chemical process was not explained until over a decade after these scientists' original hypothesis. In light of the British Antarctic Survey evidence in 1985 that there was an alarming 40% decline (from 1964 levels) in the springtime atmospheric concentration of ozone over Halley Bay, Antarctica, mounting scientific evidence was enough to motivate the major consuming and producing nations to do something about curbing the release of ozone-depleting substances.[3] This motivation was greatly bolstered by an Environmental Protection Agency (EPA) (1987a, 1987b) report that estimated that a 50% cutback in CFC emissions from 1986 levels could save the United States $64 trillion by 2075 in reduced costs associated with skin cancers. Without these reductions, skin cancer incidence was based on an annual growth of CFC use at 2.5% through 2050. The long-run costs from cutting CFC use were estimated

---

[2] On ozone's harmful effects, see de Gruijl (1995). A scientific description of the process of ozone depletion can be found in Stolarski (1988) and Toon and Turco (1991).

[3] Ironically, it was later learned that US satellites had spotted the emerging ozone hole back in 1979, but had been programmed to ignore data outside of certain predicted bounds (Barrett, 2003a, p. 224). The second-guessing of monitoring devices should be avoided.

to be between $20 and $40 billion during the 1989–2075 period, given the projected CFC use growth rates; thus US benefits from individual actions far outweighed the costs.

Limiting ozone-depleting substances is purely public to the entire world. A thicker ozone shield provides nonrival benefits to everyone worldwide; ultraviolet radiation protection afforded to people in Europe does not limit the protection derived by people in North America or any-where else. The derived benefits from a thickened layer are also nonexcludable globally. Efforts at reducing the emission of ozone-depleting compounds are cumulative, thus abiding by a summation aggregator technology in which curtailed emissions are the *sum* of all countries' control actions. The impacts on countries differ based on their geographic location with nations in the higher latitudes more at risk from ozone holes that opened in the springtime; thinning is more equally distributed worldwide later in the year through a natural equilibrating process. Given these classic properties of pure publicness, a collective action puzzle arises, because free riding on the actions of a few is anticipated; yet the world community has taken decisive actions to curb ozone-shield thinning. Why?

This decisive action is summarized in Table 10.1, which lists the major treaties and their notable accomplishments with respect to protecting the ozone layer. The middle column indicates both the date of enactment and the subsequent date of ratification for the treaties. As is standard, the process began with a convention – the Vienna Convention for the Protection of the Ozone Layer – that mandated scientific evaluation of the ozone-depleting process and its harmful consequences. Nations were committed to monitor the ozone layer, to exchange scientific findings, and to develop domestic programs for limiting ozone-depleting substances. The Vienna Convention was enacted, but not ratified, just prior to the discovery of the ozone hole by the British Antarctic Survey. Noteworthy global collective action followed with the Montreal Protocol that required progressive reductions in five CFCs and a freeze in the production and consumption of three halons. The subsequent amendments strengthened the conditions of the Montreal Protocol in three significant ways: (i) enhancing the level of cutbacks, (ii) increasing the number of controlled substances, and (iii) accelerating the time table for the cutbacks. Thus, all CFCs are now scheduled for complete elimination, and the number of controlled substances has increased from 8 in the Montreal Protocol to a total of 95 with the ratification of the Beijing Amendment in February 2002. New substances included other CFCs, halons, and bromide substances.

Table 10.1. *Treaties Controlling Ozone-Depleting Substances*

Treaty	Dates[a]	Notable Accomplishments
Vienna Convention	March 1985 September 1988	Mandated ratifiers to study the harmful effects of CFC emissions on ozone layer.
Montreal Protocol	September 1987 January 1989	Progressive cuts, rising to 50% of 1986 levels, in the consumption and production of five CFCs. The production and consumption of three halons frozen.
London Amendment	June 1990 August 1992	Cuts for 15 CFCs increased to 85% of 1986 levels and eventually eliminated. Increasing cuts imposed on three halons, carbon tetrachloride, and methyl chloroform. Nonbinding cuts on HCFCs.
Copenhagen Amendment	November 1992 June 1994	Accelerated the phasing out of 15 CFCs (by 1996), 3 halons, carbon tetrachloride, and methyl chloroform. Explicit cuts to HCFCs. HBFCs and methyl bromide entered to list of controlled substances.
Montreal Amendment	September 1997 November 1999	Phase out of methyl bromide. List of controlled depleters increased to 94.
Beijing Amendment	December 1999 February 2002	Bromochloromethane controlled. Better controls developed for ozone depleters.

[a] The first date is when the treaty was enacted, while the second date is when it was ratified.
Sources: Barrett (2003a), Fridtjof Nansen Institute (1996), and United Nations Environmental Program (2003).

The Copenhagen Amendment is particularly noteworthy in this regard because hydrochlorofluorocarbons (HCFCs) and hydrobromochlorofluorocarbons (HBFCs) were added to the list of controlled substances. Both of these substances were the original substitutes for CFCs. Their eventual phasing out means that the world community will have to rely on other substitutes such as hydrofluorocarbons (HFCs) that contain no ozone-depleting chlorine or bromine. These substitutes replaced CFCs and other compounds used in air conditioning, refrigerators, aerosols, insulating foam, the cleaning of circuit boards, and other applications.

Ratifiers of the Montreal Protocol were automatically considered to be parties to the Vienna Convention. Developing nations were given a strong inducement to ratify the Protocol in that they could delay compliance by up to ten years, gain technical and financial assistance, and escape trade sanctions. As of 22 April 2003, 185 countries had ratified the Vienna Convention; 184, the Montreal Protocol; 164, the London Amendment;

147, the Copenhagen Amendment; 94, the Montreal Amendment; and 49, the Beijing Amendment [United Nations Environmental Program (UNEP), 2003].

Many considerations supported this unprecedented global collective action.[4] One essential factor is that the number of key emitters was relatively concentrated. In 1986, just three nations – the United States, Japan, and the former Soviet Union – accounted for 46% of CFC emissions. At the time of ratification of the Montreal Protocol, just twelve countries caused over 78% of the emissions (World Resources Institute, 1992, Table 24.2). If these twelve nations were to reduce production and consumption of CFCs, significant progress toward stemming the release of ozone-depleting substances would be achieved. This follows because the other 180 or so countries did not have the collective capacity in the short or medium run to undo the cooperative efforts of these twelve countries by becoming the new producers. Moreover, such nonparticipating nations could not add sufficient consumption to offset the cutbacks of the major consumers.

Another factor that fostered international collective action involved the fact that all countries would suffer from ozone depletion. Although some countries would lose more than others, no country stood to gain from enhanced ultraviolet radiation. Even the countries with commercial interests in producing CFCs were positioned to gain from their reductions owing to the discovery of substitutes – HCFCs, HFCs, and others. Faced with mounting evidence against CFCs, the primary producers searched for substitutes and succeeded fairly quickly. The treaty-provided phasing out of CFCs allowed these producers to sell off existing CFC supplies as they began production of substitute substances. Commercial interests in CFCs were quite concentrated with just sixteen producers in 1987. A mere five firms accounted for all of US production: DuPont, 49%; Allied Signal, 25%; Pennwalt Corporation, 13%; Kaiser Chemicals, 9%; and Racon, 4% (Morrisette et al., 1990, p. 57). Moreover, most major producers, especially those in the United States, were largely diversified firms, whose CFC production accounted for a relatively small proportion of sales – for DuPont, less than 2% of sales was CFCs in 1986 (Morrisette et al., 1990, p. 15). This concentration of interests and the prospect of substitute-generated profits meant that there was

---

[4] On the diplomacy behind the Montreal Protocol, see Benedick (1991) and Morrisette et al. (1990).

little political pressure to oppose the Montreal Protocol or its subsequent amendments.

The eventual resolution of the uncertainty, with respect to both the thinning of the ozone layer and understanding the chemical process behind this thinning, paved the way to the treaty-specified limits to CFCs. This resolution not only gave the push to producers to develop substitutes but also helped the EPA compute the benefits and costs that a thinning shield would impose on the US population. Clearly, governments will not commit to costly actions unless they have sufficient information to calculate the consequences. For the United States, the EPA report demonstrated that the benefits (b_i) minus the costs (c_i) to acting alone were positive. This meant that the dominant strategy for the United States was to curb CFC emissions by 50% regardless of what the other countries did. Other major producing and consuming countries reasoned that their net benefits from curtailing emissions were also positive owing to the EPA calculation for the United States. Thus, the major emitters could "privilege" the rest of the world with reduced ozone-depleting emissions by exercising their dominant strategy. Given these nations' willingness to reduce emissions, medium-sized polluters may then view their own cutbacks, in conjunction with the gains derived from these large emitters, as providing them a net benefit.

Many of the cutbacks encoded in the Montreal Protocol would have occurred in the absence of the treaty.[5] Nevertheless, the Montreal Protocol still achieved some cooperative gains by allowing the early ratifiers to cajole others into signing through positive inducements (that is, delayed compliance for developing countries, known as Article 5 countries) and threatened punishments (that is, trade restrictions). The treaty established norms of good behavior. The Montreal Protocol also set up a framework by which the treaty-mandated emission cutbacks could be augmented quickly as substitutes improved, new information surfaced, and major polluters exceeded treaty-mandated reductions.

Perhaps, the most important boost for the collective success of the Montreal Protocol was leadership by the United States, the largest user and producer of CFCs. Scientific findings from studies at the US Department of Transportation, the Federal Task Force on Inadvertent Modification

---

[5] This implies that the Nash equilibrium is consistent with the conditions of the Montreal Protocol for the first set of ratifiers, so the extent of cooperative benefits was initially limited (Murdoch and Sandler, 1997).

of the Stratosphere, and the National Academy of Sciences convinced the EPA to prohibit the nonessential use of CFCs as aerosol propellants back in 1978 (Morrisette et al., 1990, pp. 10–12). Other nations followed the US lead: Canada banned aerosol use of CFCs in 1978, Sweden in 1979, and Norway in 1981. The European Economic Community reduced use of CFC aerosols by 30% from 1976 levels, which was more symbolic than substantive (Barrett, 2003a, p. 223). As a country responsible for almost 25% of CFC consumption, US leadership was essential; leadership by a small polluter would have virtually no effect as its reductions would do little to alleviate the problem. In addition, cutbacks by small producers and consumers can be easily offset by slight increases by big producers and emitters. US leadership became essential after the 1987 EPA report, at which time US planned action involved all uses of CFCs.

Another favorable impetus concerned intertemporal considerations regarding when actions today are able to improve the ozone shield in the future. Following the Protocol-mandated reductions in CFCs and other emissions, the ozone shield would continue to thin as earlier-emitted CFCs made their journey to the stratosphere and eventually released their chlorine. The treaty-mandated reductions indicated in Table 10.1 would allow the ozone shield to recover its pre-1980 concentration by about 2050 (World Meteorological Organization, 1998). Improvements would begin to be experienced some time after the start of the century. Thus, there are gains for the current generation from their actions; not all gains are experienced by later generations. If the latter had been the case, then collective action would have been much more difficult to achieve. So the temporal patterns of gains were in favor of reducing ozone-depleting substances.

Two additional factors supported collective action with respect to reducing CFCs and other halons. First, decision makers were more informed about the benefits than the costs from reducing ozone-depleting substances. Scientific studies appear to focus on the benefits. The news media also emphasized these benefits when taking up the case of protecting the ozone layer. The public was not well informed about the added costs from eliminating CFCs and other halons. This bias to stressing benefits over costs also fostered collective action. Second, although ozone-depleting substances had varied applications, still relatively few activities would be impacted especially when compared with the impact of a significant cutback in the emission of GHGs.

Table 10.2. *Atmospheric Concentration of Ozone-Depleting Gases*
(in parts per trillion)

Year	Carbon Tetrachloride	Methyl Chloroform	CFC-11	CFC-12	CFC-13	Total Gaseous Chlorine
1982	92	81	175	325	26	1,865
1983	93	85	182	341	28	1,939
1984	94	88	190	355	31	2,016
1985	96	92	200	376	36	2,121
1986	97	96	210	394	40	2,216
1987	99	98	221	413	48	2,322
1988	100	103	231	433	53	2,425
1989	100	107	240	452	59	2,524
1990	101	110	249	470	66	2,620
1991	101	113	254	484	71	2,685
1992	101	116	259	496	77	2,751
1993	101	112	260	503	80	2,764
1994	100	106	261	512	81	2,769
1995	99	97	261	518	82	2,753
1996	98	85	261	523	82	2,725
1997	97	73	260	528	83	2,693
1998	96	64	259	530	82	2,664

Source: World Resources Institute (2000, Table AC.3, p. 285).

Table 10.2 indicates the atmospheric concentration of ozone-depleting gases in parts per trillion. By the early 1990s, most ozone-depleting substances were falling in their atmospheric concentration or their increases were leveling off owing to a significant drop in consumption. For example, the United States, Japan, and the European Union (EU) had cut their CFC consumption by greater than half between 1986 and 1992 (Fridtjof Nansen Institute, 1996, p. 24). Thus, treaty ratifiers adhered to their commitments and usually at accelerated rates. Once it became clear that they could outdo treaty stipulations, treaty participants met to increase mandated cutbacks through amendments (see Table 10.1) that forced others to comply with these higher standards. Illegal trade in CFCs limited somewhat the success of the treaties,[6] but this is a temporary problem until the capital stock – for example, air conditioners and refrigerators – using CFCs becomes obsolete.

[6] Imposing high taxes on CFCs during their phase-out means that significant profits can be made by unscrupulous individuals who illegally trade CFCs at lower prices that do not include the tax.

Global Warming

By way of contrast, I next consider global warming which stems from a greenhouse effect as trapped gases in the earth's atmosphere let sunlight through but absorb and capture infrared radiation, thereby raising the mean temperature. Gases with this characteristic are called GHGs and include carbon dioxide (CO_2), CFCs, HFCs, methane (CH_4), nitrous oxide (N_2O), and others. The bulk of the atmosphere is comprised of oxygen and nitrogen, which do not act as GHGs. CO_2 is a by-product of the burning of fossil fuels and deforestation, while methane is largely a result of solid wastes, coal mining, oil and gas production, wet rice agriculture, and livestock. Nitrous oxide is largely derived from the use of fertilizers and energy production.

Unabated accumulation of GHGs can raise the mean temperature on earth by as much as $2°$ to $5°$ C during the next century; estimates differ widely and much uncertainty remains. The precise relationship between the accumulation of GHGs in the atmosphere and the extent of global warming is still not quantified, though improved models are being developed.[7] Offsetting influences from other pollutants are not fully understood; for example, sulfur in the atmosphere can reflect solar radiation, thus alleviating global warming. Comprehensive models are required that incorporate the influence that a warmer climate will have on the distribution of rainfall, the levels of the seas, and the distribution of the food-producing regions. Unlike most global difficulties where all nations are harmed, global warming may greatly benefit some nations by enhancing their agricultural productivity. Understandably, nations that may gain from a warmer climate and greater rainfall are reluctant to institute carbon taxes and other measures that would slow down economic activities while the true costs of a warmer atmosphere are unknown. To achieve sought-after reductions in CO_2 emissions of 50%, the world may have to allocate 2% or more of its gross national product (GNP) in perpetuity (Intergovernment Panel on Climate Change, 1990; Schelling, 1992). The world is unprepared to make such sacrifices unless the consequences of doing so are better understood.

Like limiting ozone depletion, curbing global warming is a textbook example of a purely public GPG that abides by a summation aggregator

---

[7] See the Intergovernmental Panel on Climate Change (1990), Nordhaus (1991), and the US Congressional Budget Office (1990).

Table 10.3. *Carbon Dioxide Emissions of Major Polluters, 1990, 1996*

Country	Emissions in 1990 (000 metric tons)	Emissions in 1996 (000 metric tons)	Rank in 1996	Percent of World Total 1996	Per-Capita CO_2 Emissions in 1996 (metric tons)
United States	4,823,982	5,300,991	1	22.2	19,674
China	2,401,741	3,363,541	2	14.1	2,729
Russian Federation	NA	1,579,514	3	6.6	10,681
Japan	1,070,665	1,167,666	4	4.9	9,284
India	675,261	997,385	5	4.2	1,050
Germany	NA	861,223	6	3.6	10,514
United Kingdom	563,281	556,983	7	2.3	9,532
Canada	409,628	409,353	8	1.7	13,669
South Korea	241,179	408,060	9	1.7	8,999
Italy	398,852	403,231	10	1.7	7,029
Ukraine	NA	397,291	11	1.7	7,751
France	353,184	361,820	12	1.5	6,211
Poland	347,585	356,782	13	1.5	9,229
Mexico	294,974	348,106	14	1.5	3,754
Australia	266,010	306,633	15	1.3	16,902
South Africa	291,108	292,746	16	1.2	7,678
Brazil	202,612	273,371	17	1.1	1,692
Saudi Arabia	177,096	267,831	18	1.1	14,225
Iran	212,354	266,662	19	1.1	4,201
North Korea	244,634	254,326	20	1.1	11,249
Indonesia	165,210	245,056	21	1.0	1,223
Spain	211,710	232,484	22	1.0	5,872
Total of 22		18,651,060		78.0	
World	22,361,392	23,881,952		100.0	4,157

NA stands for not available

Source: World Resources Institute (2000, Table AC.1, pp. 282–3).

technology. Cutbacks in GHGs yield benefits that are not only nonrival among nations but also nonexcludable globally. Efforts by any nations to emit fewer GHGs limit the atmospheric concentration of GHGs globally as mixing occurs in the atmosphere, therefore all countries gain. Of all of today's global challenges, global warming appears to be the most intractable. Despite the framing of the Kyoto Protocol, GHGs continue to accumulate at disturbing rates. In Table 10.3, the 22 largest emitters of CO_2 are displayed in rank order for 1996 along with their per-capita CO_2 emissions. Each emitter's percent of total CO_2 emissions is also displayed for 1996. These countries' emissions are listed for 1990 and 1996 to demonstrate that most continue to do little to abate their CO_2 despite the United Nations Framework Convention on Climate Change that entered into force in 1994. Not surprising, the Kyoto Protocol of 1997 is not yet in force, with key polluters such as the United States, accounting for almost a quarter of CO_2 emissions, unwilling to sign unless developing countries are required to curb their emissions. Table 10.3 underscores US concerns with China, India, South Korea, Mexico, Brazil, Iran, and Indonesia, which show the most rapid rates of increase. Unless these countries face limits with a protocol, the efforts of the developed countries will be offset quickly. With the exception of Mexico, the Kyoto Protocol encodes no cutbacks for these countries.

Table 10.4 provides essential contrasts between factors that support collective action for protecting the ozone shield and those that inhibit collective action for reducing global warming. Since the favorable influences for ozone depletion have already been presented, I will concentrate on the unfavorable ones for controlling GHGs. As shown in the table, the two problems have almost opposite drivers where facilitators are replaced by inhibitors. In the case of global warming, virtually every country adds to GHG emissions, with developing countries being the source of the greatest increases. Nations with large rain forest cover – for example, Brazil, Indonesia, and Zaire – add to GHGs through the destruction of large forest tracts. Agricultural countries – China, India, the United States, and the Russian Federation – add to GHGs through methane and nitrous oxide emissions (Sandler, 1997). Population pressures will continue to add GHGs through food, shelter, and energy demands, particularly in developing countries where population is growing the fastest. In short, there are many more key players for GHGs than for CFCs, and their numbers serve to limit collective action – the greater the number of participants, the poorer is the typical prognosis for collective action.

Table 10.4. *Different Collective Action Factors Affecting Ozone-Shield Depletion and Global Warming*

Ozone-Shield Depletion	Global Warming
• Emissions concentrated in relatively few countries	• Virtually every country adds to GHGs with developing countries being the source of the greatest increases
• Every country loses from a thinning ozone layer	• There are gainers and losers from global warming
• Commercial gains from substitutes	• No commercial gains from substitutes
• Resolved uncertainty in terms of process and consequences	• Unresolved uncertainty in terms of processes and consequences
• Dominant strategy for some key polluters is to curb pollutants since $b_i - c_i > 0$	• Dominant strategy for most key polluters is not to curb pollutants since $b_i - c_i < 0$
• Leadership by key polluters	• Lack of leadership by key polluters
• Some intertemporal reversibility within 50 years	• No intertemporal reversibility within 50 years
• Decision makers were more informed about benefits than costs	• Decision makers were more informed about costs than benefits
• Relatively few activities add to depletion	• Many activities add to global warming

Because some countries may gain from global warming, some interests are opposed to doing anything. Unlike CFCs, the commercial interests are not concentrated. Moreover, those who gain from GHGs are unlikely to be those who will profit from possible substitutes if such substitutes can be uncovered. In addition, significant uncertainties with respect to global warming processes and consequences persist, which keep countries from making commitments that they may want to change later as more becomes known. Except for relatively small levels of cutbacks stemming from conservation or enhanced efficiency, the costs of reducing GHGs are anticipated to exceed the benefits, so that $b_i - c_i < 0$. The dominant strategy is then not to curb GHG emissions; hence, global collective inaction follows. Since these scenarios characterize the United States (Nordhaus, 1991) and other key players, effective leadership is absent. At times, the EU has tried to assume this role, but it has not been effective thus far. Additionally, the time profile for action today to have noticeable future effects is much longer for global warming because CO_2 stays within the atmosphere for a much longer period than ozone depleters (Nordhaus, 1991). The current generation must be quite altruistic to future generations if much progress is to be accomplished. Decision makers are more informed about abatement costs than abatement benefits for global warming owing to unresolved uncertainties. Finally, myriad activities add to global warming; even taking a breath gives off carbon dioxide.

These contrasting factors mean that collective action with respect to global warming is unlikely to mimic that for the control of ozone-depleting substances. Today, this prediction is borne out by the tremendous progress with respect to the latter and the minimal progress with respect to the former. There are some ways to move forward with respect to global warming. Actions to use the Montreal Protocol as a template for the Kyoto Protocol [see the recommendation of Benedick (1991)] should be resisted. A treaty instrument for global warming needs to be designed that accounts for its unique aspects. Too generous provisions for developing countries, while effective for the Montreal Protocol because these countries were minor polluters, will keep the industrial polluters from ratifying the Kyoto Protocol. Some cutback will have to be mandated of all countries, though differentiation can allow emissions reductions to take effect at different times for ratifiers. Another essential action is to accelerate research on global warming to lessen the remaining uncertainty. Governments should subsidize research and development for alternatives to internal combustion engines. The need to curb oil consumption should follow from a concern for the environment and not from the price of fossil fuels. Additionally, countries must come to accept the usefulness of tradable permits and other market-based solutions, even though these schemes allow the rich countries to limit their cutbacks, although at a price.

Acid Rain: A Second Tale of Two Collectives

Unlike global warming and ozone holes, acid rain is a more localized RPG problem whose benefit spillovers from abatement are less far reaching. Here, I am concerned with explaining why more progress has been made in addressing sulfur-based acid rain than nitrogen-based acid rain. When sulfur and nitrogen oxide (NO_X) emissions from the generation of electricity, transportation, vehicles, and other sources combine in the lower atmosphere with water vapor and tropospheric ozone, sulfuric acid and nitric acid can form. These acids later fall with the rain and degrade lakes, rivers, coastal waters, forests, and manmade structures. This degradation can also arise from dry depositions of sulfur and NO_X that lead to increased acidity of soils and watersheds. In 1980 prior to any collective action, sources of sulfur emissions were 47.8%, power plants; 37.4%, industry; 10%, residential and commercial; 3.7%, cars and trucks; and 1%, miscellaneous. In 1980, sources of NO_X emissions were 53.6%, cars and trucks; 23.5%, power plants; 15.4%, industry; 6.1%, residential and commercial; and 1.3%, miscellaneous.[8]

Various strategies are available for the control of sulfur and NO_X emissions. Both emissions can be limited through improved efficiency, especially in the case of residential and commercial uses, and increased conservation. Sulfur pollution can also be controlled through the use of low-sulfur coal and oil as well as flue-gas desulfurization for power plants. In the case of NO_X, emissions can be reduced in power plants by installing low-NO_X burners. Pollution from mobile sources can be curtailed by setting emission standards on vehicles and by increasing the rate of turnover of vehicle fleets. New vehicles can incorporate improved emission control technologies. Both sulfur and NO_X emissions pose a transnational pollution concern, because once released into the atmosphere these pollutants can remain aloft for days and travel from their emission sources to be deposited on the territory of a downwind country. Sulfur emissions are heavier than NO_X and remain aloft for less than an hour or up to seven days, while NO_X can remain airborne from two to eight days (Alcamo and Runca, 1986, p. 3). On average, sulfur pollutants travel shorter distances than NO_X pollutants and land nearer to home. Although the publicness properties of these two forms of acid rain are quite similar to one another, they differ greatly from the two GPGs considered earlier. Once airborne, these pollutants are *deposited* downwind in a *rival fashion*: a ton deposited on Belgium is a ton that cannot be deposited elsewhere. In total, pollutants sent airborne must end up somewhere though some may land at sea. Some emissions will be deposited at home: the larger the country, the more that lands at home. Efforts to control acid-rain-inducing emissions are therefore rival based on where emissions will be deposited. However, control efforts yield nonexcludable benefits insofar as those countries destined for deposition gain whether or not they support the efforts.

A weighted-sum aggregator technology characterizes these control efforts. This is best illustrated by examining Figure 10.1, which displays a *transport matrix*. In this matrix, the columns designate the emitters,

---

[8]   The figures in this paragraph come from the Organization of Economic Cooperation and Development (OECD) (1990).

$$
\begin{array}{c}
\text{Emitters} \\
\begin{array}{c c c c c c c c c}
 & 1 & 2 & 3 & 4 & 5 & 6 & 7 & 8
\end{array} \\
\text{Recipients}
\begin{array}{c}
1 \\ 2 \\ 3 \\ 4 \\ 5 \\ 6 \\ 7 \\ 8
\end{array}
\begin{bmatrix}
A_{11} & A_{12} & \cdot & \cdot & \cdot & & & A_{18} \\
A_{21} & A_{22} & \cdot & \cdot & \cdot & & & A_{28} \\
\cdot & & \cdot & & & & & \cdot \\
\cdot & & & \cdot & & & & \cdot \\
\cdot & & & & \cdot & & & \cdot \\
 & & & & & & & \\
 & & & & & & & \\
A_{81} & A_{82} & \cdot & \cdot & \cdot & & & A_{88}
\end{bmatrix}
\end{array}
$$

Figure 10.1. Transport matrix

while the rows list the recipients. Because each country is both an emitter and a recipient to some sulfur or NO_X pollution, each country must be assigned to both a row and a column. The numbers 1 through 8 denote the eight countries used for illustration purposes. In practice, the matrix should include all possible emitters and recipients, so the matrix for Europe would include western and eastern European countries. The matrix entries A_{ij}s indicate the percentage of country j's emissions deposited on country i. If all relevant countries are included, then the column totals should add to 100% as all of a country's emissions are eventually deposited on countries including itself in the region. The diagonal A_{ii}s represent self-pollution and captures an essential localized benefit from addressing the acid rain problem, since less emissions means less self-pollution.[9] The A_{ij}s are the weights in the weighted-sum technology. That is, the reduction in country i's pollution equals the sum of the countries' cutbacks weighted by the appropriate A_{ij}s – for example, country k's cutback is multiplied by A_{ik} to identify how its efforts reduce depositions in country i. If, for instance, A_{ik} equals 30% and country k reduces sulfur by 100 tons, then country i receives 30 fewer tons of sulfur pollution as a public good spillover.

In 1977, the Cooperative Program for Monitoring and Evaluation of the Long-Range Transmission of Air Pollutants in Europe (henceforth, EMEP) was initiated to measure these transport matrices for sulfur and NO_X (Eliassen and Saltbones, 1983). This EMEP matrix measurement was an important precursor to subsequent treaties involving sulfur and

[9] If all A_{ij}s were 100, then the good would be purely public with every country receiving all of a producer's output. If, instead, all A_{ii}s were 100 and all off-diagonal entries were zero, then the good would be a private good with just the provider receiving the good's benefits.

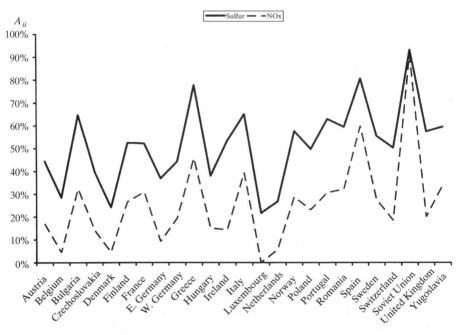

Figure 10.2. Self-pollution percentages for 1990

NO_X emissions, because it removed uncertainty as to the pattern of emissions and depositions. For example, downwind countries in the east learned that they had much to gain from a treaty that limited depositions coming from their western neighbors. Countries also began to understand that they had much to gain from limiting their own emissions, particularly in the case of sulfur. This is illustrated in Figure 10.2, which displays the self-pollution percentages (the A_{ii}s) for sulfur and NO_X for 1990.[10] As shown, sulfur has uniformly greater percentages of self-pollution than NO_X. Moreover, larger countries experience greater self-pollution – see, for example, the former Soviet Union and Spain.

On 13 November 1979, the Long Range Transboundary Air Pollution (LRTAP) Convention was adopted at a high-level meeting of the UN Economic Commission for Europe on the Protection of the Environment. Like the Vienna Convention on ozone depleters, the LRTAP

[10] The representation in Figure 10.2 is not to imply a continuous relationship; each country's percentage is unrelated to that of the other countries. On average, these A_{ii}s do not change by much each year. I chose 1990 because it corresponds to when the NO_X cutbacks, mandated by the Sofia Protocol, were to go into effect.

Convention mandated scientific investigation and evaluation of the problem. This evaluation was made possible by EMEP measurement of sulfur, NO_X, and volatile organic compounds (VOCs) (hydrocarbons which cause surface ozone). The Convention was subsequently ratified on 16 March 1983 by Austria, Belgium, Bulgaria, Canada, Czechoslovakia, Denmark, Finland, France, East Germany, West Germany, Greece, Hungary, Iceland, Ireland, Italy, Liechtenstein, Luxembourg, Netherlands, Norway, Poland, Portugal, Romania, Soviet Union, Spain, Sweden, Switzerland, Turkey, the United Kingdom, the United States, and Yugoslavia (UNEP, 1991). On 8 July 1985, the Helsinki Protocol to the LRTAP Convention was adopted and committed ratifiers to reduce sulfur emissions by 30%, based on 1980 levels, as soon as possible or by 1993. The Protocol entered into force on 2 September 1987. In the case of NO_X emissions, protocols have been much slower and less stringent. On 31 October 1988, the Sofia Protocol was signed, requiring reductions in NO_X to return emissions to 1987 levels by 31 December 1994 (UNEP, 1991). This Protocol did not enter into force until 14 February 1991.

More recently, the Oslo Protocol of 14 June 1994 mandated further reductions in sulfur emissions beyond those of the Helsinki Protocol for most nations.[11] This Protocol, entered into force on 5 August 1998, tailors emissions reductions for the treaty parties based on their costs of abatement so that across-the-board cuts are no longer applied to each nation (Finus and Tjøtta, 2003). By tailoring these reductions to a country's marginal abatement costs, the Oslo Protocol can achieve cost minimization; that is, countries with small marginal abatement costs are assigned greater mandated cutbacks than those with larger marginal abatement costs. This tailoring practice gives the treaty instrument greater flexibility in ensuring that each party perceives a net gain from its participation, despite different dependencies on fossil fuels and diverse abilities to curb emissions. As a consequence, treaty participation is wider.

In the case of VOCs, the Geneva Protocol of 18 November 1991 required ratifiers to reduce annual emissions of select VOCs by at least 30% by 1999, using a chosen year between 1984 and 1990 for calculating the baseline emissions. A few ratifiers – Bulgaria, Greece, and Hungary – were allowed to choose 1999 for the baseline level (UNEP, 2003). This Protocol entered into force on 29 September 1997, just over ten years after the Helsinki Protocol.

---

[11] Information on these treaties and their ratification status can be found in UNEP (2003).

Table 10.5. *Percentage Reductions in Voluntary Sulfur and NO$_x$*
Emissions by Country

Country	%SUL85	%SUL90	%NO$_x$87	%NO$_x$90
1. Austria	50.75	47.39	4.88	5.13
2. Belgium	45.41	16.38	32.81	−12.46
3. Bulgaria	−12.88	−28.54	0.00	9.62
4. Czechoslovakia	10.32	−8.79	16.28	2.08
5. Denmark	23.89	30.18	−11.72	7.21
6. Finland	34.59	25.48	−2.27	−7.41
7. France	55.96	32.25	10.59	−7.36
8. East Germany	−25.58	−41.63	−13.56	5.97
9. West Germany	24.98	40.57	1.78	11.17
10. Greece	−25.00	−55.00	0.00	0.00
11. Hungary	13.97	8.11	−1.10	13.77
12. Ireland	36.94	−5.68	−57.53	−17.39
13. Italy	34.11	12.63	−14.86	−3.59
14. Luxembourg	33.33	3.33	17.39	0.00
15. Netherlands	40.77	25.36	−2.01	1.27
16. Norway	28.57	31.43	−25.14	−1.75
17. Poland	−4.88	−8.29	−2.00	16.34
18. Portugal	25.56	−6.69	30.12	−5.17
19. Romania	0.00	−30.00	0.00	0.00
20. Spain	34.04	0.24	11.68	0.00
21. Sweden	43.85	37.31	−2.86	6.26
22. Switzerland	23.81	20.79	−2.04	8.00
23. Soviet Union	13.05	3.12	−23.44	−7.84
24. United Kingdom	23.97	−7.05	−10.03	−7.27
25. Yugoslavia	−14.88	−43.34	−25.71	4.55
Average	20.59	3.98	−2.75	0.84

%SUL85 = % reduction in total sulfur emissions from 1980 to 1985 as a percent of 1980 emissions.
%SUL90 = % reduction in sulfur emissions, *beyond the* 30% *target reduction*, from 1980 to 1990 as a percent of 1980 emissions.
%NO$_x$87 = % reduction in total NO$_x$ emissions from 1980 to 1987 as a percent of 1980 emissions.
%NO$_x$90 = % reduction in total NO$_x$ emissions from 1987 to 1990 as a percent of 1987 emissions.
Source: Data in Sandnes (1993).

The sequence and character of the regional collective action embodied in these protocols to the LRTAP Convention are easily explained. Given the greater localized benefits to sulfur, it is no wonder that treaties emerged quicker and were more constrained for sulfur than for NO$_X$. Table 10.5 indicates the percentage reduction in sulfur in 1985 (%SUL85) prior to the formulation of the Helsinki Protocol. Mean reductions in sulfur from 1980 levels were already 20.59%. Projections over the next couple of years indicated that most potential ratifiers would exceed reductions of 30% *prior* to the treaty's date of ratification in 1987 (Murdoch, Sandler, and Sargent, 1994, 1997). In Table 10.5, average sulfur cutbacks were almost 4% over the treaty-mandated cutbacks by 1990 (see %SUL90). Recall that nations had until 1993 to achieve the 30% reductions. Thus, the Helsinki Protocol largely encoded cutbacks that most ratifiers would have achieved in the absence of the treaty – that is, the treaty-encoded Nash noncooperative behavior.[12] The treaty did serve to bring along some stragglers and this achieved some cooperative gains. As ratifiers of the Helsinki Protocol exceeded mandated cutbacks, these nations framed the Oslo Protocol with individualized cutbacks tailored to what signers anticipated they could do – that is, further encoding of Nash behavior. At the time of the framing of the Sofia Protocol, the average reduction of NO_X emissions was less than one percent (i.e., 0.84%) of 1987 emissions (see the %NO_X90 column in Table 10.5). This anticipated failure to make much progress in curbing NO_X pollution influenced the modest goals set forth in the Sofia Protocol for which noncooperative Nash behavior again became the encapsulated standard in the treaty.

Other aspects differentiate these two alternative tales of collective action. Compared to sulfur, a much greater portion of NO_X emissions was never deposited on parties to the Sofia Protocol but fell at sea or outside of the treaty region (Sandnes, 1993). This meant that potential participants would perceive more limited benefits from an NO_X agreement than from a sulfur treaty. In addition, information on NO_X transportation took longer to develop so that uncertainty was resolved more slowly in the case of NO_X. Sulfur emissions arose primarily from public utilities – electric plants – that can be more easily controlled than the many owners of vehicles in the case of NO_X emissions. For sulfur, publicly sanctioned monopolies had to be regulated, while for NO_X the behavior of private citizens within each nation as well as among nations had to be regulated. The latter presents a greater collective action problem.

Similar factors delayed progress on the Geneva Protocol on curbing VOCs. For example, VOCs were not monitored until years after sulfur and NO_X. Polluters include a large and diverse set of emitters, similar to

---

[12] Proof of this provocative statement is provided through statistical analysis in Murdoch, Sandler, and Sargent (1997) and Murdoch, Sandler, and Vijverberg (2003).

those associated with NO_X emissions. A collective action inhibitor unique to VOCs was the large number of hydrocarbon compounds that required evaluation and control. Before any treaty could be framed, potential participants to a treaty had to agree upon which VOC compounds to limit the emissions of. This required potential treaty participants to learn about more than one pollutant: in particular, how much progress they had made in curbing emissions to date, and how much progress they anticipated in the near future. Each additional VOC included in the treaty could inhibit agreement, especially if equal reductions applied to all VOCs and some VOCs were easier to control than others. When more than one pollutant is included in the same treaty, a *bundling* problem may arise where the toughest pollutant to control becomes the weakest link that holds up progress on the entire treaty.

Some Policy Recommendations

Some policy insights can be gleaned from these two tales of collective action. First, one should not look for a panacea where "one pill cures all diseases." Even seemingly similar GPGs and RPGs may imply quite different collective action outcomes so that treaties for each need a good deal of tailoring. Benedick's (1991) view that the Montreal Protocol should provide the model for other environmental treaties has been influential but not helpful. If one looks at the wording of protocols since the Montreal Protocol on ozone-depleting substances, treaty framers have used the latter's text as a template as Benedick recommended. The action has, I believe, inhibited progress on global warming where special status for developing countries will greatly limit the Kyoto Protocol's eventual accomplishments, if ever ratified, while keeping key polluters from signing. For ozone protection, developing countries did not, nor were they expected to, emit many ozone-depleting substances. For GHGs, the same is not true.

Second, the Helsinki Protocol was wise not to include cutbacks in NO_X and VOCs, where less was known and collective action considerations were less supportive. Rather than providing greater grounds for negotiation as hypothesized by Barrett (2003a), bundling different pollutants into the same treaty instrument can delay progress to that for the pollutant where the least is known or that is the hardest to control. In the absence of bundling, any added-in transaction costs are apt to be made up in increased efficiency for quicker and more decisive action on the easier to control substances.

Third, uncertainty needs to be resolved more quickly. Both the underlying process of how the pollutant performs its insidious effects and its distribution of impacts must be understood. Problems that are more rapidly reversible are easier to address. For the acid rain problem, pollutants did not remain in the atmosphere for long in contrast to CFCs and GHGs; thus, the acid rain problem is comparatively easier to address. One means for streamlining the treaty formation process is for the global community to permanently maintain a body of scientists, social scientists, statisticians, and medical experts to evaluate pending environmental concerns. Such a body would be comparatively inexpensive but could save the world community billions of dollars or more in facilitating faster and more decisive action when warranted. By eliminating the need to create problem-specific panels, my proposal would allow for faster action. In some cases, the convention stage can be bypassed, so that a protocol to take action can be considered immediately. Faster responses may mean that nations will have to do less than when a problem had been longer term, and this smaller commitment also favors reaching an agreement quicker.

Fourth, the sequence of amendments for the Montreal Protocol indicates that successful treaties can begin modestly so that nations become committed and a framework for collective action is initiated. From this platform, greater levels of commitment can be achieved over time as warranted. If, instead, the initial treaty tries for too much cooperation at the outset, then the protocol may not be ratified. The process behind efforts to reduce CFCs and sulfur emissions are in the nature of a repeated game whereby greater commitments are attained when participants come to realize that short-run gains from cheating are overwhelmed by longer-term losses from missed opportunities to cooperate.

Finally, the differences between the sulfur and nitrogen acid rain difficulties underscore that collective action concerns may be multilayered. For NO_X, successful collective action at the supranational level meant that each nation then had to address a more difficult collective action problem at home where many small polluters had to be controlled. For sulfur, success at the supranational level pretty much implied success at the national level where state-regulated utilities could be easily controlled. Similarly, supranational agreements with respect to CFCs created a nation-based cheating problem as smugglers tried to profit from the rising price of CFCs during their phase-out period.

Although the three properties of publicness have much to say about the prognosis and form for collective action, other considerations may also play an essential role. By choosing to examine two GPGs and two RPGs with nearly identical properties of publicness but vastly different collective action prospects, I have established this key insight into modern global collective action.

11

The Final Frontier

On 1 February 2003, the fiery end of space shuttle *Columbia*, a mere 16 minutes prior to its scheduled landing, underscored the perils of space travel and exploration. This tragedy came just over 17 years after the explosion of space shuttle *Challenger*, which disintegrated some 73 seconds after liftoff on 28 January 1986. In many ways, outer space represents the final frontier for globalization and commercial activities. As the earth's carrying capacity is surpassed with greater population pressures,[1] outer space offers alternative resource supply sources and even habitats for a stressed planet. The main constraint is getting there – it is costly to escape the earth's atmosphere and dangerous to reenter it. Launch cost remains a prime determinant of the economic feasibility for the utilization of outer space and its associated resources.

Global collective action issues abound in outer space. Myriad satellites that ring the globe present various externalities from signal interference to collisions if insufficiently spaced. As large satellites or space laboratories fall back to earth as their orbits deteriorate, these objects pose a hazard to people or property in their debris path. Observation from outer space offers public goods in many forms: monitoring the health of the planet, surveying the earth's resources, warning earth of collision with asteroids and comets, tracking the path of hurricanes, and discovering the origins of the universe. Space observations also allow for a better understanding of the risks and damage to satellites from solar flares. Cooperative research aboard the International Space Station (ISS) can further our understanding of global warming, the dispersion of pollutants, the laws

---

[1] The carrying capacity indicates the limit to which an ecosystem can support activities and still recover its natural attributes. Once this carrying capacity is surpassed, activities will have a lasting degrading impact on the ecosystem.

235

of quantum mechanics, the role of gravity on human physiology, and the physics of combustion. Zero gravity can aid in the formation of perfect protein crystals that can improve the quality of insulin and pharmaceutical drugs.[2]

The purpose of this chapter is to investigate both the market opportunities and market failures associated with the exploration and exploitation of outer space. Market opportunities take the form of surveying, communication, and navigation from satellite-provided services that can be withheld from nonpayers and sold on a per-unit basis. In developing these products, governments often provide the expensive research and development (R&D) in pursuit of some public benefits – for example, defense and communication needs – before giving access to private firms for the commercialization of the jointly produced excludable outputs. Manufacturing in outer space also offers market possibilities if launch and landing costs become reasonable.

Market failures arise from the externalities and public goods associated with the use of the common-property resources of outer space. For example, the allocation of the electromagnetic spectrum and orbital slots to satellites presents property rights issues that must be addressed if these resources are to be assigned to their most-valued use (Macauley, 1998; Sandler and Schulze, 1981, 1985; Wilhborg and Wijkman, 1981). Should these two resources be allocated separately or together as once had been the case? Given the large fixed costs associated with space activities, underinvestment is anticipated, especially when intergenerational public good benefits are recognized. Governmental efforts to subsidize the development of space technologies and exploration are also unlikely to account for benefits conferred on other countries, so that too little investment results. The leading countries in outer space – the United States and Russia – can determine what aspects of their discoveries they choose to share, thereby limiting spillover benefits and global welfare. Participation in the ISS breaks this monopoly in exploration and can promote a greater distribution of benefits. China's launch of a manned spacecraft on 16 October 2003 also serves to expand international participation in space exploration; nevertheless participants remain small in number. Owing to their limited technological capacities, most countries will gain only belatedly, if at all, from space discoveries. Therefore, this final market frontier is

---

[2] These and other benefits from ISS are described by National Aeronautics and Space Administration (NASA) (2003).

anticipated to widen the income gap among nations. The high investment cost associated with many space-based technologies will mean that natural monopoly elements are present owing to decreasing per-unit cost as a larger market is served, thereby conferring a competitive advantage on the initial producer. Noncompetitive influences may also arise from markets that may profitably support only a few competitors. For launch vehicles, Japan's H2-A rocket is anticipated to capture little of the annual $2 billion market for launches (Space.com, 2003), which is served by NASA, the European Space Agency (ESA), Orbital Sciences, and the Russian Space Agency. Today's market for launches may be too small to support yet another competitor.

Why Is Outer Space Scarce?

A glance at the heavens gives the impression of infinite resources and, hence, no need for economics to allocate resources to their most-valued use; but, in fact, many key resources in outer space are quite scarce. Consider orbital slots in geostationary space, some 22,300 miles [36,000 kilometers (km)] above the equator. At this altitude, satellites orbit the earth in the same time interval that the earth rotates about its axis so that satellites remain stationary over a fixed point on the surface of the earth. This stationary position is particularly desirable for communication satellites because only a single earth-station receiver, located directly beneath, is needed to communicate with each satellite. At this high altitude, a mere three satellites are required to provide point-to-multipoint service almost everywhere on earth except near the poles (Edelson, 1977). Without station-keeping devices, which limit a satellite's drift (about 100 miles in orbit), approximately 1700 evenly spaced satellites can populate the geostationary orbital band before collisions become a concern. Since most transoceanic communications occur between North America and Europe, the most desirable orbital slots are some 375 positions over the Atlantic unless costly station-keeping devices are used to limit drift (Wihlborg and Wijkman, 1981). These orbital slots are in danger of eventually being exhausted. At each orbital band, economic trade-offs involve the size and number of satellites, as well as the drift of satellites. For example, station-keeping devices not only increase satellite cost and weight (the latter raises launch costs) but also may shorten the satellite's lifetime owing to energy supply considerations.

The scarcity of these orbits is even more apparent when the external effects of interference are examined with respect to the electromagnetic spectrum whose radiation is used by satellites to transmit signals. Interference occurs when satellites using the same frequency band for transmissions are too close together, thus leading to noise in the form of undecipherable signals. To limit this interference, regulators separate satellites from 800 to 1,600 miles, thereby greatly reducing available geostationary orbit slots (Macauley, 1998, p. 743). In recent years, the allocation of greater bandwidth to satellites is mitigating this concern, but this allocation reduces the bandwidth that can be assigned to other uses.

Other plum orbital slots exist that are ideal for some purposes. For example, sun-synchronous orbits are polar orbits (that is, passing over earth's polar regions from north to south) at an altitude of between 373 miles (600 km) to 497 miles (800 km), where the satellite is continually illuminated by the sun. These positions are useful for solar or earth observation because data can be continually transmitted to earth-based receivers. Other desirable positions are the so-called stable Lagrange points – L-4 and L-5 – at which the gravitational forces exerted by the sun, moon, and earth are in balance. This balance means that a satellite or space colony placed at L-4 or L-5 will remain fixed with respect to these three celestial bodies. If the resources from the moon are eventually mined, then space colonies placed at these Lagrange points will facilitate interchanges of crew and resources between moon and earth (O'Neill, 1977). Low-earth orbits between 99 miles (160 km) and 621 miles (1000 km) altitude are useful for remote sensing, military purposes (for example, targeting), and manned spaceflights or space laboratories. The lower the orbit, the more satellites needed for continuous communication with a limited number of earth-based receivers – 20 to 50 satellites may be required to cover the globe depending on the orbital altitude and number of earth-based receivers. Once again, a trade-off exists: the number of satellites in a given orbital band can be substituted for more earth-based receivers. The large number of satellites needed for global coverage means that collision and interference externalities are also a risk in these more plentiful low-earth orbits. There is simply no escaping the realization that favorable positions in outer space are scarce and must be allocated through economic-based decisions.

The so-called "orbit spectrum" resource consists of two separate resources: the orbital slot and the bandwidth assigned to a parked satellite.

In the past, the International Telecommunication Union (ITU) assigned user rights to orbits and electromagnetic spectrum on a first-come, first-served basis for an indefinite time period (Wihlborg and Wijkman, 1981, p. 40), which gave potential windfall gains to those who secured these rights. Moreover, the rights to these two resources were assigned as a package, which failed to account for the substitution possibilities where the number of satellites (hence, orbital slots) can be traded off against greater bandwidth allocation. This action to assign two resources as though they were one inhibited the workings of markets, thereby resulting in inefficiency. In recent years, bandwidth for satellite use is being auctioned to the highest bidder – an action that promotes greater efficiency. For example, the Federal Communication Commission recently auctioned off bandwidth ideal for mobile phones and broadband services.

Even though these actions are a step in the right direction, markets for the orbit spectrum are far from efficient because many bandwidths are secured by governments for military, intelligence, and emergency applications. There is no necessary reason why this allocation reflects the true underlying valuation of the public goods derived from these bandwidth assignments. In addition, the ITU merely hands out orbital slots to those who request them so that the valuation of the requester for these slots does not play a role in their assignments. The exchange of the orbit-spectrum resource must also contend with distortions arising from collisions between nearby satellites and interference externalities. In short, the orbit-spectrum resource is not allocated in a complete market where all costs and benefits are reflected in the price. If those who obtain the orbit slot from the ITU are later able to sell it to the highest bidder, then market efficiency is enhanced because the resource will be directed to its highest-valued application by the trading process. This outcome requires the ITU to vest the user with long-term ownership rights, including the right to trade. Economic efficiency is improved still further if the ITU auctions property rights to orbital slots.

Outer Space, Collective Action, and Market Failure

The exploitation of outer space is associated with a host of market failures. Because outer space has a large discovery component, an intergenerational public good of knowledge creation is involved. As with many discovery pursuits, a best-shot public good is germane in which the greatest effort is often the most likely to end in success. Not surprisingly, a few rich countries will be the primary participants in this discovery process. The growing inequality among countries, especially in terms of technological knowledge, will limit participation still further in the future. European Union (EU) members have wisely chosen to participate in this discovery by pooling their resources with the creation of the ESA. Although Russia is still a participant, its reduced economic well-being in the post-Cold War era has meant that it has had to pool much of its discovery activities with the United Sates and others in the ISS.

The ISS serves to represent both global collective action and inaction. Action stems from the unprecedented cooperation between NASA, ESA, the Russian Space Agency, the National Space Development Agency of Japan (NASDA), and other countries (for example, Israel). Inaction arises because government officials are anticipated to underinvest in R&D projects that yield long-term benefits only after years of efforts (Cohen and Noll, 1986). Legislators and other elected officials will demonstrate impatience by foreshortening the R&D period to achieve results quickly that can be translated into constituent support during the next election. This impatience is aptly illustrated by NASA's now-defunct philosophy to do things faster and cheaper. After two Mars missions failed because of foolish errors (for example, a unit of measurement error) that could have been avoided with quality control, NASA dropped this philosophy. Government officials are also reluctant to assume the risks associated with bold new projects. The combination of impatience and risk aversion has led to the reliance on the Space Shuttle as the sole reusable launch vehicle (RLV) well past its intended lifetime. The recent loss of *Columbia* has greatly limited activity in the ISS as efforts are undertaken to avoid another shuttle disaster.

Military uses of outer space have also produced some significant public goods. First, the pursuit of a strategic nuclear deterrent during the Cold War created breakthroughs in launch vehicles that later allowed satellites to be put into orbit for communication and other peaceful purposes that benefit everyone. The current generation of expendable launch vehicles (ELVs) are direct descendants of intercontinental ballistic missiles (ICBMs) and, in some recent launches, are modified ICBMs discarded owing to disarmament treaties. Second, the military developed the Internet, which has transformed communication in wondrous ways. Third, the US military developed the Global Positioning System (GPS) for targeting and other logistical purposes. GPS allows for the guidance of smart bombs and precision-guided munitions to their targets, thereby limiting collateral civilian casualties during conflict. The associated commercial application of GPS is fast revolutionizing navigation at sea and on land and has a vast market potential (*The Economist*, 2003c; Zervos, 2003). Commercial revenues in 2002 from GPS are thought to be $12 billion and growing by over 20% each year (Braunschvig, Garwin, and Marwell, 2003, p. 158). Given the control that the military exercised over these technologies, including choosing the timing of their release, the associated public benefits have been limited.[3]

The Pentagon spent $20 billion constructing the GPS system and ringing the globe with satellites in low-earth polar orbit (12,000 miles altitude) to supply worldwide coverage (*The Economist*, 2003c). For GPS, the military initially made available an *inferior* signal for commercial users owing to strategic concerns (that is, an enemy's use of GPS for logistical purposes). Because the Pentagon viewed the marginal cost of supplying the GPS signal to commercial users as zero, the Pentagon provided the less accurate GPS signal for free. Recent demands by commercial interests and ESA's current development of Galileo – an improved navigation signal for commercial users – have induced the US military to release an improved GPS signal for the general public in the United States and elsewhere. This improved signal is now available because the US military developed the means to jam the signal to potential enemies; signal exclusion can also be applied to commercial users.

There is a significant contrast between the approach that the EU is taking with respect to the commercialization of Galileo versus that of the United States with respect to GPS. For Galileo, the EU will put in the initial investment during the development stage (2001–5) that includes in-orbit testing of some satellites and construction of some ground stations (€1.1 billion).[4] Deployment then takes place during 2006–7 when 30 satellites are launched and the earth-based network of signal receivers are completed (€2.1 billion with just €0.6 billion provided publicly). During deployment, a public–private partnership is formed for financing and operational purposes. In the third and final operational stage (2008 and beyond), the annual cost of €0.2 billion is borne by the private interest

---

[3] GPS produces joint products: a public good from defense applications and excludable public and private benefits from GPS commercial applications. Civilian users outnumber military users by 100 to 1.

[4] On the background on Galileo, see the interesting and informative paper by Zervos (2003) and references therein.

managing Galileo. Fees will be charged to those who utilize the navigation signal based on a toll arrangement like that of a club. This framework contrasts greatly with the US GPS arrangement where commercial applications of the GPS signal earn revenues but users of the signal pay nothing to defray development cost or upgrade the system overtime.

If the marginal cost of the signal is truly zero – that is, there is no crowding or diminution of the signal from use *and* the system capacity is adequate to serve all users now and into the future, then the US arrangement is efficient contrary to critics (for example, *The Economist,* 2003c). Charging for an excludable, nonrival good is inefficient – recall Figure 3.2 and surrounding discussion. If, in contrast, the system has limited capacity so that military use rivals commercial applications in the strength of the signals, then critics are correct in pointing to Galileo as a more efficient arrangement since fees will internalize such nonzero crowding externalities. Moreover, the US Department of Defense (DOD) would be better able to calculate the true valuation of commercial (jointly produced) private benefits when upgrading the system if it were to share in the revenues. Currently, GPS needs to be upgraded to inhibit hostile jamming and meet current standards for air-traffic control and other applications (Braunschvig, Garwin, and Marwell, 2003). A share of the revenues from such applications would greatly assist DOD in designing the capacity and capabilities of the next generation of GPS.

Suppose that the GPS arrangement remains unchanged, but that Galileo provides a more accurate alternative service in 2008 as planned. Commercial users will decide between the two systems based on their marginal willingness to pay: those users with a high valuation for signal accuracy will choose Galileo over GPS. The current arrangement is apt to promote efficient collective action as high-valuation users partition themselves from low-valuation users by their choice of system. This is no different than in Washington, DC, and other places where some people choose the parallel toll road to the more congested (lower-quality-of-service) free highway. Such choice can often rectify a potential market failure by matching a user's valuation with a desired level of service. As a consequence, Galileo does much more than reinvent the wheel with its enhanced radio navigation service; it also ameliorates potential inefficiencies associated with GPS.

A future potential intergenerational public good could come from the use of outer space to sequester plutonium and other highly radioactive elements. For example, these substances can be placed into low-earth orbit from which they can then be shot either into the sun or beyond the solar system. The main worry is to find a launch vehicle that is virtually 100% reliable; an explosion of a launcher transporting plutonium into orbit would have catastrophic consequences. Clearly, the Space Shuttle is not such a vehicle. In the case of a launch accident, the risk of a radiation release could be made negligible if the payload encasement can withstand the consequences of a failure. Thus, payload encasement reliability can be traded off against launcher reliability.

Market failures in outer space may arise from externalities. Signals transmitted by satellites may not only interfere with other satellites but also with space probes (for example, *Voyager*), whose signals when beamed back to earth may be blocked by satellites in their transmission's pathway. When receiving or transmitting signals, satellites may interfere with one another not only in the same altitude band but also in different altitude bands. Because satellite interference often implies some kind of reciprocal externality, there is an incentive among satellite operators to reach an accommodation. For satellite collisions, there is the added impetus for a negotiated outcome since potential accidents only involve one or two nearby satellites unlike signal interference, which may affect many satellites at different orbital bands.

To internalize the externality associated with a satellite or a space station that crashes back to earth, an enforceable liability assignment must be instituted whereby the satellite or station owner is made to compensate victims on earth. Clearly, the owner of such space debris is easy to identify so that the difficult collective action problem is devising an enforcement mechanism. There are, of course, perverse incentives for those nations with large objects in orbit to assume liability once an accident occurs. Article VII of the so-called "Outer Space Treaty" (entered into force on 10 October 1967) assigns international liability for damages caused by satellites and other orbital objects to the nation or organization launching and operating them.[5] Nevertheless, when a Soviet satellite crashed in the north of Canada in the late 1970s and spread radioactive fallout over a large debris field, the Soviet Union assumed no responsibility. The

---

[5] The full name of this treaty is "Treaty on Principles Governing the Activities of States in the Exploration and Use of Outer Space Including the Moon and Other Celestial Bodies."

United States assisted Canada in locating and cleaning up the radioactive material. Thus, in its first real test, the provisions of the Outer Space Treaty were neither abided by nor enforced.

Launch Vehicle

The feasibility of activities in outer space depends in large part on the costs of lifting payloads into orbit. In 1981, the costs of placing one pound of payload in low-earth orbit, geostationary orbit, and on the moon were $1,100, $4,000, and $8,000, respectively (Sandler and Schulze, 1981). Although these costs have fallen somewhat, they are still reasonable proxies. An additional cost is the insurance needed to cover an accident on launch that would destroy the payload or put it in a useless orbit. Until the successful launch of the first Ariane rocket launcher (Ariane 1) on Christmas Eve of 1979, only three countries had launch capability – the United States, the Soviet Union, and China. The ESA's Ariane ELV has grown in importance; Ariane 4 has made over 113 successful launches from 15 June 1988 through 15 February 2003 and served 50% of the commercial launch market.[6] Ariane 5 with a larger payload has been operational since its first successful launch on 30 October 1997.

There are now three primary providers of ELVs for putting satellites into orbit – the United Sates, the ESA, and the Russian Space Agency. In the United Sates, NASA and Orbital Sciences (a private firm) supply commercial launches. Japan also has recently developed a commercial launcher – the H2-A – which can place satellites into low-earth or geostationary orbit. Table 11.1 indicates currently operational ELVs along with the company or developer, the country or international organization in charge of launches, and whether the launcher can put a payload in geostationary orbit. These launchers can lift a variety of different sized payloads; for example, Orbital Sciences' ELVs specialize in small payloads. China's CZ-2C space launcher was first launched in July 1975. Since then, it has averaged only one or two launches per year of satellites for China (Federation of American Scientists, 2003), thus, China is not yet a real player in the commercial launch market. China's Shezhou 5 launch of a manned spacecraft in October 2003 may bolster customer confidence in its commercial launch vehicles, which experienced a series of failures in the 1990s.

[6] On Ariane, see European Space Agency (2003).

Table 11.1. *Currently Operational Expendable Launch Vehicles (ELVs)*

Vehicle	Company/Developer	Country	Geostationary Orbit Capability
Athena	Lockheed Martin	United States	No
Titan 2	Lockheed Martin	United States	No
Atlas 2; 3; 5	Lockheed Martin	United States	Yes
Tital 4B	Lockheed Martin	United States	Yes
Delta 2; 3; 4	Boeing	United States	Yes
Delta 4 Heavy	Boeing	United States	Yes
Minotaur	Orbital Sciences	United States	No
Pegasus	Orbital Sciences	United States	No
Taurus	Orbital Sciences	United States	No
Zenit 3SL	Sea Launch	Ukraine-Russia[a]	Yes
Ariane 4	Aerospatiale, Arianespace	France, ESA	Yes
Ariane 5	Aerospatiale, Arianespace	France, ESA	Yes
H2-A	NASDA[b]	Japan	Yes
Proton	Russian Space Agency	Russia	Yes
Soyuz	Russian Space Agency	Russia	No
Vosok	Russian Space Agency	Russia	No
Zenik	Russian Space Agency	Russia	No

[a] In a commercial partnership with Boeing.
[b] National Space Development Agency of Japan.
Source: Federal Aviation Administration (2003) on US vehicles; European Space Agency (2003) on Ariane 4 and 5; NASDA (2003) on H2-A; and Russian Space Web (2003) on Russian launchers.

The current race in outer space is for the development of the next generation of RLVs to replace the aging Space Shuttle, the only currently operational RLV. In Table 11.2, some of the current contenders in this competition are listed with their developer and key features. As shown, the next generation being developed may be vertically launched, horizontally launched like a plane, or air-launched from atop a plane. Currently, it is unclear which propulsion system and design will prove successful. The development of the next set of operational RLVs is a better-shot public good, where alternative designs can provide greater service reliability when a crash grounds one type of RLV as the cause is being investigated. Thus, even a second-best technology has something to offer in terms of enhanced reliability and increased diversity.

Given the tremendous uncertainty as to what is the best RLV design, efforts should not be pooled. The high degree of randomness associated with finding the next RLV favors a number of teams working

Table 11.2. *Reusable Launch Vehicles (RLVs) in Development*

Alternative RLVs	Developer	Features
Orbital Space Plane	NASA	A crew-return craft launched atop an ELV that can transfer limited sized cargoes to the ISS in low-earth orbit.
Responsive Access, Small Cargo, and Affordable Launch (RASCAL) Vehicle	Department of Defense	A two-stage air-launched vehicle that puts small 220-lb payloads in low-earth orbit. The first stage will be an aircraft that flies to 100,000 feet, at which point a rocket is launched to achieve the orbit.
Astroliner	Kelly Space and Technology	A horizontal takeoff system in which a modified Boeing 747 tows a space plane to 20,000 feet, where the space plane is released and its rocket engine fired to carry it into low-earth orbit.
Black Armadillo	Armadillo Aerospace	A single-stage space plane that can transport three persons into an orbit of 62 miles and then return them to earth.
K-1	Kistler Aerospace	This crewless vehicle launches vertically like an ELV. Its two stages are recoverable through an integrated parachute and airbag system. This reusable rocket system is intended to launch payloads of 3,460 lbs into low-earth orbit or geosynchronous transfer orbit.
Pathfinder	Pioneer Rocketplane	A two-pilot crew takes off on a horizontal runway. At an altitude of 19,685 feet, Pathfinder is refueled with liquid oxygen from a tanker plane. Pathfinder's rocket engine then fires to lift it to a 70-mile-high orbit.
SA-1	Space Access	A crewless RLV space plane with hybrid propulsion system that can use air and liquid hydrogen. This space plane takes off and lands horizontally on conventional runways.

Source: Federal Aviation Administration (2003, pp. 17–25).

independently on diverse design concepts to increase the likelihood of success. These multiple efforts are being encouraged by the X-Prize Foundation, a nonprofit corporation that is offering a $10 million reward for the first developer who launches a space vehicle that carries the equivalent payload of three persons into a suborbital altitude of 62 miles and repeats the flight within two weeks with the same craft [Federal Aviation Administration (FAA), 2003, pp. 24–5]. The prize is intended to encourage an RLV that allows for rapid turnaround and reuse. In the case of the Space Shuttle, the turnaround was not only slow but unpredictable; consequently, the Shuttle's ability to exploit economies of scale was very limited. Cost per launch would have been smaller if a greater number of launches could have spread the large fixed development cost over more flights. Current contenders for the X-Prize include the *Astroliner*, the *Black Armadillo*, and the *Pathfinder* (see Table 11.2). Some of the other RLV designs in development are not for manned flight and so are not in competition for the X-Prize. To encourage private R&D, NASA is also awarding grants to private developers.

A craft being developed by AeroVironment (a private company) with NASA's assistance is the unmanned aerial vehicle (UAV) that ascends to an altitude of just 12.4 miles (20 km) where it can remain over the same spot on earth for many months (*The Economist*, 2003d, pp. 70–1). A UAV resembles a wing with solar cells on its upper side that power its flight and movement. To achieve the required flight duration, a better energy storage device must be developed so that daytime-collected solar power can be used to power the UAV at night. UAVs have many advantages over satellites. Their nearness to earth means that surveillance can be done with better resolution than from satellites in low-earth or geostationary orbit. Placing these unmanned platforms into their stationary positions is very inexpensive compared with satellites. Their low altitude also means that, when used for communications, UAV transmitters and receivers do not have to be very powerful. Moreover, UAVs can fulfill many chores where proximity is advantageous including security against terrorism, surveying the planet, monitoring the troposphere, and providing broadband communications. Although UAVs can supply some satellite services, they cannot replace satellites – their low altitude gives them very limited coverage compared with satellites, especially those in geostationary space. If used for defense purposes, UAVs are relatively easy targets compared with low-earth satellites, which are higher and not stationary.

Conflict and Outer Space

Article IV of the Outer Space Treaty outlaws the placement of nuclear weapons and other weapons of mass destruction (WMD) in orbit. The Treaty also inhibits the establishment of military bases on the moon or celestial bodies. Although these actions have not materialized, outer space is increasingly being utilized for military purposes. The GPS system guides cruise missiles and smart bombs, and navigates warships, troops, and vehicles on the battlefield while limiting friendly fire. GPS targeting has increased greatly in recent years: 3% of the bombs were guided by GPS during the Kosovo War compared with 60% during the 2003 Iraq War (Braunschvig, Garwin, and Marwell, 2003). Targets can be viewed at various frequencies along the electromagnetic spectrum, including infrared, visual, and radio. During the Kosovo War, US planes could see through clouds to guide their munitions to their targets, which was not the case for British and French planes. What can be seen – no matter the frequency – can be targeted, and what can be targeted can be annihilated. Given the massive size of new conventional weapons and their enhanced ability to cause horrific destruction, the use of outer space platforms for targeting purposes violates the spirit of the Outer Space Treaty.

President George W. Bush's abrogation of the 1972 Antiballistic Missile (ABM) Treaty, which limits the number of ABM deployment sites, launchers, and interceptors, opens outer space still further to an arms race. With its reliance on satellites for targeting, surveillance, and other military purposes,[7] the United States will eventually have to consider defensive measures around its satellites and this will mean the deployment of weapon platforms in space. The United States has already tested defense systems to destroy satellites.

There is also the issue of "Star Wars," a missile defense system to make the United States impregnable to attack. Such a system would have many space-based components for tracking and targeting incoming missiles. President Ronald Reagan first pushed the deterrent umbrella concept of using a global satellite system to shield the United States from a nuclear attack by the Soviet Union. The US alleged (and misrepresented) superiority in the Star Wars technology may have ended the Cold War by convincing the Soviets that to overcome the US technological advantage

---

[7] Pike (2002) reviews the military uses of outer space and gives a list of satellites with military purposes.

would require increased resource allocations during a time when the Soviets were already assigning more than they could afford. President George W. Bush is pushing the national missile defense system as a means of protecting against missiles fired by rogue states or terrorists. The cost of such a system, if feasible, will be astronomical; nevertheless, the Bush administration is going ahead with R&D.

The development of a national missile defense is the ultimate best-shot public good where the greatest and most sustained effort has the greatest likelihood of success, given the technological complexities. Once the system is deployed, the United States has no choice but to protect virtually everyone: once a missile is fired, there is almost no time to determine if US territory or its interests abroad are the intended target. Globalization has dispersed US people, property, and interest sufficiently that any missile from a rogue state or terrorist group would have to be taken as a threat and destroyed. If the missile releases decoys early in its flight as is true of Russian and American ICBMs, then this makes it even more imperative to destroy the missile during the initial three to four minute boost stage. Thus, US allies and other nations can merely free ride on the US system if developed; nations would have no incentive to buy into the systems.

Markets and Clubs

Outer space gives one the impression of nonexcludable and nonrival goods. Surely, the light show displayed by an exploding star has both of these classic properties of a public good, as does a solar flare that disrupts satellite and terrestrial communications. In fact, outer space presents many market and club opportunities that can achieve near-efficient outcomes. Markets are particularly suited to space manufacturing as in the case of pharmaceuticals whose crystalline structure is enhanced in zero-gravity conditions. For space manufacturing to be profitable, there must be a high value to weight because launch and reentry costs are so high. Space manufacturing will become more feasible once launch costs are reduced.

Satellite launches have become a lucrative market, which is now becoming saturated. As the lifetime of satellite applications have been extended, the number of launches per application have fallen. This is also due to the capacity of communication satellites being increased so that today's communication satellites can handle more phone lines and television stations. The laying of fiber optic cables has reduced the growth of satellite-based communications. New satellite applications will, however, come along and expand the market. In this regard, the Galileo navigation system will require 30 satellites to provide global coverage and this will increase the number of launches as the system is deployed. If the required technological breakthroughs are achieved, then the national missile defense system will also require vast numbers of new satellites.

An excellent example of a club arrangement in outer space is the International Telecommunication Satellite Organization (INTELSAT), which took its permanent structure in 1973. INTELSAT began on an interim basis in 1964 after the 1963 launch of the Early Bird telecommunication satellite (INTELSAT, 1993). INTELSAT currently carries more than half of all international telephone calls and virtually all transoceanic television broadcasts.[8] In recent years, INTELSAT accounts for 31% of the transmissions for high-speed Internet connections. INTELSAT also transmits cellular phone calls. Today, the system contains 25 geostationary satellites: 12 over the Atlantic Ocean, 8 over the Indian Ocean, 1 over the Asian-Pacific region, and 4 over the Pacific Ocean. Because the largest flow of messages is across the Atlantic Ocean, this region requires more satellites than elsewhere. As in an ideal club, the shared good's capacity and provision level is tailored to the level of utilization or the size of the market. Of the 25 satellites, some serve as spares thereby increasing the system's reliability to better than a 99.99% effectiveness rate. An INTELSAT satellite receives weak radio signals in the megahertz frequency band from earth-station transmitters. After receiving these signals, the satellite amplifies and retransmits them in the gigahertz band to earth-station receivers. Between the 18,000 earth stations and other ground points, signals travel via microwave links and cables.

Economies of scale in transmission have been achieved by increasing the capacity of the different generations of INTELSAT satellites. Thus, the investment per circuit year dropped from $30,000 to $800 as the size of INTELSAT satellites increased from Series I to V (Edelson, 1977). For example, INTELSAT IV-A satellites contain 6,000 circuits, where each circuit consists of two one-way telephone channels, so that 6,000 simultaneous telephone conversations can be conducted by each satellite. INTELSAT V satellites have 12,000 circuits and can transmit two television stations. INTELSAT VI satellites have 24,000 circuits and can

---

[8] Some of the facts in this paragraph come from INTELSAT (2003).

transmit three television stations. Subsequent generations of INTELSAT satellites use digital circuits to increase their capacity and clarity.

The INTELSAT communication system represents a club good since network access is restricted by coding or scrambling signals. Additionally, the network can be simultaneously used by its 400 members, which include countries, Internet service providers, telecommunication companies, broadcasters, corporate networks,[9] and international organizations. Members' use can be monitored and tolls charged accordingly. As utilization of the system increases, the benefits per signal transmitted diminish owing to congestion as an increased volume of signals share the same frequency band. A club arrangement can allocate utilization rates efficiently based on congestion-based toll charges (see Chaps. 2 and 3). Every user pays the same toll per unit of utilization as reflected by, say, a second of transmission or reception using the network. The toll *values the congestion imposed* on the membership from this unit of use. Users' total toll payments are then based on their number of units of transmission or reception times the toll. Those members who transmit and receive more signals pay more in total tolls as their utilization rate reveals their true preferences for the network.

The current structure of INTELSAT conforms closely to that of an economic club where members pay fees according to their utilization on a per-unit basis, and voting at meetings of the Board of Governors is weighted based on the members' utilization rates and investment share.[10] The latter is itself based on a member's percentage of utilization of the network. Although the other bodies of INTELSAT (for example, the Assembly of Parties, the Meeting of Signatories, and the Manager) make policy recommendations, the Board of Governors is the ultimate decision-making body. A utilization-weighted voting scheme is consistent with efficiency because heavier users (for example, a telecommunication company) will be serving more individuals whose interests must be reflected, and consequently these heavier users will support a greater share of the costs resulting from policy changes. Toll revenues support the system and underwrite investment in upgrades and increased capacity. This club structure does

---

[9] For example, airline companies use INTELSAT for their intercontinental booking arrangements; newspapers transmit their editions via INTELSAT for printing and distribution in other countries.

[10] On the institutional structure of INTELSAT, see Edelson (1977) and INTELSAT (1973, 1993, 1995).

not necessitate nations sacrificing their political autonomy to the wishes of the majority; members determine their own levels of utilization and can choose to leave the system if they wish.

Many satellite applications lend themselves to a club arrangement because of the ability to exclude nonpayers and the congestion costs associated with utilization. LANDSAT is another example where users are charged according to the amount of surveying requested. These fees can then be used to support and upgrade the system. In the case of LANDSAT, the US government developed the technology and initially constructed the satellite network before selling it to a commercial firm. Information from weather satellites can also be sold to subscribers – for example, broadcasting networks – in a club arrangement.

Space Exploration

As with most discoveries, outer space exploration has a strong public good component. The Hubble telescope's observation of evidence related to the origin of the universe and other phenomena enlightens all people. Scientists from many countries participate in analyzing data from the telescope and building theories to explain them. Even though the United States built and launched this telescope, other countries have added to the project through their scientists' expertise. The United States receives private benefits through prestige and the ability to assign observation times to others as they choose. More distant observations have come from space probes sent to nearby asteroids, the sun, comets, and other planets as a means to augment our understanding of the solar system. The United States, Russia, Japan, and the EU have launched such probes. Given that the payoffs from these probes are in the future and benefit everyone, a suboptimal amount of this exploratory effort is anticipated.

The underlying aggregation technology for space exploration is best shot where efforts may be best pooled for activities in which known thresholds must be surpassed. In other instances, the discovery process may be less easily chartered so that multiple diverse efforts are needed to stumble on the discovery – for example, is there life on Mars? For the ISS, a huge expenditure is required, so a pooled effort is probably more fruitful than numerous independent small stations. When sending unmanned probes to Mars, much less investment is required; therefore, multiple efforts with diverse designs are more likely to yield a wider range of discoveries than pooling efforts with a single complex probe. Multiple approaches also minimize the risk of failure – for example, the failure of ESA's Beagle 2 to communicate after landing on Mars in December 2003.

The ISS is noteworthy as a supreme instance of global collective action that involves many different kinds of contributions from numerous countries. The United States plays a crucial leadership role in terms of technological knowledge, financial resources, and launch and reentry capabilities. This collective action was also fostered by the relatively small number of key countries needed at the outset for the endeavor – just the United States and Soviet Union – which limited transaction costs. Later other important participants – most notably, the ESA – joined the project. All participants receive some nation-specific benefits that serve to motivate participation; for example, the ISS allowed the Russians to maintain a space laboratory during the difficult economic times following the collapse of the Soviet Union. The Russians provided the United States with technical knowledge that they had gained from their earlier space laboratory and allowed the Americans to jointly occupy this laboratory prior to the construction of the ISS. Additionally, the Russians had a Soyuz reentry vehicle to serve as a backup to the Space Shuttle; Soyuz proved essential following the crash of the *Columbia* and the grounding of the shuttle fleet. Global collective action for the ISS was also promoted because the earlier space laboratory took away a lot of the uncertainty about the feasibility and the potential gains from a human presence in space. All participants would gain; there would be no losers from participation. The international presence reduced the likelihood that the colony would be diverted to military purposes. Once the major expenditures were covered by the United States, future participants could easily achieve a net positive benefit since cost would be small. Thus, the ISS possesses many of the factors that bolster collective action at the global level. As the major stakeholder in the ISS, the United States could influence which countries participated and their level of involvement, which is a crucial US-specific benefit. Bush's plan to refocus NASA's exploration program, announced in January 2004, jeopardizes the long-run future of the ISS.

Space Wanderers and Collisions

When one examines the moon's surface, the number of impact craters from planetesimals – comets and asteroids – is a prominent feature. On earth, there are only a few notable examples of impact craters such as Meteor Crater in central Arizona, because erosion and weathering hide the scars of the past. Unlike the moon, the earth's thicker atmosphere destroys small and medium-sized planetesimals in a fiery display, dubbed shooting stars. Nevertheless, the earth has been frequently bombarded with asteroids and comets, and in the future, such bombardments could have cataclysmic consequences.[11] The March 1996 encounter with Comet Hyakutake within a mere ten million miles, which is close by astronomical standards, underscores the perils that the earth faces. The collision between fragments of the Shoemaker–Levy 9 comet and Jupiter beginning on 16 July 1994 gives a vivid picture of the consequences of such encounters: the plume from the first impact shot 3,000 km above the clouds of Jupiter. An impact spot at ground zero on Jupiter was the size of the earth (Levy, Shoemaker, and Shoemaker, 1996, p. 89). Although a past impact with a comet is widely believed to have caused the extinction of the dinosaur, these collisions have also been crucial for life on our planet. The earth's oceans are believed to have been brought to the planet by comets after the earth had cooled and solidified. Any water on the planet would have evaporated during the molten lava stage when the earth was hot, so water had to have been reintroduced by comets. In fact, observations from satellites indicate that small pieces from passing comets still bring water to our planet.

Once in every 300,000 years on average, an asteroid or comet larger than a kilometer across strikes the earth. The impact would be devastating, equivalent to a million times the energy released by the atom bomb at Hiroshima. The ensuing explosion would throw-up dirt and debris that would obscure the sun, resulting in a "nuclear winter" with subzero temperatures, violent windstorms, massive destruction to settlements, and huge loss of life.

Taking action against such a pending collision is the quintessential best-shot public good with intergenerational benefits. If given sufficient warning – a hundred years or more, humankind could conceivably avert the pending disaster by arming a vessel with explosives and sending it on a distant rendezvous in space with the intruder. At a great enough distance from earth, the necessary explosion would be fairly small to divert the object, because even a small jolt might result in a deviation in the

---

[11] The material in this subsection draws from Gehrels (1996) and Levy, Shoemaker, and Shoemaker (1995). Also some of the material comes from Sandler's (1997, pp. 209–10) *Global Challenges* and is reprinted with the kind permission of Cambridge University Press.

comet's or asteroid's trajectory sufficiently large to miss the earth. The greater the mass of the menacing planetesimal, the sooner it must be discovered, so that the rendezvous with an explosive-laden probe is farther from the earth. Moreover, the required explosion must be greater. Unlike a Hollywood movie, the technology to divert such objects must be developed well in advance and not weeks before a pending event. The key to success is advanced warning and an averting technology in hand. Advanced warning requires that asteroids and comets that could come into the earth's path be mapped to provide the earth sufficient warning; NASA is currently engaged in a spacewatch operation to map such objects. This vigilance must be ongoing because asteroids and comets can be hurled toward the inner solar system from the Oort Cloud and Kuiper Belt (both of which include remnants from the formation of the solar system) as the sun passes near other celestial bodies in its movement in the galaxy. In late April 1996, a comet was discovered that has a 50% chance of striking the earth in some 100,000 years.

Both the process of discovering the menace and the development of the averting technology require a pooling of effort. The United States is expending much of the discovery activity, and some observations are being made by astronomers from other countries in their normal viewing of the heavens. The more problematic action is to be technologically ready to divert the asteroid or comet if the threat ever materializes. Thus far, there is no formal cooperative arrangement among countries with launch capabilities to develop the technology. Perhaps, the hope is that the technology being developed to probe the solar system can be readily converted to carry out the diversion mission. Clearly, the relatively low probability of the event works against a concerted effort to be prepared.

Concluding Remarks

Outer space offers the next market frontier for a globalizing world as well as a new set of market failures to address. Given the ever-widening technological gap between the United States and other countries, the world has little choice but to rely on the United States to provide the best-shot public goods associated with space exploration and protection of the planet. In both cases, underprovision is anticipated as benefits to other countries' residents and future generations are undercounted or left out of the US decision calculus. A basic message of this chapter is that market opportunities do exist in outer space and will grow greatly as launch costs are reduced through technological breakthroughs and competition. Another message is that clubs represent a low-cost and essential institutional form for promoting allocative efficiency for satellite networks and applications. A third message is that the widening gap between the rich and poor countries will become larger through the exploitation of outer space.

Many of the technologies utilized by outer space clubs and markets have been developed by governments and later given to commercial ventures. As a consequence, their initial pricing structure does not reflect long-run marginal cost including development expenditure. Until the *Challenger* disaster, NASA charged customers for satellite launches way below their marginal cost, which implies an efficiency loss estimated by Toman and Macauley (1989, p. 91) to total $2.5 billion. As these commercial ventures later used their revenues to upgrade the next generation of satellites, pricing began to incorporate development cost and to be characterized by greater efficiency. Thus, the public–private partnerships in space need not have a long-term efficiency loss if future development cost is incorporated in the venture's pricing. Whether a conscious choice or not, INTELSAT has gravitated to an institutional form that appears appropriate and efficient. This same club structure is appropriate for Galileo's radio navigation system, which should foster allocative efficiency by providing a higher quality product than GPS for those prepared to pay the price.

12

Future Conditional

In 2000, I made a career change when I accepted an endowed chair in the School of International Relations (SIR) at the University of Southern California. Although I still have an appointment in economics, my primary affiliation and responsibilities are in international relations, an ideal discipline to apply my economic methods to the study of international policy. My efforts to focus on international political economy meant my return to the roots of economics as embodied in the works of Adam Smith, David Ricardo, Thomas Robert Malthus, and the other founders of economics. Since joining SIR, I have discovered from my colleagues that my characterization of agents as rational actors who seek their best outcome subject to constraints is a *realist* approach.[1] The application of noncooperative game theory to understand nations' actions also follows this tradition. My view that nations will remain the main agents in addressing transnational externalities and global public goods (GPGs) is also consistent with the realist representation. These nations will resist sacrificing their autonomy unless the perceived benefits from treaties and membership in supranational institutions, which circumscribe nations' freedom of actions, outweigh the high value that nations place on this freedom. Despite the impediment to transnational collective action, there are notable instances – for example, the Montreal Protocol to curb ozone-depleting substances, initial actions to control al-Qaida following 9/11, and

---

[1] An alternative to realism is liberalism, which views agents as cooperating for mutual gain when selfish behavior results in a suboptimal outcome. Consider the Prisoners' Dilemma. A realist sees the players as exercising their dominant strategy and ending up at the suboptimal Nash equilibrium. A liberalist predicts that the players will eventually cooperate to attain the social optimum. More recently, there is a partial convergence of these two approaches in the guise of neorealism and neoliberalism. Other approaches to international relations also exist.

global efforts to control Severe Acute Respiratory Syndrome (SARS) – where exigencies have been collectively addressed. For some responses, caution is needed to distinguish real from imagined progress; the latter stems from actions that would have occurred even without an agreement. By understanding past successes and failures, we can gain insight into a realist-based view as to what motivates nations to eschew autonomy for the sake of the collective. With this knowledge, the world community can encourage a response by creating favorable preconditions.

My basic message is that to comprehend how to address the myriad global challenges, one must master the modern concepts of collective action. That is, both the simple rules of thumb (for example, small groups tend to achieve more efficient outcomes than larger groups) and the grounds for exceptions (for example, supportive ties between individual contributions and the overall level of provision) must be understood. Transnational externalities and transnational public goods (TPGs) are behind many global concerns. Subtle differences among these issues – for example, in terms of the three dimensions of publicness – can lead to vastly different policy prescriptions. Nevertheless, public good properties are not always sufficient for the proper assessment of global collective action: two public goods may possess virtually identical properties of publicness, yet may have quite different collective action prognoses, as shown for global warming and ozone-depleting substances (Chap. 10). In other instances, global challenges drawn from diverse areas of concern may share similar collective action principles and policy recommendations. The key insight is to know when to generalize and when to discriminate among collective action issues. As such, political, strategic, temporal, institutional, and other considerations play a role.

In a surprising number of cases, the international community does not have to resort to elaborate supranational structures. For global communication, INTELSAT demonstrates nicely that a simple institutional arrangement, adhering to club principles, can achieve efficient results while limiting transaction costs and maintaining participants' autonomy. The search for uncomplicated structures and remedies holds out the best hope for successful global collective action.

Key Considerations for Success

Global collective action is best initiated by a limited set of essential nations that have a *significant* ameliorating influence on the problem. If too many key players are excluded, then gains achieved by the collective can be annihilated by those outside acting at cross-purposes (Buchholz, Haslbeck, and Sandler, 1998). For example, large emitters of greenhouse gases (GHGs) that do not agree to cutbacks may make matters worse by increasing economic activities or offering a safe haven to polluting industries. If, however, framers of an agreement try to be too inclusive, then transaction costs will be high, cooperation will be delayed, and an agreed-upon standard of cooperation may not result in much of an improvement. When putting together the cooperating nations, homogeneous participants – in terms of income, tastes, and their relationship to the problem – are best included initially to limit transaction costs. As much as possible, uncertainty should be resolved with respect to understanding the genesis of the challenge and the implications of various levels of collective action prior to approaching potential participants. Simple collective agreement should be applied first.

Highlighting associated localized or country-specific benefits encourages collective action as potential cooperators realize that these gains can only be achieved by contributing; they cannot sit back and free ride on others to obtain such benefits. Localized benefits thus provide some property rights to participants that engage in collective action. Leadership by key nations can set the proper example and induce others to participate. Cutbacks already achieved in ozone-depleting emissions were emphasized by treaty ratifiers to motivate others to support the Montreal Protocol and its subsequent amendments. Once a sufficient threshold of participation is surpassed, it becomes easier to extend cooperation because nations prefer to abide by largely held norms.

When deciding which challenges to tackle first, it is best to take on those where everyone can gain from the action. As global warming illustrates, problems with both gainers and losers are particularly difficult to address. Unbundling global challenges that involve multiple issues means that the level of cooperation achieved need not gravitate to that associated with the hardest issue to solve. The Long-Range Transboundary Air Pollution Convention made rapid progress on curbing sulfur emissions by framing one protocol for sulfur and other protocols for nitrogen oxides and volatile organic compounds, for which measurement took longer and less abatement progress had been achieved. Global concerns with favorable temporal profiles – where efforts today begin to reap payoffs for the agents in the not-too-distant future – are easier to address. If benefits realized are temporally separated by over a generation, then the prognosis for collective action is not as good. The more generations of separation, the less favorable the outcome. Public goods that abide by some aggregation technologies – for example, weakest link and threshold – are more conducive to a successful resolution. If collective action can influence the underlying aggregate technology, then efforts can encourage success by instituting a more favorable technology.

Institutional design can also enhance global collective action. Institutions based on cost-sharing promote desirable outcomes by making individual choices and their consequences more aligned with group welfare; that is, this institutional innovation eliminates the motives for free riding because benefits from contributing now outweigh costs. If threshold levels of action must be obtained, then refundability of cost prior to these thresholds being attained can make contributing a dominant strategy (Chap. 4). Institutional design that makes others more aware of an agent's actions also fosters collective action. Thus, Olson (1965) argued for national institutions being federated, where much of the participation is done at the local level where action gets noticed. The emerging movement to disperse some of the funding from the World Bank to the regional development banks applies this same principle of federalism to the global level. If the underlying collective good is either excludable or generates contributor-specific joint products, then club and market-like structures can promote collective action at low transaction costs.

What Will the Future Bring?

As a realist, I view the nation-state as remaining the primary player in addressing transnational interdependencies. Nations will sacrifice autonomy in only the most desperate circumstances and then to regional and multilateral organizations that do not greatly impinge on their autonomy. Increased cross-border flows will bring nations into more frequent negotiations over transnational concerns. With time and experience, nations will come to appreciate the interrelationship among some of these global exigencies. For example, the world community will learn that civil wars may adversely influence global health as such conflicts provide a favorable environment for HIV (often spread by soldiers), malaria, and other opportunistic microbes. By lessening inequality and raising the opportunity costs of conflict, foreign assistance can curtail civil wars and enhance security. Air pollution weakens a population, making individuals more vulnerable to diseases; thus, environmental concerns are connected to health and security issues. The current piecemeal approach to addressing global challenges will eventually be replaced by a more holistic approach.

Until recent years, there has been a reliance on a couple of multilateral organizations to provide GPGs and regional public goods (RPGs). These organizations also finance national public goods (NPGs) as a complementary activity required to enable developing countries to acquire the capacity to absorb and contribute RPGs and GPGs (World Bank, 2001). As globalization, new technologies, and the breakup of nations create new TPGs, these multilaterals have assumed an ever-growing set of issues by either assigning new chores to the organization or creating a new agency within the organization. Mission creep has resulted where cost savings from economies of scope are becoming exhausted. The presence of so many activities in these organizations also raises concerns over diseconomies of scale – increases in per-unit costs arising from communication and other institutional bottlenecks. There is also the worry over conflicts and incompatibilities among various activities of these multilaterals – for example, environmental policies may conflict with development policies.

To address some of these and related concerns, there is a movement to decentralize some activities of the global multilaterals by assigning them to regional institutions. With increased funding, the regional development banks can provide a greater range of RPGs. This arrangement effects a closer application of the principle of subsidiarity (see Chap. 4), where activities are assigned to institutions with jurisdictions that best match the benefit range of public goods or externality spillovers. Subsidiarity assumes that the regional institutions are better able to reflect local tastes and foster ownership as nations have a greater influence on regional than global institutions. If this reliance on regional development banks is to succeed, these banks must also alter some of their practices. One theoretical argument favors grants to underwrite purely public goods and loans for those activities with relatively large shares of recipient-specific benefits,[2] such as NPGs (World Bank, 2001). Thus, RPGs and GPGs should be financed by grants. The World Bank has implemented this financing

---

[2] In the case of GPGs, the recipient country is providing a good that benefits the global community; thus, grants from this community allow those who receive these benefits to underwrite the cost. When, however, a significant share of recipient-specific benefits is present, the recipient has a motivation for accepting some of the support in the form of a loan that must later be paid back.

division (World Bank, 2001); the regional development banks should mimic this division.

There is also the question about those public goods that are more than an RPG but less than a GPG. For example, the control of river blindness involves portions of Africa, the Arabian peninsula, and Latin America. Some environmental public goods may influence widely dispersed regions on the same continent – for example, river basins and coastal states – or on different continents – such as, air pollutants that transverse an ocean. Knowledge-based RPGs may apply to more than one region, say, with similar climatic conditions. To provide sufficient coverage for these inter-regional public goods, networks of *regional* organizations are advisable and may be a better alternative than assigning yet another task to the World Bank or United Nations. These networks are quite flexible and can add or subtract linkages among regional partners as needed. As such, networks can be designed to reflect the range of spillovers, thus account-ing for the preferences of those impacted by the public good. This tailor-ing ability of the networks saves on transaction costs, which are wasted by a "one-size-fits-all" global institution. Networks – such as the Global Environment Facility and the Consultative Group for International Agri-cultural Research – will grow in number to deal with interregional public goods.

Another hallmark of future global collective action, already evident in the last decade, is the increase in the types and prevalence of nonstate agents – that is, nongovernmental organizations (NGOs), consortiums, charitable foundations, partnerships, regional institutions, and commer-cial firms. The appearance of these new players often means new sources of funds that do not crowd out other contributions. As these organiza-tions gain successes in promoting the supply of some TPGs, other similar institutions will be encouraged to enter the international arena to push other TPGs. Moreover, multilaterals will become more adept at interact-ing with these new players. The downside of these new players is that they have their own agenda, which has a healthy dose of organization-specific benefits. Another downside involves a new form of crowding out where TPGs crowd out one another, unlike the standard crowding out of contri-butions to the same TPG. These institutions are at times in competition for funding; hence, given the size of world GDP, there are limits to which these new players can draw additional sources of funding.

In recent years, the share of funding spent on environmental public goods has declined in favor of health and security public goods (Willem te Velde, Morrissey, and Hewitt, 2002). This redistribution of shares is anticipated to increase, especially in light of SARS and many deadly civil wars (for example, the Congo). More interest will also be shown in governance TPGs because of their potentially large spillover benefits for wealthy nations that desire economic strength and stability in emerging markets for trading partners and investment opportunities. Developing countries have little choice but to adopt and underwrite these governance TPGs if they are to integrate into the world community and attract greater commerce. Knowledge-based TPGs will continue to lag behind the other categories, especially those financed through foreign assistance. This follows because these TPGs are unlikely to have many spillovers for more technically advanced donor countries. Even geographical differences – tropics versus nontropics – inhibit some benefit spillovers from knowledge-based health TPGs. In general, such TPGs have a high degree of intergenerational spillovers and this also works against their provision because future beneficiaries are not present to make their effective demand known. The world community must devise means for promoting more far-sighted support of intergenerational public goods to foster health breakthroughs, exploration, inventions, and innovations. Novel patent arrangements may help in some instances.

Tomorrow's Hot Issues

Numerous GPGs and RPGs will be the key concerns for tomorrow's global challenges; current issues that are particularly intractable are apt to be prime candidates. Based on its many impediments (see Chap. 10), global warming deserves to be high on the list of tomorrow's problems. There is little to favor effective action against the buildup of GHGs short of the recognition of some catastrophic consequences from inaction. The best hope for curbing GHGs is the discovery of an alternative to the internal combustion engine or its significant modification to achieve better fuel efficiency with less emitted GHGs. Another possible fix is to find additional reservoirs for the sequestration of carbon in new forests or underground holding tanks (for example, in formations that once held oil or gas underground). Geoengineering may play a key role.

Security issues are associated with a number of TPGs that will continue to occupy the global community's attention. Transnational terrorism is a major concern for the United States and the global community. As terrorists learn new attack tactics, they will try to outdo the most heinous past operations in their competition to capture media attention. Even before 9/11, terrorists had an increased reliance on suicide missions that are hard to protect against and particularly destructive as the terrorists choose the moment of maximum carnage. On average, suicide attacks are 13 times more deadly than the average terrorist incident. The current wave of suicide bombings in public places in northern Africa, the Middle East, and Sri Lanka will surely come to the United States and Europe, since these attacks create an atmosphere of heightened anxiety, far out of proportion to their true threat. When faced with suicide campaigns, governments experience greater pressure to capitulate to some of the terrorists' demands. Owing to their logistical simplicity, the wider reliance on suicide missions is more likely than terrorists' use of weapons of mass destruction (WMD). With few exceptions, modern-day terrorists have relied on bombs and simple means of attack. By getting the authorities to believe in WMD attacks, terrorists have greatly succeeded in their goal of creating an atmosphere of fear, while making governments expend billions of dollars in security and protection.

As a misguided policy, the new homeland security terrorist-alert system probably does more harm than good because the terrorists know that they can set it off with sufficient Internet chatter, thereby costing governments millions of dollars. By keeping silent, the terrorists can bring down the threat level and provide a less-vigilant environment in which to conduct attacks. This system provides a strategic advantage to the terrorists, who are kept informed by the government about its level of vigilance. Governments have to be far more clever than this alert system to curb the terrorist threat. As shown in Chapter 8, greater international cooperation is needed to prevent global terrorist networks from exploiting the inevitable weakest link. This is an area where governments will have to concede some autonomy if they are to be more effective.

Another growing security concern is cyberspace security where insidious viruses and worms can attack computers, computer programs, servers, or computer networks. Cyberspace security is truly a global collective action problem that can be mitigated, but not eliminated, by individual action (for example, the purchase of virus protection software). In an effort to disrupt the US and other economies, terrorists may also resort to cyberspace attacks. To date, however, terrorists have used the Internet to organize, communicate, and mount attacks, but have not turned to spreading cyberspace viruses to cause mass disruption (Arquilla and Ronfeldt, 2001). Although protection against new viruses can be developed, there is still a real cost incurred following their dissemination prior to the institution of countermeasures. To minimize the threat, countries must punish those who create and distribute cyberspace viruses. If perpetrators are not punished, they will continue creating new viruses. Unless a global standard of enforcement and vigilance is adopted, a weakest-link situation applies where the overall safety from attack is determined by the country with the least effort to curb viruses. Hackers will merely locate in a permissive environment from which they can attack computers and servers worldwide.

Global health will remain an area of heightened interest because standards of healthcare will vary greatly, thereby giving microbes opportune populations to infect. This weakest-link problem will never be corrected and the variation in standards will increase as income inequality widens. Realistically, the rich countries will not bring poorer countries up to an acceptable level of healthcare, so opportune hosts are ever-present. The likely scenario is that the richest countries will address health exigencies in developing countries only when there are negative consequences for them, and then only after the fact. If populations continue to expand at current rates in poor countries and conflicts plague many of these countries, then health risks will continue to originate there. As globalization progresses, the time required for diseases to disperse widely will continue to shrink. Thus, the current mindset of most nations to wait until a problem surfaces or some other nation takes action may mean that new diseases can gain a stronger foothold globally than in the past before the world acts. During the SARS crisis, China began experiencing the disease in November 2002, but the world community did not start mobilizing efforts until March 2003 (*The Economist*, 2003a). A future virus that spreads more easily than SARS could spell graver consequences with a similar delay.

Another global health challenge arises from the aging of the baby-boom generation in the rich industrial countries. This generation will demand life-prolonging and life-enhancing drugs that will divert R&D funds to noncommunicable diseases of old age and away from diseases of greater concern to developing countries. There is an irony in this diversion because this growing elderly population is the most vulnerable to diseases that may come from the developing world. For example, SARS posed the greatest risk of death to older patients. Changing demographics make it even more imperative to maintain the health of the population in developing countries to protect the growing share of elderly in the developed countries.

A widening gap between the rich and poor nations implies that challenges that adhere to a weakest-link or weaker-link technology in the health, governance, environmental, intelligence, and security areas will in the future present greater potential risks to the global community. Increasing inequality has its negative consequences as a more interconnected world must maintain acceptable standards of risks. On the positive side, greater inequality provides an advantage to the world community when it must tackle best-shot and better-shot TPGs. Thus, the overall net influence of enhanced inequality hinges on whether future TPG contingencies abide by aggregator technologies that favor or do not favor inequality. Although this characterization of future TPGs is impossible to predict, an educated guess can be made contingent on how the functional categories of TPGs increase in number. If, for example, health and governance TPGs grow relative to other categories, greater income inequality *will then be a concern* as these categories contain a relatively large portion of weakest-link and weaker-link public goods where inequality poses provision difficulties.

Pollution spillovers will remain a major problem as human pressures on the planet surpass environmental carrying capacities by ever-wider margins. Chapter 10 emphasized that some of these environmental problems provide the right incentives for action, so there are hopeful aspects for environmental protection. On the less optimistic side, the growth of the developing countries will place greater future stresses on earth's ecosystems. These countries' development is, of course, essential for reducing poverty, fostering security, and ameliorating health and other problems. If, therefore, other global challenges are to be addressed, then this development is absolutely necessary. Means for allowing greater economic activities with reduced environmental impact are essential, and industries that provide this managed environmental consequence constitute a growth sector of tomorrow. Unquestionably, regional and global collective action for preserving environmental quality will continue to increase in importance. The world community must address how to meet these contingencies while allocating a greater share of foreign assistance to nonenvironmental TPGs – the inflow of funding from new participants is crucial.

Related to environmental concerns is the increased demand on natural resources, especially in terms of arable land and water. Both of these scarce resources are an increasing worry because of population pressures. I am more optimistic about the arable land problem because agricultural technology has met this challenge throughout the last two centuries and will continue to meet it. The dire prediction of Malthus about famine and the so-called negative checks (for example, diseases) to population growth never really materialized, because Malthus never factored in the tremendous advances that have been achieved in agriculture. Genetic engineering, new farming methods, novel pest control, and other advances will continue to stay ahead of global food needs. Water is more problematic, not so much because of its scarcity as to its unequal distribution. But here too, the challenge can be addressed even though temporary crises may develop; for example, property rights to some international rivers (those flowing through more than one country) will be contentious and may on rare occasion lead to conflict. Humankind has the technologies to redistribute water to where it is needed and to tap underground water reservoirs. An economical means for converting seawater to drinking water will be found when the need is sufficiently great.

A final hot issue will continue to be the threat of states that do not follow the norms of the world community and that acquire WMD to threaten others (Chap. 7). US actions in Iraq exacerbated the problem by exaggerating the exigency and signaling to the world community that it can be expected to be "privileged" by US initiatives in dealing with alleged rogue states. Thus, nations will come to expect a free ride and will position themselves accordingly by doing little to prepare their own forces to address such a contingency. This free-riding mindset then spills over to other global collective action problems and may sour negotiations on other issues involving the United States and the rest of the world community. In many ways, the real global collective concern associated with rogue nations is more basic, but no easier to solve. How to inhibit nations, firms, and individuals from assisting rogue states with their acquisition of WMD and large military forces? On this score, the United States is as guilty as other nations because of its short-sighted support of "convenient" allies (for example, US support of Iraq in its war against Iran or US assistance of the Afghan rebels including bin Laden).

This list of tomorrow's issues is *not* meant to convey the impression that there are crises everywhere and that global challenges spell disaster. I do not hold this viewpoint; in fact, I view many global challenges as self-correcting or exaggerated. The contingencies highlighted here are those where *incentives for self-correcting collective action* are often perverse. For such challenges, nations need to devise some appropriate policies that foster collective action. Those policies that save on transaction costs by utilizing minimalist institutions that harness the participants' self-interested motives work best.

Future of Globalization

The growth of cross-border flows of all kinds will continue. World War I ended the globalization of the late 1800s, but the current round of globalization will expand further. There are still actions that can be instituted not only to increase commodity flows but also to augment input flows, especially in terms of labor, which, in contrast to the earlier era of globalization, remains largely immobile (Rodrik, 1997, 1999). Greater labor mobility may greatly improve social welfare by removing a key impediment to free trade. There are externalities both within and among nations that are created by globalization. Augmented cross-border exchanges have losers (for example, immobile low-skilled labor) and gainers (for example, highly skilled labor) so that the associated uncompensated interdependencies must be addressed for globalization to progress further. Social programs are needed to lessen the inequality impacts of globalization within nations. Globalization makes it more difficult for workers to maintain their benefits owing to more competitive labor markets, where generous benefit packages either create unemployment as in Europe or shift the burden of the packages onto the workers as in the United States (Rodrik, 1997, pp. 16–22). Except through foreign assistance, which faces numerous difficulties (see Chap. 6), there is no way to redress the inequality among nations that follows from globalization.

Increased travel and trade also aid in the transfer of invasive species that can decimate plants and animals in receiving ecosystems. These invasive species represent a leading threat to biodiversity. Efforts to protect biodiversity – an intergenerational GPG – have not been very successful as countries do not have either the means or the interest to protect indigenous species unless benefits, such as ecotourism, figure prominently.

Globalization would progress at a faster pace if the supranational infrastructure were more highly developed to promote financial stability, dispute settlement, banking conventions, and accounting standards. Other necessary functions of this infrastructure are to control organized crime, institute labor standards, improve global health institutions, and augment environmental quality. The world community is addressing some of these needs – for example, the Basle Accord institutes international banking practices to improve bank solvency and reduce financial risks. Further progress in creating a sound supranational infrastructure is an undersupplied GPG.

A final concern for the future of globalization is the world's reliance on the US economy as an engine of growth for the global economy. Such reliance makes for too much instability, where the fortunes of a single economy can greatly influence global GDP growth. A more diversified engine of growth is advisable for stability purposes. The growing economic influence of the European Union, China, and India may eventually offer this diversity.

Concluding Remarks

When preconditions and incentives are right, nations can achieve successful collective action at a regional and even global level. Greater future success follows once these preconditions and incentives are identified and then bolstered through informed policy and institutional design. The purpose of the book has been to identify these factors in the hopes of improving global collective action. Even for those situations where a treaty merely codifies action that the initial ratifiers would have taken anyway, some positive additional action may stem from the ratifiers cajoling others to adopt a higher standard of behavior. The Montreal Protocol and its amendment on the control of ozone-depleting substances is a prime example where preconditions and incentives were right for action; even modest progress grew to significant gains as the initial framers induced almost global adherence to the treaty's stringent regulations. The Kyoto Protocol is equally instructive because of its failure to date. These cases teach us a lot provided that we do not generalize too much and recognize the special circumstances that promote and inhibit global collective action. By examining a host of problems from diverse applications, I have tried to provide this lesson.

Technology, trade, and progress will continue to make political borders more porous. Though nations will maintain the artificial distinction of the nation-state, cross-border flows and the need for collective action to manage their consequences will grow in importance. The issues raised and elucidated in this book are essential for understanding how nations interact today and tomorrow.

References

Akerlof, George A. (1970), "The Market for 'Lemons': Quality Uncertainty and the Market Mechanism," *Quarterly Journal of Economics*, 84(3), 488–500.

Alcamo, Joseph M. and Eliodora Runca (1986), "Some Technical Dimensions of Transboundary Air Pollution," in Cees Flinterman, Barbara Kwiatkowska, and Johan G. Lammers (eds.), *Transboundary Air Pollution: International Legal Aspects of the Cooperation of States* (Dordecht: Martinus Nijhoff), 1–17.

Alexander, Yonah, Marjorie Ann Browne, and Allan S. Nanes (1979), *Control of Terrorism: International Documents* (New York: Crane Russak).

Alexander, Yonah and Dennis Pluchinsky (1992), *Europe's Red Terrorists: The Fighting Communist Organizations* (London: Frank Cass).

Anderson, Roy M. and Robert M. May (1991), *Infectious Diseases of Humans: Dynamics and Control* (Oxford: Oxford University Press).

Anderton, Charles H. (2000), "An Insecure Economy under Ratio and Logistic Conflict Technologies," *Journal of Conflict Resolution*, 44(6), 822–37.

Anderton, Charles H., Roxanne A. Anderton, and John R. Carter (1999), "Economic Activity in the Shadow of Conflict," *Economic Inquiry*, 37(1), 166–79.

Andreoni, James (1988), "Privately Provided Public Goods in a Large Economy: The Limits of Altruism," *Journal of Public Economics*, 35(1), 57–73.

Andreoni, James and Martin C. McGuire (1993), "Identifying the Free Riders: A Simple Algorithm for Determining Who Will Contribute to a Public Good," *Journal of Public Economics*, 51(3), 447–54.

Arce M., Daniel G. (2001), "Leadership and the Aggregation of International Collective Action," *Oxford Economic Papers*, 53(2), 114–37.

Arce M., Daniel G. and Todd Sandler (2001), "Transnational Public Goods: Strategies and Institutions," *European Journal of Political Economy*, 17(3), 493–516.

Arce M., Daniel G. and Todd Sandler (2002), *Regional Public Goods: Typologies, Provision, Financing, and Development Assistance* (Stockholm: Almqvist and Wiksell International Expert Group on Development Issues, Swedish Ministry for Foreign Affairs).

Arce M., Daniel G. and Todd Sandler (2003), "Health-Promoting Alliances," *European Journal of Political Economy*, 19(3), 355–75.

271

Arhin-Tenkorang, Dyna and Pedro Conceição (2003), "Beyond Communicable Disease Control: Health in the Age of Globalization," in Inge Kaul, Pedro Conceição, Katell Le Goulven, and Ronald U. Mendoza (eds.), *Providing Global Public Goods: Managing Globalization* (New York: Oxford University Press), 484–515.

Arquilla, John and David Ronfeldt (2001), *Networks and Netwars: The Future of Terror, Crime, and Militancy* (Santa Monica, CA: RAND).

Arrow, Kenneth J. (1974), "General Economic Equilibrium: Purpose, Analytic Techniques, Collective Choice," *American Economic Review*, 64(3), 253–72.

Axelrod, Robert (1984), *The Evolution of Cooperation* (New York: Basic Books).

Bagnoli, Mark and Michael McKee (1991), "Voluntary Contribution Games: Efficient Private Provision of Public Goods," *Economic Inquiry*, 29(2), 351–66.

Barrett, Scott A. (1994), "Self-Enforcing International Environmental Agreements," *Oxford Economic Papers*, 46(4), 878–94.

Barrett, Scott A. (1999), "Montreal versus Kyoto: International Cooperation and the Global Environment," in Inge Kaul, Isabelle Grunberg, and Marc A. Stern (eds.), *Global Public Goods: International Cooperation in the 21st Century* (New York: Oxford University Press), 192–213.

Barrett, Scott A. (2002), "Supplying International Public Goods: How Nations Can Cooperate," in Marco Ferroni and Ashoka Mody (eds.), *International Public Goods: Incentives, Measurement, and Financing* (Boston: Kluwer Academic Publishers), 46–79.

Barrett, Scott A. (2003a), *Environment and Statecraft: The Strategy of Environmental Treaty-Making* (New York: Oxford University Press).

Barrett, Scott A. (2003b), "Global Disease Eradication," *Journal of European Economic Association*, 1(2–3), 591–600.

Benedick, Richard E. (1991), *Ozone Diplomacy* (Cambridge, MA: Harvard University Press).

Bergstrom, Theodore C., Lawrence Blume, and Hal Varian (1986), "On the Private Provision of Public Goods," *Journal of Public Economics*, 29(1), 25–49.

Binmore, Ken (1992), *Fun and Games* (Lexington, MA: D.C. Health).

Braunschvig, David, Richard L. Garwin, and Jeremy C. Marwell (2003), "Space Diplomacy," *Foreign Affairs*, 82(4), 156–64.

Breton, Albert (1965), "A Theory of Government Grants," *Canadian Journal of Economics and Political Science*, 31(2), 147–57.

Brophy-Baermann, Bryan and John A. C. Conybeare (1994), "Retaliating against Terrorism: Rational Expectations and the Optimality of Rules versus Discretion," *American Journal of Political Science*, 38(1), 196–210.

Bruce, Neil (1990), "Defense Expenditures by Countries in Allied and Adversarial Relationships," *Defence Economics*, 1(2), 179–95.

Bruce, Neil (2001), *Public Finance and the American Economy*, 2nd Ed. (Reading, MA: Addison-Wesley).

Buchanan, James M. (1965), "An Economic Theory of Clubs," *Economica*, 32(1), 1–14.

Buchholz, Wolfgang, Christian Haslbeck, and Todd Sandler (1998), "When Does Partial Cooperation Pay?" *Finanz Archiv*, 55(1), 1–20.

Buira, Ariel (2003), "The Governance of the International Monetary Fund," in Inge Kaul, Pedro Conceição, Katell Le Goulven, and Ronald U. Mendoza (eds.), *Providing Global Public Goods: Managing Globalization* (New York: Oxford University Press), 225–244.

Burnside, Craig and David Dollar (2000), "Aid, Policies, and Growth," *American Economic Review*, 90(4), 847–68.

Bush, William C. and Lawrence S. Mayer (1974), "Some Implications of Anarchy for the Distribution of Property," *Journal of Economic Theory*, 8(4), 401–12.

Carlsson, J. (1998), "Swedish Aid for Poverty Reduction: A History of Policy and Practice," Working Paper 107, Overseas Development Institute, London, in collaboration with Nordic Africa Institute, Uppsala, Sweden.

Centers for Disease Control (CDC) (2003), "Update on Severe Acute Respiratory Syndrome," available at http://www.cdc.gov/od/oc/media/transcripts/t030414.htm.

Chamberlin, John (1974), "Provision of Collective Goods as a Function of Group Size," *American Political Science Review*, 68(2), 707–16.

Chen, Lincoln C., Tim G. Evans, and Richard A. Cash (1999), "Health as a Global Public Good," in Inge Kaul, Isabelle Grunberg, and Marc A. Stern (eds.), *Global Public Goods: International Cooperation in the 21st Century* (New York: Oxford University Press), 284–304.

Clarke, Edward H. (1971), "Some Aspects of the Demand-Revealing Process," *Public Choice*, 29(supplement), 37–49.

Coase, Ronald H. (1960), "The Problem of Social Cost," *Journal of Law and Economics*, 3(1), 1–44.

Cohen, Linda R. and Roger G. Noll (1986), "Government R&D Programs for Commercializing Space," *American Economic Association Papers and Proceedings*, 76(2), 269–73.

Collier, Paul (1997), "The Failure of Conditionality," in Catherine Gwin and Joan M. Nelson (eds.), *Perspectives on Aid and Development*, Policy Essay No. 22 (Washington, DC: Overseas Development Council), 51–77.

Collier, Paul and Anke Hoeffler (1998), "On the Economic Causes of Civil Wars," *Oxford Economic Papers*, 50(4), 563–73.

Collier, Paul and Anke Hoeffler (2002a), "Greed and Grievance in Civil War," WPS 2002–01, Centre for Study of African Economics, University of Oxford, Oxford, UK.

Collier, Paul and Anke Hoeffler (2002b), "On the Incidence of Civil Wars in Africa," *Journal of Conflict Resolution*, 46(1), 13–28.

Collier, Paul and Nicholas Sambanis (2002), "Understanding Civil War: A New Agenda," *Journal of Conflict Resolution*, 46(1), 3–12.

Collier, Paul, Anke Hoeffler, and Mans Soderbom (2003), "On the Duration of Civil War," unpublished manuscript, University of Oxford, Oxford, UK.

Commission on Macroeconomics and Health (CMH) (2001), "Macro-economics and Health: Investing for Health," available at http://www.cid.harvard.edu/cidcmh/CMHReport.pdf.

Congleton, Roger D. (1992), "Political Institutions and Pollution Control," *Review of Economics and Statistics*, 74(3), 412–21.

Cook, Lisa D. and Jeffrey Sachs (1999), "Regional Public Goods in International Assistance," in Inge Kaul, Isabelle Grunberg, and Marc A. Stern (eds.), *Global Public Goods: International Cooperation in the 21st Century* (New York: Oxford University Press), 436–49.

Cornes, Richard (1993), "Dyke Maintenance and Other Stories: Some Neglected Types of Public Goods," *Quarterly Journal of Economics*, 108(1), 259–71.

Cornes, Richard and Todd Sandler (1981), "Easy Riders, Joint Production, and Collective Action," Working Paper No. 060 in Economics and Econometrics, Australian National University, Canberra.

Cornes, Richard and Todd Sandler (1984), "Easy Riders, Joint Production, and Public Goods," *Economic Journal*, 94(3), 580–98.

Cornes, Richard and Todd Sandler (1985), "The Simple Analytics of Pure Public Good Provision," *Economica*, 52(1), 103–16.

Cornes, Richard and Todd Sandler (1994), "The Comparative Static Properties of the Impure Public Good Model," *Journal of Public Economics*, 54(3), 403–21.

Cornes, Richard and Todd Sandler (1996), *The Theory of Externalities, Public Goods, and Club Goods*, 2nd Edition (Cambridge: Cambridge University Press).

Dando, Malcolm (1994), *Biological Warfare in the 21st Century* (London: Brassey's).

de Gruijl, Frank R. (1995), "Impacts of a Projected Depletion of the Ozone Layer," *Consequences: The Nature & Implications of Environmental Change*, 1(2), 13–21.

Devlin, Robert and Antoni Estevadeordal (2001), "What's New in the New Regionalism in the Americas? Integration and Regional Programs Department," Working Paper No. 6, Inter-American Development Bank, Washington, DC.

Dodds, Klaus (1998), "The Geopolitics of Regionalism: The Valdivia Group and Southern Hemispheric Environmental Co-Operation," *Third World Quarterly*, 19(4), 725–43.

Dorn, William (1998), "Regional Peacekeeping Is Not the Way," *Peacekeeping and International Relations*, 27(4–5), 3–4.

Durch, William J. (1993), "Paying the Tab: Financial Crisis," in William J. Durch (ed.), *The Evolution of UN Peacekeeping: Case Studies and Cooperative Analysis* (New York: St. Martin's Press), 39–55.

Easterly, William (2002), *The Elusive Quest for Growth: Economists' Adventures and Misadventures in the Tropics* (Cambridge, MA: The MIT Press).

Easterly, William and Ross Levine (1998), "Troubles with the Neighbors: Africa's Problem, Africa's Opportunity," *Journal of African Economies*, 7(1), 120–42.

The Economist (2002a), "For 80 Cents More," *The Economist*, 364(8286), 17 August, 20–2.

The Economist (2002b), "Hope for the Best. Prepare for the Worst," *The Economist*, 364(8281), 13 July, 65–8.

The Economist (2003a), "China Wakes Up," *The Economist*, 367(8321), 18–19.

The Economist (2003b), "The Global Menace of Local Strife," *The Economist*, 367(8325), 23–5.

The Economist (2003c), "GPS and Galileo: Navigating the Future," *The Economist*, 367(8330), 66.

The Economist (2003d), "Unmanned Aerial Vehicles," *The Economist*, 368(8331), 70–1.

Edelson, Burton I. (1977), "Global Satellite Communications," *Scientific American*, 236(2), 58–73.

Elbadawi, Ibrahim A. and Njuguna Ndung'u (2000), "External Indebtedness, Growth, and Investment in Conflict and Post-Conflict African Countries," unpublished manuscript, The World Bank, Washington, DC.

Elbadawi, Ibrahim A. and Nicholas Sambanis (2001), "External Interventions and the Duration of Civil Wars," unpublished manuscript, The World Bank, Washington, DC.

Elbadawi, Ibrahim A. and Nicholas Sambanis (2002), "How Much War Will We See? Explaining the Prevalence of Civil War," *Journal of Conflict Resolution*, 46(3), 307–34.

Eliassen, Anton and Jørgen Saltbones (1983), "Modelling of Long-Range Transport of Sulphur over Europe: A Two-Year Model Run and Some Model Experiments," *Atmospheric Environment*, 17(8), 1457–73.

Enders, Walter and Todd Sandler (1993), "The Effectiveness of Antiterrorism Policies: A Vector-Autoregression-Intervention Analysis," *American Political Science Review*, 87(4), 829–44.

Enders, Walter and Todd Sandler (1995), "Terrorism: Theory and Applications," in Keith Hartley and Todd Sandler (eds.), *Handbook of Defense Economics, Vol. I* (Amsterdam: North-Holland), 213–49.

Enders, Walter and Todd Sandler (1996), "Terrorism and Foreign Direct Investment in Spain and Greece," *Kyklos*, 49(3), 331–52.

Enders, Walter and Todd Sandler (1999), "Transnational Terrorism in the Post-Cold War Era," *International Studies Quarterly*, 43(1), 145–61.

Enders, Walter and Todd Sandler (2000), "Is Transnational Terrorism Becoming More Threatening? A Time-Series Investigation," *Journal of Conflict Resolution*, 44(3), 307–32.

Enders, Walter and Todd Sandler (forthcoming), "What Do We Know about the Substitution Effect in Transnational Terrorism?," in Andrew Silke and G. Ilardi (eds.), *Researching Terrorism: Trends, Achievements, Failures* (Ilford, UK: Frank Cass).

Enders, Walter, Gerald F. Parise, and Todd Sandler (1992), "A Time-Series Analysis of Transnational Terrorism: Trends and Cycles," *Defence Economics*, 3(4), 305–20.

Enders, Walter, Todd Sandler, and Jon Cauley (1990a), "UN Conventions, Technology and Retaliation in the Fight against Terrorism: An Econometric Evaluation," *Terrorism and Political Violence*, 2(1), 83–105.

Enders, Walter, Todd Sandler, and Jon Cauley (1990b), "Assessing the Impact of Terrorist-Thwarting Policies: An Intervention Time Series Approach," *Defence Economics*, 2(1), 1–18.

Enders, Walter, Todd Sandler, and Gerald F. Parise (1992), "An Econometric Analysis of the Impact of Terrorism on Tourism," *Kyklos*, 45(4), 531–54.

English, Robert D. (2000), *Russia and the Idea of the West: Gorbachev, Intellectuals and the End of the Cold War* (New York: Columbia University Press).

Environmental Protection Agency (EPA) (1987a), *Assessing the Risks of Trace Gases That Can Modify the Stratosphere*, 7 vols. (Washington, DC: EPA).

Environmental Protection Agency (EPA) (1987b), *Regulatory Impact Analysis: Protection of Stratospheric Ozone*, 3 vols. (Washington, DC: EPA).

European Space Agency (ESA) (2003), website at http://www.esa.int/export/esaLA/ASEKLU0TCNC_launchers_2.html.

Federal American Scientists (2003), "Chinese Space Launch Vehicles," available at http://www.fas.org/spp/guide/china/launch/cz-2c.htm.

Federal Aviation Administration (FAA) (2003), *2003 US Commercial Space Transportation Developments and Concepts: Vehicles, Technologies, and Spaceports* (Washington, DC: FAA) and available at http://ast.faa.gov/files/pdf/newtech03_final.pdf.

Ferroni, Marco (2002), "Regional Public Goods in Official Development Assistance," in Marco Ferroni and Ashoka Mody (eds.), *International Public Goods: Incentives, Measurement, and Financing* (Boston: Kluwer Academic Publishers), 157–86.

Ferroni, Marco and Ashoka Mody (eds.) (2002), *International Public Goods: Incentives, Measurement, and Financing* (Boston: Kluwer Academic Publishers).

Finus, Michael and Sigve Tjøtta (2003), "The Oslo Protocol and Sulfur Reduction: The Great Leap Forward?" *Journal of Public Economics*, 87(9–10), 2031–48.

Fridtjof Nansen Institute (1996), *Green Globe Yearbook of International Cooperation on Environment and Development 1996* (New York: Oxford University Press).

Gehrels, Tom (1996), "Collisions with Comets and Asteroids," *Scientific American*, 274(3), 49–54.

Gleditsch, Nils Petter, Peter Wallensteen, Mikael Eriksson, Margareta Sollenberg, and Håvard Strand (2002), "Armed Conflict 1946–2001: A New Dataset," *Journal of Peace Research*, 39(5), 615–37.

Global Fund (2003), website at http://www.globalfundatm.org.

Gompert, David C. and E. Stephen Larrabee (eds.) (1997), *America and Europe: A Partnership for a New Era* (Cambridge: Cambridge University Press).

Green, Jerry R. and Jean-Jacques Laffont (1977), "Characterization of Satisfactory Mechanisms for the Revelation of Preferences for Public Good," *Econometrica*, 45(2), 427–38.

Grossman, Herschel I. (1991), "A General Equilibrium Model of Insurrections," *American Economic Review*, 81(4), 912–21.

Grossman, Herschel I. (1992), "Foreign Aid and Insurrections," *Defence Economics*, 3(4), 275–88.

Grossman, Herschel I. (1994), "Production, Appropriation, and Land Reform," *American Economic Review*, 84(3), 705–12.

Grossman, Herschel I. (1995), "Insurrections," in Keith Hartley and Todd Sandler (eds.), *Handbook of Defense Economics*, Vol. 1 (Amsterdam: North-Holland), 191–212.

Grossman, Herschel I. (1999), "Kleptocracy and Revolutions," *Oxford Economic Papers*, 51(2), 267–83.

Hardin, Russell (1982), *Collective Action* (Baltimore, MD: Johns Hopkins University).

Hardin, Russell (1995), *One for All: The Logic of Group Conflict* (Princeton, NJ: Princeton University Press).

Hartley, Keith and Todd Sandler (2003), "The Future of the Defence Firm," *Kyklos*, 56(3), 361–80.

Heckathorn, Douglas D. (1989), "Collective Action and the Second-Order Free-Rider Problem," *Rationality and Society*, 1(1), 78–100.

Held, David and Anthony McGrew (2003), "Political Globalization: Trends and Choices," in Inge Kaul, Pedro Conceição, Katell Le Goulven, and Ronald U. Mendoza (eds.), *Providing Global Public Goods: Managing Globalization* (New York: Oxford University Press), 185–99.

Hettne, B., A. Inotai, and O. Sunkel (eds.) (1999), *Globalism and the New Regionalism* (London: Macmillan).

Hill, Stephen M. and Shahin P. Malik (1996), *Peacekeeping and the United Nations* (Aldershot, UK: Dartmouth).

Hirshleifer, Jack (1983), "From Weakest-Link to Best-Shot: The Voluntary Provision of Public Goods," *Public Choice*, 41(3), 371–86.

Hirshleifer, Jack (1991), "The Paradox of Power," *Economics and Politics*, 3(3), 177–200.

Hoffman, Bruce (1997), "The Confluence of International and Domestic Trends in Terrorism," *Terrorism and Political Violence*, 9(2), 1–15.

Hoffman, Bruce (1998), *Inside Terrorism* (New York: Columbia University Press).

Hoffman, Bruce (2002), "Rethinking Terrorism and Counterterrorism Since 9/11," *Studies in Conflict & Terrorism*, 25(5), 303–16.

Im, Eric I., Jon Cauley, and Todd Sandler (1987), "Cycles and Substitutions in Terrorist Activities: A Spectral Approach," *Kyklos*, 40(2), 238–55.

Intergovernmental Panel on Climate Change (IPCC) (1990), *Climate Change: The IPCC Scientific Assessment* (Geneva: World Meteorological Organization and UN Environmental Program).

International Institute for Strategic Studies (IISS) (2002), *The Military Balance 2002–2003* (London: Oxford University Press for IISS).

International Telecommunication Satellite Organization (INTELSAT) (1973), *Agreement Relating to the International Telecommunications Satellite Organization "INTELSAT"* (Washington, DC: INTELSAT).

INTELSAT (1993), "Fact Sheet" Washington, DC: INTELSAT.

INTELSAT (1995), *INTELSAT in the '90s* (Washington, DC: INTELSAT).

INTELSAT (2003), website at http://www.intelsat.com.

Isaac, R. Mark, Kenneth F. McCue, and Charles R. Plott (1985), "Public Goods Provision in an Experimental Environment," *Journal of Public Economics*, 26(1), 51–74.

Isaac, R. Mark, James M. Walker, and Susan H. Thomas (1984), "Divergent Evidence on Free Riding: An Experimental Examination of Possible Explanations," *Public Choice*, 43(2), 113–49.

Itaya, Jun-ichi, David de Meza, and Gareth D. Myles (1997), "In Praise of Inequality: Public Good Provision and Income Distribution," *Economic Letters*, 57(3), 289–96.

Kammler, Hans (1997), "Not for Security Only: The Demand for International Status and Defence Expenditure; An Introduction," *Defence and Peace Economics*, 8(1), 1–16.

Kanbur, Ravi (2002), "IFI's and IPG's: Operational Implications for the World Bank," Working Paper WP 2002–17, Department of Applied Economics and Management, Cornell University, Ithaca, NY.

Kanbur, Ravi, Todd Sandler, and Kevin Morrison (1999), *The Future of Development Assistance: Common Pools and International Public Goods*, Policy Essay No. 25 (Washington, DC: Overseas Development Council).

Kaul, Inge and Katell Le Goulven (2003), "Financing Global Public Goods: A New Frontier of Public Finance," in Inge Kaul, Pedro Conceição, Katell Le Goulven, and Ronald U. Mendoza (eds.), *Providing Global Public Goods: Managing Globalization* (New York: Oxford University Press), 329–70.

Kaul, Inge, Pedro Conceição, Katell Le Goulven, and Ronald U. Mendoza (eds.) (2003), *Providing Global Public Goods: Managing Globalization* (New York: Oxford University Press).

Kaul, Inge, Isabelle Grunberg, and Marc A. Stern (eds.) (1999), *Global Public Goods: International Cooperation in the 21st Century* (New York: Oxford University Press).

Khanna, Jyoti and Todd Sandler (1997), "Conscription, Peacekeeping and Foreign Assistance: NATO Burden Sharing in the Post-Cold War Era," *Defence and Peace Economics*, 8(1), 101–22.

Khanna, Jyoti, Wallace E. Huffman, and Todd Sandler (1994), "Agricultural Research Expenditures in the US: A Public Goods Perspective," *Review of Economics and Statistics*, 76(2), 267–77.

Khanna, Jyoti, Todd Sandler, and Hirofumi Shimizu (1998), "Sharing the Financial Burden for UN and NATO Peacekeeping: 1976–1996," *Journal of Conflict Resolution*, 42(2), 176–95.

Khanna, Jyoti, Todd Sandler, and Hirofumi Shimizu (1999), "Demand for UN Peacekeeping, 1975–1996," *Kyklos*, 52(3), 345–68.

Kirby, Stephen and Nick Hooper (eds.) (1991), *The Cost of Peace: Assessing Europe's Security Options* (Chur, Switzerland: Harwood Academic Publishers).

Klare, Michael T. (1995), *Rogue States and Nuclear Outlaws: America's Search for a New Foreign Policy* (New York: Hill and Wang).

Klare, Michael T. (2001), *Resource Wars: The New Landscape of Global Conflict* (New York: Metropolitan Books).

Ko, Il-Dong, Harvey Lapan, and Todd Sandler (1992), "Controlling Stock Externalities: Flexible versus Inflexible Pigovian Corrections," *European Economic Review*, 36(6), 1263–76.

Kremer, Michael (2002), "Pharmaceuticals and the Developing World," *Journal of Economic Perspectives*, 16(4), 67–90.

Krueger, Alan B. and Jitka Maleckova (2002), "Education, Poverty, Political Violence and Terrorism: Is There a Causal Connection?," National Bureau of Economic Research Working Paper 9074, Cambridge, MA.

Kuran, Timur (1989), "Sparks and Prairie Fires: A Theory of Unanticipated Political Revolution," *Public Choice*, 61(1), 41–74.

Kuran, Timur (1991a), "The East European Revolution of 1989: Is It Surprising That We Were Surprised?," *American Economic Review*, 81(2), 121–5.

Kuran, Timur (1991b), "Now Out of Never: The Element of Surprise in the East European Revolution of 1989," *World Politics*, 44(1), 7–48.

Kuznets, Simon (1955), "Economic Growth and Income Inequality," *American Economic Review*, 45(1), 1–28.

The Lancet (editorial) (2000), "Donor Responsibilities in Rolling Back Malaria," *The Lancet*, 356(9229), 521.

Lapan, Harvey E. and Todd Sandler (1988), "To Bargain or Not to Bargain: That Is the Question," *American Economic Association Papers and Proceedings*, 78(2), 16–20.

Lapan, Harvey E. and Todd Sandler (1993), "Terrorism and Signalling," *European Journal of Political Economy*, 9(3), 383–97.

Levy, David H., Eugene M. Shoemaker, and Carolyn S. Shoemaker (1995), "Comet Shoemaker–Levy 9 Meets Jupiter," *Scientific American*, 273(2), 85–91.

Lichbach, Mark I. (1996), *The Cooperator's Dilemma* (Ann Arbor, MI: University of Michigan Press).

Macauley, Molly K. (1998), "Allocation of Orbit and Spectrum Resources for Regional Communications: What's at Stake?," *Journal of Law and Economics*, 41(2) (Part 2), 737–64.

Mansfield, Edward D. and Helen V. Milner (1999), "The New Wave of Regionalism," *International Organization*, 53(3), 589–627.

McGuire, Martin C. (1974), "Group Size, Group Homogeneity, and the Aggregate Provision of a Pure Public Good under Cournot Behavior," *Public Choice*, 18(1), 107–26.

McGuire, Martin C. and Mancur Olson (1996), "The Economics of Autocracy and Majority Rule," *Journal of Economic Literature*, 34(1), 72–96.

Mickolus, Edward F. (1980), *Transnational Terrorism: A Chronology of Events 1968–1979* (Westport, CT: Greenwood Press).

Mickolus, Edward F., Todd Sandler, and Jean M. Murdock (1989), *International Terrorism in the 1980s: A Chronology of Events*, 2 vols. (Ames, IA: Iowa State University Press).

Mickolus, Edward F., Todd Sandler, Jean M. Murdock, and Peter Flemming (1989), *International Terrorism: Attributes of Terrorist Events, 1978–1987* (ITERATE 3) (Dunn Loring, VA: Vinyard Software).

Mickolus, Edward F., Todd Sandler, Jean M. Murdock, and Peter Flemming (1993), *International Terrorism: Attributes of Terrorist Events, 1988–1991* (ITERATE 4) (Dunn Loring, VA: Vinyard Software).

Mills, Susan R. (1990), "The Financing of UN Peacekeeping Operations: The Need for a Sound Financial Basis," in Indar Jit Rikhye and Kjell Skjelsback (eds.), *The United Nations and Peacekeeping: Results, Limitations and Prospects: The Lessons of 40 Years of Experience* (Houndmills, UK: Macmillan), 91–110.

Morrisette, Peter M., Joel Darmstadter, Andrew J. Plantiga, and Michael A. Toman (1990), "Lessons from Other International Agreements for a Global CO_2 Accord," Discussion Paper ENR91–02, Resources for the Future, Washington, DC.

Most, Benjamin A. and Harvey Starr (1980), "Diffusion, Reinforcement, Geopolitics, and the Spread of War," *American Political Science Review*, 74(4), 932–46.

Murdoch, James and Todd Sandler (1997), "The Voluntary Provision of a Pure Public Good: The Case of Reduced CFC Emissions and the Montreal Protocol," *Journal of Public Economics*, 63(2), 331–49.

Murdoch, James C. and Todd Sandler (2002a), "Economic Growth, Civil Wars and Spatial Spillovers," *Journal of Conflict Resolution*, 46(1), 91–110.

Murdoch, James C. and Todd Sandler (2002b), "Civil Wars and Economic Growth: A Regional Comparison," *Defence and Peace Economics*, 13(6), 451–64.

Murdoch, James C. and Todd Sandler (2004), "Civil Wars and Economic Growth: Spatial Dispersion," *American Journal of Political Science*, 48(1), 137–50.

Murdoch, James C., Todd Sandler, and Keith Sargent (1994), "A Tale of Two Collectives: Sulfur versus Nitrogen Oxides Emission Reduction in Europe," Institute for Policy Reform Working Paper No. IPR98, Institute for Policy Reform, Washington, DC.

Murdoch, James C., Todd Sandler, and Keith Sargent (1997), "A Tale of Two Collectives: Sulphur versus Nitrogen Oxides Emission Reduction in Europe," *Economica*, 64(2), 281–301.

Murdoch, James C., Todd Sandler, and Wim P. M. Vijverberg (2003), "The Participation Decision versus the Level of Participation in an Environmental Treaty: A Spatial Probit Analysis," *Journal of Public Economics*, 87(2), 337–62.

National Aeronautics and Space Administration (NASA) (2003), "Space Station Benefits," available at http://spaceflight.nasa.gov/station/benefits/index.html.

National Space Development Agency of Japan (NASDA) (2003), website at http:www.nasda.go.jp/projects/rocket-result_e.html.

NATO Press Release (2002), "Financial and Economic Data Relating to NATO Defence," M-DPC-2(2002)139, 20 December, NATO, Brussels.

Nordhaus, William D. (1991), "The Cost of Slowing Climate Change: A Survey," Cowles Foundation Paper No. 775, Yale University, New Haven, CT.

North, Douglass C. (1990), *Institutions, Institutional Change and Economic Performance* (Cambridge: Cambridge University Press).

Oklahoma City National Memorial Institute for the Prevention of Terrorism (2002), website at http://db.mipt.org.

Olson, Mancur (1965), *The Logic of Collective Action* (Cambridge, MA: Harvard University Press).

Olson, Mancur (1969), "The Principle of 'Fiscal Equivalence': The Division of Responsibilities among Different Levels of Government," *American Economic Review*, 59(2), 479–87.

Olson, Mancur (1991), "Why Hasn't Saddam Hussein Been Assassinated?," *The Wall Street Journal*, February 22, editorial page.

Olson, Mancur (1993), "Dictatorship, Democracy, and Development," *American Political Science Review*, 87(3), 567–76.

Olson, Mancur and Richard Zeckhauser (1966), "An Economic Theory of Alliances," *Review of Economics and Statistics*, 48(3), 266–79.

Olson, Mancur and Richard Zeckhauser (1967), "Collective Goods, Comparative Advantage, and Alliance Efficiency," in Roland McKean (ed.), *Issues of Defense Economics* (New York: National Bureau of Economic Research), 25–48.

O'Neill, Gerald K. (1977), *The High Frontier: Human Colonies in Space* (New York: William Morrow & Co.).

Organization for Economic Cooperation and Development (OECD) (1990), *Control Strategies for Photochemical Oxidants across Europe* (Paris: OECD).

Ostrom, Elinor, Roy Gardner, and James Walker (1994), *Rules, Games, and Common-Pool Resources* (Ann Arbor, MI: University of Michigan Press).

Overgaard, Per B. (1994), "Terrorist Attacks as a Signal of Resources," *Journal of Conflict Resolution*, 38(3), 452–78.

Padoan, P. C. (1997), "Regional Agreements as Clubs: The European Case," in Edward D. Mansfield and Helen V. Milner (eds.), *The Political Economy of Regionalism* (Cambridge: Cambridge University Press), 107–33.

Palfrey, Thomas R. and Howard Rosenthal (1984), "Participation and the Provision of Discrete Public Goods: A Strategic Analysis," *Journal of Public Economics*, 24(2), 171–93.

Palin, Roger H. (1995), *Multinational Military Forces: Problems and Prospects*, Adelphi Paper 294, International Institute for Strategic Studies (Oxford: Oxford University Press).

Pearl, M. A. (1987), "Terrorism – Historical Perspective on US Congressional Action," *Terrorism*, 10(2), 139–43.

Pearson, Lester P. (1969), *Partners in Development: Report of the Commission on International Development* (Westport, CT: Paeger).

Pike, John (2002), "The Military Uses of Outer Space," in Stockholm International Peace Research Institute (SIPRI) (ed.), *SIPRI Yearbook 2002: Armaments, Disarmament and International Security* (New York: Oxford University Press), 613–64.

President of the United States (2003), website at http://www.whitehouse.gov.

Quillen, Chris (2002a), "A Historical Analysis of Mass Casualty Bombers," *Studies in Conflict & Terrorism*, 25(2), 279–92.

Quillen, Chris (2002b), "Mass Casualty Bombings Chronology," *Studies in Conflict & Terrorism*, 25(5), 293–302.

Raffer, Kunibert (1999), "ODA and Global Public Goods: A Trend Analysis of Past and Present Spending Patterns," Office of Development Studies Background Paper, United Nations Development Program, New York.

Ratner, Steve R. (1995), *The New UN Peacekeeping: Building Peace in Lands of Conflict after the Cold War* (New York: St. Martin's Press).

Reinicke, Wolfgang H. (1998), *Global Public Policy: Governing Without Government?* (Washington, DC: The Brookings Institute).

Reuveny, Rafael (2002), "Economic Growth, Environmental Scarcity, and Conflict," *Global Environmental Politics*, 2(1), 83–110.

Rodrik, Dani (1997), *Has Globalization Gone Too Far?* (Washington, DC: Institute for International Economics).

Rodrik, Dani (1999), *The New Global Economy and Developing Countries: Making Openness Work*, Policy Essay No. 24 (Washington, DC: Overseas Development Council).

Rostow, W. W. (1960), *The Stages of Economic Growth: A Non-Communist Manifesto* (Cambridge: Cambridge University Press).

Runge, C. Ford (1984), "Institutions and the Free Rider: The Assurance Problem in Collective Action," *Journal of Politics*, 46(1), 154–81.

Russian Space Web (2003), "Rockets: Launchers," available at http://www.russianspaceweb.com/rockets_launchers.html.

Sandler, Todd (1977), "Impurity of Defense: An Application to the Economics of Alliances," *Kyklos*, 30(3), 443–60.

Sandler, Todd (1978), "Interregional and Intergenerational Spillover Awareness," *Scottish Journal of Political Economy*, 25(3), 273–84.

Sandler, Todd (1992), *Collective Action: Theory and Applications* (Ann Arbor, MI: University of Michigan Press).

Sandler, Todd (1993), "The Economic Theory of Alliances," *Journal of Conflict Resolution*, 37(3), 446–83.

Sandler, Todd (1997), *Global Challenges: An Approach to Environmental, Political, and Economic Problems* (Cambridge: Cambridge University Press).

Sandler, Todd (1998), "Global and Regional Public Goods: A Prognosis for Collective Action," *Fiscal Studies*, 19(3), 221–47.

Sandler, Todd (1999), "Intergenerational Public Goods: Strategies, Efficiency, and Institutions," in Inge Kaul, Isabelle Grunberg, and Marc A. Stern (eds.), *Global Public Goods: International Cooperation in the 21st Century* (New York: Oxford University Press), 20–50.

Sandler, Todd (2001), *Economic Concepts for the Social Sciences* (Cambridge: Cambridge University Press).

Sandler, Todd (2003a), "Global Challenges and the Need for Supranational Structures," in Omar Azfar and Charles Cadwell (eds.), *Market-Augmenting Government: The Institutional Foundations for Prosperity* (Ann Arbor, MI: University of Michigan Press), 269–94.

Sandler, Todd (2003b), "Assessing the Optimal Provision of Public Goods: In Search of the Holy Grail," in Inge Kaul, Pedro Conceição, Katell Le Goulven, and Ronald U. Mendoza (eds.), *Providing Global Public Goods: Managing Globalization* (New York: Oxford University Press), 131–51.

Sandler, Todd (forthcoming), "Regional Public Goods: Demands and Institutions," in Antoni Estevadeordal, Brian Frantz, and Tam Nguyen (eds.), *Regional Responses to Globalization: Regional Public Goods and Development Assistance* (Washington, DC: Inter-American Development Bank and Asian Development Bank).

Sandler, Todd and Daniel G. Arce M. (2002), "A Conceptual Framework for Understanding Global and Transnational Public Goods for Health," *Fiscal Studies*, 23(2), 195–222.

Sandler, Todd and Daniel G. Arce M. (2003), "Pure Public Goods versus Commons: Benefit–Cost Duality," *Land Economics*, 79(3), 355–68.

Sandler, Todd and John F. Forbes (1980), "Burden Sharing, Strategy, and the Design of NATO," *Economic Inquiry*, 18(3), 425–44.

Sandler, Todd and Keith Hartley (1999), *The Political Economy of NATO: Past, Present, and into the 21st Century* (Cambridge: Cambridge University Press).

Sandler, Todd and Keith Hartley (2001), "Economics of Alliances: The Lessons for Collective Action," *Journal of Economic Literature*, 39(3), 869–96.

Sandler, Todd and Harvey E. Lapan (1988), "The Calculus of Dissent: An Analysis of Terrorists' Choice of Targets," *Synthese*, 76(2), 245–61.

Sandler, Todd and James C. Murdoch (2000), "On Sharing NATO Defence Burdens in the 1990s and Beyond," *Fiscal Studies*, 21(3), 297–327.

Sandler, Todd and John W. Posnett (1991), "The Private Provision of Public Goods: A Perspective on Neutrality," *Public Finance Quarterly*, 19(1), 22–42.

Sandler, Todd and William Schulze (1981), "The Economics of Outer Space," *Natural Resources Journal*, 21(2), 371–93.

Sandler, Todd and William Schulze (1985), "Outer Space: The New Market Frontier," *Economic Affairs*, 5(4), 6–10.

Sandler, Todd and Kevin Siqueira (2003), "Global Terrorism: Deterrence versus Preemption," unpublished manuscript, University of Southern California, Los Angeles, CA.

Sandler, Todd and John Tschirhart (1980), "The Economic Theory of Clubs: An Evaluative Survey," *Journal of Economic Literature*, 18(4), 1481–1521.

Sandler, Todd and John Tschirhart (1997), "Club Theory: Thirty Years Later," *Public Choice*, 93(3–4), 335–55.

Sandnes, Hilde (1993), *Calculated Budgets for Airborne Acidifying Components in Europe, 1985, 1987, 1989, 1990, 1991, and 1992*, EMEP/MSC-W Report 1/93 (Oslo: Norske Meterologiske Institutt).

Schelling, Thomas C. (1992), "Some Economics of Global Warming," *American Economic Review*, 82(1), 1–14.

Sen, Amartya K. (1967), "Isolation, Assurance, and the Social Rate of Discount," *Quarterly Journal of Economics*, 81(1), 112–24.

Shibata, Hirofumi (1971), "A Bargaining Model of Pure Theory of Public Expenditure," *Journal of Political Economy*, 79(1), 1–29.

Shimizu, Hirofumi and Todd Sandler (2002), "Peacekeeping and Burden-Sharing, 1994–2000," *Journal of Peace Research*, 39(6), 651–68.

Singer, J. David and Melvin Small (1993), *Correlates of War Project: International and Civil War Data, 1816–1992* (ICPSR 9905), Interuniversity Consortium of Political Science Research, Ann Arbor, MI.

Siverson, Randolph M. and Harvey Starr (1990), "Opportunity, Willingness, and the Diffusion of War," *American Political Science Review*, 84(1), 47–67.

Skaperdas, Stergios (1991), "Conflict and Attitudes toward Risk," *American Economic Review*, 81(2), 160–4.

Skyrms, Brian (1996), *Evolution of the Social Contract* (Cambridge: Cambridge University Press).

Solow, Robert M. (1957), "Technical Change and the Aggregate Production Function," *Review of Economics and Statistics*, 39(3), 312–20.

Space.com (2003), "Japan Rethinks Its Space Program," available at http://www.space.com/missionlaunches/japan_space_030405.html.

Stålgren, Patrick (2000), "Regional Public Goods and the Future of International Development Cooperation. A Review of the Literature," Working Paper 2000:2, Expert Group on Development Issues, Ministry for Foreign Affairs, Stockholm, Sweden.

Starr, Harvey and Benjamin A. Most (1983), "Contagion and Border Effects on Contemporary African Conflict," *Comparative Political Studies*, 16(1), 92–117.

Starr, Ross M. (1997), *General Equilibrium Theory: An Introduction* (Cambridge: Cambridge University Press).

Stiglitz, Joseph E. (2000), "The Contributions of the Economics of Information to Twentieth Century Economics," *Quarterly Journal of Economics*, 105(4), 1441–78.

Stiglitz, Joseph E. (2002a), "Information and the Change in Paradigm in Economics," *American Economic Review*, 92(3), 460–501.

Stiglitz, Joseph E. (2002b), *Globalization and Its Discontents* (New York: W.W. Norton).

Stockholm International Peace Research Institute (SIPRI) (2000), *SIPRI Yearbook 2000: Armaments, Disarmament and International Security* (New York: Oxford University Press).

Stockholm International Peace Research Institute (SIPRI) (2002), *SIPRI Yearbook 2002: Armaments, Disarmament and International Security* (Oxford: Oxford University Press).

Stolarski, Richard S. (1988), "The Antarctic Ozone Hole," *Scientific American*, 258(1), 30–6.

Terrell, Stanley S. (2002), "The HIV/AIDS Problem in Central America Contained and Controlled," presented at Inter-American Development Bank's Conference on Regional Public Goods & Regional Development Assistance, November 6–7, 2002, Washington, DC.

Toman, Michael A. and Molly K. Macauley (1989), "No Free Launch: Efficient Space Transportation Pricing," *Land Economics*, 65(2), 91–9.

Toon, Owen R. and Richard P. Turco (1991), "Polar Stratospheric Clouds and Ozone Depletion," *Scientific American*, 264(1), 68–74.

Tullock, Gordon (1974), *The Social Dilemma: The Economics of War and Revolution* (Blacksburg, VA: University Publications).

United Nations (2003), website at http://www.un.org/Depts/dpko/dpko/home.shtml.

United Nations Development Program (1999), *Human Development Report 1999* (New York: Oxford University Press).

United Nations Environment Program (UNEP) (1991), *Selected Multilateral Treaties in the Field of the Environment*, Vol. 2 (Cambridge: Grotius Publications).

United Nations Environment Program (UNEP) (2003), website at http://www.unep.ch/ozone/ratif.shtml.

United Nations High-Level Panel (2001), "Recommendations of the High-Level Panel on Financing Development," United Nations, New York.

United Nations Population Fund (1994), *The State of World Population 1994: Choices and Responsibilities* (New York: UN Population Fund).

United States Congressional Budget Office (1990), *Carbon Charges as a Response to Global Warming: The Effects of Taxing Fossil Fuels* (Washington, DC: Congressional Budget Office).

United States Congressional Budget Office (1997), "The Role of Foreign Aid in Development," Congressional Budget Office Study, Washington, DC.

United States Department of State (various years), *Patterns of Global Terrorism* (Washington, DC: US Department of State).

van de Walle, Nicolas and Timothy A. Johnston (1996), *Improving Aid to Africa*, Policy Essay No. 21 (Washington, DC: Overseas Development Council).

Vicary, Simon (1990), "Transfers and the Weakest-Link: An Extension of Hirshleifer's Analysis," *Journal of Public Economics*, 43(3), 375–94.

Vicary, Simon and Todd Sandler (2002), "Weakest-Link Public Goods: Giving In-Kind or Transferring Money," *European Economic Review*, 46(8), 1501–20.

Warr, Peter G. (1983), "The Private Provision of a Public Good Is Independent of the Distribution of Income," *Economics Letters*, 13(2), 207–11.

Wihlborg, Clas G. and Per Magnus Wijkman (1981), "Outer Space Resources in Efficient and Equitable Use: New Frontiers for Old Principles," *Journal of Law and Economics*, 24(1), 23–43.

Wilkinson, Paul (1986), *Terrorism and the Liberal State*, rev. ed. (London: Macmillan).

Wilkinson, Paul (2001), *Terrorism Versus Democracy: The Liberal State Response* (London: Frank Cass).

Wilkinson, Paul (2002), "Editorial," *Terrorism and Political Violence*, 13(4), vii–x.

Willem te Velde, Dirk, Oliver Morrissey, and Adrian Hewitt (2002), "Allocating Aid to International Public Goods," in Marco Ferroni and Ashoka Mody (eds.), *International Public Goods: Incentives, Measurement and Financing* (Boston: Kluwer Academic Publishers), 119–56.

Wintrobe, Ronald (2001), "Can Suicide Bombers Be Rational?," unpublished manuscript, University of Western Ontario, London, Ontario.

Wolfensohn, James D. (1999), "A Proposal for a Comprehensive Development Framework," Memorandum to Staff of the World Bank Group, January 21, World Bank, Washington, DC.

World Bank (1998), *Assessing Aid: What Works, What Doesn't, and Why* (New York: Oxford University Press).

World Bank (1999), *International Bank for Reconstruction and Development: Financial Statements, June 30, 1999* (Washington, DC: World Bank), available at www.worldbank.org/html/extpb/annrep99.

World Bank (2001), *Global Development Finance: Building Coalitions for Effective Development Finance* (Washington, DC: World Bank).

World Bank CDF Secretariat (2000), *Comprehensive Development Framework: Country Experience, March 1999–July 2000* (Washington DC: World Bank).

World Bank CDF Secretariat (2001), "Comprehensive Development Framework, Meeting the Promise? Early Experience and Emerging Issues," September 17, World Bank, Washington, DC.

World Bank CDF Secretariat (2003), *Toward Country-Led Development: A Multi-Partner Evaluation of the Comprehensive Development Framework* (Washington, DC: World Bank).

World Bank Partnership Group (1998), "Partnership for Development: Proposed Actions for the World Bank," Discussion Paper, May 20, World Bank, Washington, DC.

World Health Organization (WHO) (2001), *World Health Report 2001* (Geneva: WHO).

World Health Organization (WHO) (2002), *Coordinates 2002: Charting Progress against AIDS, TB and Malaria* (Geneva: WHO).

World Meteorological Organization (1998), *Scientific Assessment of Ozone Depletion: 1998*, WMO Global Ozone Research and Monitoring Project, Report No. 44, Geneva.

World Resources Institute (1992), *World Resources 1992–93* (New York: Oxford University Press).

World Resources Institute (2000), *World Resources 2000–01* (New York: Oxford University Press).

Zacher, Mark W. (1996), *Governing Global Networks: International Regimes for Transportation and Communications* (Cambridge: Cambridge University Press).

Zacher, Mark W. (1999), "Global Epidemiological Surveillance: International Cooperation to Monitor Infectious Diseases," in Inge Kaul, Isabelle Grunberg, and Marc A. Stern (eds.), *Global Public Goods: International Cooperation in the 21st Century* (New York: Oxford University Press), 266–83.

Zervos, Vasilis (2003), "Can Commercial Space Programs End the Post-Cold War Space Race? A Theoretical Model Applied to Galileo Public–Private Partnerships," unpublished manuscript, Nottingham University Business School, Nottingham, UK.

Author Index

Akerlof, George A., 160
Alcamo, Joseph M., 226
Alexander, Yonah, 173, 186
Anderson, Roy M., 105
Anderton, Charles H., 145
Anderton, Roxanne A., 145
Andreoni, James, 34
Arce M., Daniel G., 9, 34, 56, 60, 61, 75, 81, 85, 88, 90, 104, 107, 112, 116, 125, 137, 138, 148, 150, 177
Arhin-Tenkorang, Dyna, 107
Arquilla, John, 166, 264
Arrow, Kenneth J., 45
Axelrod, Robert, 30

Bagnoli, Mark, 64, 94
Barrett, Scott A., 5, 27, 76, 95, 111, 214, 216, 219, 232
Benedick, Richard E., 5, 10, 44, 217, 225, 232
Bergstrom, Theodore C., 34, 61
Binmore, Ken, 22
Blume, Lawrence, 34, 61
Braunschvig, David, 241, 242, 248
Breton, Albert, 85
Brophy-Baermann, Bryan, 187
Browne, Marjorie Ann, 186
Bruce, Neil, 39, 47, 77, 86, 119
Buchanan, James M., 37
Buchholz, Wolfgang, 93, 259
Buira, Ariel, 95
Burnside, Craig, 127
Bush, William C., 19

Carlsson, J., 125
Carter, John R., 145

Cash, Richard A., 107
Cauley, Jon, 168, 183, 184, 185, 186
Centers for Disease Control (CDC), 99
Chamberlin, John, 33
Chen, Lincoln C., 107
Clarke, Edward H., 48
Coase, Ronald H., 70
Cohen, Linda R., 240
Collier, Paul, 126, 193, 194, 199, 200
Commission on Macroeconomics and Health (CMH), 104, 119
Conceição, Pedro, 75, 107, 137
Congleton, Roger D., 10
Conybeare, John A.C., 187
Cook, Lisa D., 88, 90
Cornes, Richard, 24, 37, 38, 41, 48, 61, 69

Dando, Malcolm, 155
Darmstadter, Joel, 217, 219
de Gruijl, Frank R., 214
de Meza, David, 140
Devlin, Robert, 88
Dodds, Klaus, 7, 88
Dollar, David, 127
Dorn, William, 202
Durch, William J., 205, 209

Easterly, William, 124, 125, 201
The Economist, 1, 99, 100, 108, 193, 194, 241, 242, 247, 265
Edelson, Burton I., 250, 251
Elbadawi, Ibrahim A., 193, 194, 200
Eliassen, Anton, 227
Enders, Walter, 4, 165, 168, 169, 170, 173, 174, 179, 183, 184, 185, 186, 190
English, Robert D., 197

287

Subject Index